*Pra*

# Looking ــ Angels

*Looking for Angels* is *the* definitive book on who or what angels truly are across all spiritual traditions and on how to call on them, recognize them, and work with them (even if you never thought you could). No other book on angels is as comprehensive or as practical.

—*Katy Koontz, editor of* Unity Magazine

A balanced and well-researched account of the history and science of angels that is palatable to skeptics and believers alike.

—*Lina Eliasson, PhD Cpsychol*

The authors embrace the concept of angels through a well-woven thread through different religions and perspectives. It's a beautifully evoked, candid, and powerful look at angels and is an insightful and fascinating read.

—*Bindi Shah, MD*

A delightful, informative deep dive into the realm of angels. Scott and Nichole guide the reader through human perspectives, angel mythology, modern-day visitations and so much more! *Looking for Angels* is a must read for those of us who are eager to identify and work with the angelic energies.

—*Jill Stanley,* Common Mystics Podcast

# Looking for Angels

For more information, visit *lookingforangelsbook.com*
or the authors' websites:
Scott Guerin, PhD: *angelintraining.org*
Nichole Bigley: *apsychicsstory.com*

ISBN: 979-8-9879918-0-0

Cover design by Jeremy Mayes and Hailee Pavey
Interior design and layout by Hailee Pavey: *paveydesign.com*

---

## *Disclaimers to Readers*

This book is designed to provide information and inspiration to its readers,
with the understanding that the authors do not intend to render any type of
emotional, legal, medical, mental, psychological, religious, or any other kind
of professional advice, nor prescribe the use of any technique or practice as a
form of treatment. Neither the publishers nor the authors shall be liable for any
commercial, emotional, financial, physical, psychological, or spiritual damages, including but not limited to special, incidental, consequential, or other
damages. The authors, publishers, and any other associated parties assume no
responsibility for your actions and their consequences accrued from the information in this book.

Always consult a physician or therapist when considering using the techniques
listed within this book. Always make sure to practice the meditations, intentions, prayers, or exercises in an environment that is safe to do so. Do not engage
in these activities while driving a car or operating any kind of machinery.

---

# Looking for Angels

## A Guide to Understanding and Connecting with Angels

Scott Guerin, PhD
& Nichole Bigley

# Dedication

This book is dedicated to God, Universe, and Source (GUS), as well as the archangels, ascended masters, spirit guides, and loved ones who make up our spirit team. We owe eternal gratitude for your divine love, guidance, and support as we continue to awaken and grow on our spiritual paths.

This book is also dedicated to you, dear reader. Picking this book isn't by accident. Your angels led you here. Let them continue to guide you forward. Be proud of yourself and know this is a sign that your angels are already working with you.

# Contents

# Preface: Our Stories

## Nichole Bigley

One day as I was sitting at home preparing for a client session and praying, I received a message from my angels that I should write about them—what a person's "spirit team" consists of, who the archangels are and what they do, how guardian angels and spirit guides differ, and how people can connect with them. The primary reason for this, they explained, was so that people could refer back to this information on a regular basis and wouldn't require a session with someone like me.

My first thought was "That's amazing! I'd love to." And that thought was quickly followed by overwhelming frustration. I have a full-time public relations job, which is my nine-to-five (or should I say my eight-to-six?). After that, I typically hold client readings or energy healings in the evenings during the week and all day on Saturdays. Sundays are reserved for my podcast work, which includes guest interviews, editing, and content writing—you get the idea. Each and every time I would ask for guidance on when I could take something off my plate, I'd be told, "Not yet," and/or the Universe would add something else for me to do. So, the thought of writing a book at that time just felt impossible. However, the urgency from Spirit was so strong that I said:

> *If you want me to do this, I will absolutely honor your request. But I ask that you provide me with the resources to do it—either a person to help me write it,*

*the funding to self-publish, or a publisher to guide me through the process. I am open to all the possibilities the Universe has to offer for the best and highest good of myself and others—at the right time.*

Fast forward to two days later, I received an email:

*Subject: Hello and Query about Book Collaboration*

*Hi Nichole, I first learned about you through your podcast and have listened to many of your episodes ...*

*I am working on a book with the primary focus to serve as a strong introduction and encouragement to how we can interact with angels to help us in our spiritual journey and to possibly better help others ...*

*Just throwing this out there if you would be interested in a collaboration ...*

*Dr. Scott Guerin*

Now, I am all for receiving messages and signs from God, Universe, and Source (GUS). I'm blessed to have been getting them throughout my life. But at times like this, even I can't help but still be utterly amazed and grateful that we have a spirit team, and that the Universe truly has our back in the moments we need it.

## *Everyone Has a Spirit Team*

Every single one of us has a spirit team. Our teams consist of archangels, ascended masters, deities, guardian angels, spirit guides, and loved ones from the other side. They exist with the *soul* (not sole) purpose of helping us stay connected to the Divine—where we came from and where we will ultimately go back to—and guiding us in times of need as we navigate this physical dimension and earthly life. If you are reading this book, I suspect you know this and have felt the need to understand who your spirit team is and how you can connect and communicate with them.

That's where this book comes in. You are being called or led by something greater than you can ever imagine. I do not have all the answers—you and your angels do. But I will certainly help facilitate the process as my angels have for me.

When I was five, I was bummed I didn't seem to have any imaginary friends. Many of the kids around me would talk about and seemingly interact with their imaginary friends. They would describe what they looked like and even have full conversations. I definitely felt left out because I couldn't see or hear anything. Then one day, a word began to take shape in my mind. At first, it felt and sounded like a thought, but as it formed, I realized it had a different quality somehow. It was separate from my own thoughts but still felt as if it were coming through me. As I embraced it, the message was unmistakable.

I let my mind focus on the name, and suddenly I could not only energetically feel him near me but also see him in my mind's eye. I saw an extremely tall being that emanated bright white light. As the light expanded, the outer edges turned to a golden shimmering energy. When I tried to focus on more detail, I could sense him painting a picture for me. This was when a handsome, kind face came into focus, along with a white robe over a more human type of body, something you would typically see in today's depiction of angels. However, there was no halo, nor were there wings. The experience felt very familiar. I felt safe and oh so loved.

This was the beginning of a beautiful and lifelong connection with who I now know to be Archangel Michael.

## *Why Now?*

My angels and guides were insistent that this book was to be written and that it was to be done *right now*. There is a reason for that, just as there is a reason you are reading this book at this time. Spirit has been waking us up all over the world at rapid speed and calling people to their higher purpose; the Universe doesn't want you to feel like you have to do it alone. These are tense times, and having a spirit team in your corner is exactly what you need to help you along your path. Despite everything that is going on in the world and your personal life, you have the capacity to connect with your spirit team through your intuition. Each of us has the ability to connect intuitively once we know how to activate that power. That part of the process is trust, ask, act (TAA). There is more about this process in Chapter 15, "Connecting with Your Spirit Team." But also, knowing how to connect with your angels and guides in order to fulfill what it is you came here to do makes it all the easier.

As a global community, we are being called to spiritually awaken, strengthen our connection to the other side, and in doing so, remember our connection to the Divine. We came here in a vibratory state of love, and if we can tap into and hold on to that state as often as possible, we have the chance to not only shift ourselves and our souls individually, but also get the collective to a state of awareness and love to heal the world. Everyone has an innate knowing within them—a forgotten ability just waiting to be recalled. It is our spiritual right to tap our spirit team for guidance along the way.

The opportunity I was given to work with Archangel Michael and my other angels and guides growing up allowed me to communicate with them every moment of every day—like breathing. This automatic response is something that this book will get you closer to doing on your own, tapping into that state of BE-ing and the support system that is there before you right now.

# Scott Guerin

Not too long ago, I rented a booth at a local spiritual holistic expo. It was the first time for me; I was promoting my books on spiritual development and online courses. It was a grueling three-day event with thousands of visitors and hundreds of booths offering readings, crystals, and oils, among other spiritual tools and services.

I was sitting across the aisle from a tarot card reader, and we spoke a few times when traffic was low. She was a short, roundish woman, probably in her mid-fifties, with long black hair with streams of gray. Her booth was set up nicely, with a large banner on the back wall, a card table for her sessions, and a long, narrow table at the front with books and tarot card decks, along with other items for sale. She spoke quickly and to the point. I wondered how that would play with clients because it seemed she was rushing but, at the same time, conveyed a large amount of information. At the end of the weekend, we were talking about the event and the people we met when I asked her what she thought of my minimally appointed booth.

She replied, "It looks nice, professional, but ..."

"But what?" I asked.

"It's too academic. You have a poster about a new book on angels, but you don't have any images of angels, figurines, or statues."

"Great point, thank yo—" I tried to respond.

"Also, it would be good to have a female voice included in your work. Do you know of anyone?" she asked abruptly.

"No, I don't kno—" I attempted to reply when she interrupted again.

"Yes, that would be good."

I thanked the woman and left the expo, thinking about who I could ask. I had discovered Nichole's *A Psychic's Story* podcast a few months earlier and had listened to several episodes while on bike rides. I was impressed by the breadth and depth of her guests and her masterful interviewing style. So about two days later, I took a chance and sent the above email to Nichole, and off we went. Even the most skeptical side of me had a hard time thinking this was a coincidence. This marked a new chapter in my spiritual journey, which began decades ago in traditional religious settings.

I was raised in a Lutheran Church, then turned to conservative Christian nondenominational organizations, and then the Presbyterian Church. Beginning when I was a teenager, whatever church I attended, I was all in. Any service, education, sacrament, or practice available, I threw myself into 110 percent. I was the head of our Christian organization during college, went to dozens of Christian retreats, attended seminary for a master's degree in theology, taught Sunday School for more than ten years, and was ordained an elder in the Presbyterian Church. Unfortunately, despite my devotion to my religion, my life fell apart, and I entered a dark and depressing time during which I felt that God was missing in action.

Then one day, in the midst of my depression, I woke up. Driven by my deep passion for a spiritual life, I abandoned everything religion had taught me and started from zero. I spent the next several years investigating spirituality from a scientific and psychological perspective to answer basic questions about God, spirituality, and how I related to them. This journey brought me through two master's degrees and a doctorate in psychology, focusing on human and spiritual development.

During this time, my personal experiences deepened as well, and as a result, I started to experience Spirit in a new way. My academic path quickly led me to the practice of meditation; like every other spiritual and religious practice, I dove into learning how to quiet my mind through various meditation techniques. However, the most profound experience for me was participating in the ten-day silent Vipassana meditation retreat and a follow-up three-day session.

Looking back over my life, I can see where I have had possible angel encounters—for example, surviving a head-on collision with an eighteen-wheeler, ending with a totaled car and not a scratch on me. Many times over the last few years, I would be developing a manuscript or article, and looking back at a paragraph I just wrote, I had no memory of writing it. Other signs also appeared, like seeing repeated numbers on digital clocks dozens of times during the week. Recently, I have had unusually strong connections with my high school teacher, coach, and friend who passed in 2015.

A more dramatic event occurred recently, after I read about spirit animals. The article described how many of us have spirit animal guides to support and protect us in life. At the end of the article, the author suggested that anyone could ask to see and meet their spirit animal by simply asking God or Spirit to provide. The morning after I asked, in my mind appeared a relatively large leopard on my right side, sometimes sitting and other times walking next to me. I call her Shera, and she is so real to me that sometimes I unconsciously reach my hand over to pet her head.

Also, lately, I have had a growing sense of a group of guides behind and around me. One in particular is a male figure standing or walking alongside me, sometimes poking my right shoulder, almost throwing me off balance at times. During these experiences, I get the clear message to keep writing. Nichole and another psychic friend say it is Archangel Gabriel; their strength is communication.

In any case, I am pleased to be working with Nichole. I joke with her that I thank her and *blame* her for helping me take giant steps in my spiritual journey, which can be a bit uncomfortable at times. After six and a half decades of walking this planet, passionately seeking a greater connection with Spirit through religion, academia, and direct experience, this book reflects a new phase in spiritual development for me. And, hopefully, it comes at precisely the right time for you.

# *Introduction*

*Looking for Angels* is divided into five parts. While the authors collaborated on the entire book, Parts One and Two were written by Dr. Scott Guerin, and Parts Three and Four were written by Nichole Bigley, with both authors collaborating on Part Five.

First, to better understand where humanity initially learned about angels, Part One provides an overview of how angels are depicted in the world's largest religions—Christianity and Judaism, Islam, Hinduism, and Buddhism. Together, these faiths comprise approximately 80 percent of the world's population.

For the scientifically minded, Part Two explores the physical challenges of seeing angels and capturing images of them. We discuss the psychological aspects of how we experience angels and how clinicians approach clients who say they have angelic encounters. We also address why interest in angels has decreased since ancient times and why there may be a resurgence of attention to these spiritual beings.

Parts Three and Four cover the practical aspects of connecting with angels. We review types of spiritual practitioners, along with providing an explanation of spirit teams, how they work with us, and what psychic senses we each innately have.

Part Five organizes the intentions and meditations presented throughout the book for your convenience. In addition, we include ways to identify and locate the most appropriate spiritual being for your needs.

It is our intention to provide you with enough information about angels so that you feel safe, comfortable, and empowered to connect with them and take your spiritual journey to a new level.

# Part One

# Angels in Religion

Scott Guerin, PhD

In religious texts, angels are rarely named or brought to the forefront of divine activity. Though an integral part of how Scripture shows God's will being carried out on Earth, the heavenly host's service operates like a computer program running in the background. As we'll see, there are exceptions, and they are significant.

—*Michael Heiser, PhD,* Angels

# Chapter 1

# Christianity and Judaism: A Starting Point

*"We do not have to walk on the edge of an infinite void to feel the brush of the wings of angels in the starlight."*
—*Thomas Merton*

If a movie were made focusing on how angels are portrayed in the Hebrew and Christian Bibles, it would rival any action movie ever made. The range of characters would include large multi-winged creatures with many faces, animal arms, and legs descending in a cloud of smoke and fire to terrify audiences. Angels with superpowers of flight and strength engaging in massive battles would compete with any character that Marvel or DC Comics has to offer. Other family friendly angels would be depicted as regular people, offering comfort and guidance, or proclaiming good news to all humankind. This may seem dramatic, but as you will see, it comes close to the descriptions found in many of the world's ancient sacred texts.

For some of you, the ideas in this book will present a drastically different perspective of angels from what you have known. We propose that humankind is moving into a new phase of spiritual development. This phase will not be centered on a new spiritual leader or spiritual practice. It will not occur through a dramatic storm of change, but rather through a gentle breeze impacting vast numbers of people throughout the world at the individual level. People will become aware that they are fully human and fully divine, and they will experience this through more in-depth interactions with angels and their spirit teams.

Before we present how we can have modern-day relationships with these divine beings, a good place to start is to briefly review what the world's great religions have taught us about the spirit world.

To begin, the Hebrew and Christian Bibles reference angels, spirits, and related terms hundreds, if not thousands, of times. The word *angel* is mentioned approximately three hundred times in the Bible. The English word *angel* is translated from the Hebrew word *mal'ak* and the Greek word *angelos*, both meaning "messenger." The Hebrew Bible was primarily written in Hebrew and is referred to as the Old Testament by Christians. The New Testament was mainly written in Greek. The number of angels mentioned is actually much higher because other terms refer to angel-like beings: for example, the Hebrew words *rûah,* meaning "spirit," or *šamayim,* meaning "heavenly ones."

It is important to know that the Hebrew Bible (identified as the Old Testament for Christians) and the New Testament span both of these faiths because Christians and Jews accept the Old Testament books. There is a long and winding history of how each of the sixty-six books of the Christian Bible was accepted or canonized as the authentic word of God, which is too detailed to review here. In addition, many other books and documents present content related to the books of the Bible but are not included in the canonized biblical collection. Most organized religions have texts that fit into this category and are called apocryphal texts. The word *apocrypha* means "hidden." The Catholic Apocrypha is one example. In approximately AD 1500, the Catholic Church accepted seven additional Old Testament books into its Bible that were written during the five hundred years between the Old and New Testament times. In addition to these books, many other writings authored by prominent Jewish theologians such as Josephus and Philo, while not canonized, were deemed reliable enough to shed light on what was happening during the intertestamental period. In addition, the Septuagint, a Greek translation of the Old Testament, was developed during this time.

## The Celestial Hierarchy

*God loves in the Seraphim as charity, knows in the Cherubim as truth, is seated in the Thrones as equity, reigns in the Dominions as majesty, rules in the Principalities as principle, guards in the Powers as salvation, acts in the Virtues as strength, reveals in the Archangels as light, assists in the Angels as piety.*
*—St. Bernard (1090–1153), Mellifluous Doctor*

Before we discuss how angels are depicted in the Old and New Testaments, let's first look at the work of Pseudo-Dionysius, a Greek author and theologian who lived in the late fifth century. He wrote several books and letters on Christian theology, including an overview of the angelic realm generally accepted by theologians and biblical scholars, entitled *The Celestial Hierarchies*.[1] In this book, the author presents descriptions of three orders and nine choirs, or groups, of angels, each with specific characteristics.

| First Order | Second Order | Third Order |
|---|---|---|
| Seraphim | Dominions | Principalities |
| Cherubim | Virtues | Archangels |
| Thrones | Powers | Angels |

The first order includes seraphim, meaning "those who make hot" and "closest to God." Cherubim relate to knowledge and wisdom (see further descriptions below). The thrones represent the nearness and openness to God, uncorrupted by any earthly influence. Ophanim and galgalim are creatures that function as the actual chariots of God, driven by the cherubs; the throne of God is usually shown to be moved by wheels, containing many eyes, as in the vision of Daniel 7:9. This designation is the highest of all others because of ophanim's and galgalim's proximity to God.[2]

The second order includes dominions, which dominate the lower groups or choirs at the direction of higher hierarchies and govern the universe. Virtues work miracles, oversee the movements of the universe, and are connected with the planets, elements, and nature. Powers are warrior angels tasked to uphold the natural order and fight against demonic choirs with powers over the Devil.

The third order is the lowest of the three and includes principalities, who have direct power over angels and care for and guard communities, kingdoms, and states. They also are involved with transitions of power. Archangels are the bearers of messages and are assigned to communicate and carry out divine plans for humanity. Archangel Michael is the only named archangel in the Bible. However, several more archangels are identified in the apocryphal texts (see further descriptions below). The angels are the closest choir to the material world and humans. They are generally associated with the idea of guardian angels.[3]

## Notable Angels of the Judeo-Christian Bible

### The Angel of the Lord

The most important and highest level of angel presented in the Bible is the Angel of the Lord, first mentioned in Genesis 16. The identity of this angel ranges from being a mystery to being the representation of God in human form.[4] There is ample evidence suggesting this angel is God in the form of a human and also speaks to the divine Godhead (God as being more than one person).[5]

The Angel of the Lord speaks as God in the first person several times throughout the Old Testament, providing direction to the Israelites and announcing what He would do. For example, He directed Abraham not to sacrifice his son Isaac when they were in the wilderness, He announced to Moses in a burning bush that He would liberate the Jews from the Egyptians, and He forgave the sins of the Old Testament figure Joshua.

When discussing the Godhead and God in human form, it is a good place to speak briefly about the identity of Jesus Christ. When associating Jesus with the Godhead, it acknowledges Him as part of the Holy Trinity: God the Father, Son, and Holy Spirit. Christianity views Jesus as God's son and equal to the Father and the Holy Spirit. One analogy of the Holy Trinity that I always thought interesting was comparing it to the three forms of water: solid, liquid, and gas. Certainly, the precise identity of Jesus has been debated for thousands of years. Ascribing Jesus as equal to God the Father is the core of Christianity, and many believe that is the reason why He was crucified. Other religions, such as Judaism and Islam, view Jesus not as God but as a good rabbi and prophet. Still others identify Jesus as an ascended master, a category not mentioned in the Bible that will be discussed in Part Three.

## Archangels

Of the three hundred mentions of angels in the Bible, the only names that appear are Michael and Gabriel.[6] Both are frequently ascribed the title of archangels, meaning high-ranking angels. However, some view Archangel Michael as the one and only archangel since the canonized scriptures only attribute this title to him. The qualifications of archangels vary across the literature, and they are generally depicted as leaders of other angels or as having specific duties or responsibilities. The number of named archangels expands by five in the Jewish intertestamental book of Enoch, with the addition of Archangels Uriel, Reuel, Remiel, Sariel, and Raphael to the list.[7] Other sources include Archangels Jophiel, Azrael, and Chamuel.[8]

The duties of archangels vary greatly, with several mentions of them leading spiritual battles, directing other angels in the worship of God, praying for those on Earth, and expelling demons. For example, Archangel Michael led the battle that expelled the angel Lucifer from heaven. Most agree that Lucifer is the being identified as the dragon in the New Testament book of Revelation 12:7-9:

> *And there was a war in heaven. Michael and his angels fought back against the dragon, and the dragon and his angels fought back. But he was not strong enough, and they lost their place in heaven. The great dragon was hurled down—that ancient serpent called the devil or Satan, who leads the world astray. He was hurled to the earth, and his angels with him.*

Gabriel is the only other named angel in canonized scriptures, though they are not identified as an archangel. Sometimes Archangel Gabriel represents a woman and sometimes a man. So we refer to Archangel Gabriel as "they." Many ascribe this title to them based on Jewish apocryphal texts. They appeared to Daniel and foretold the coming of the Messiah and the destruction of Jerusalem. They are most often remembered for their role in appearing to the Virgin Mary to tell her she would be the mother of the Son of God, as told in the book of Luke 1:26-31:[9]

> *In the sixth month of Elizabeth's pregnancy, God sent the angel Gabriel to Nazareth, a town in Galilee, to a virgin pledged to be married to a man named Joseph, a descendant of David. The virgin's name is Mary. The angel went to her and said, "Greetings, you who are highly favored! The Lord is with you."*
>
> *Mary was greatly troubled by his words and wondered what kind of greeting this might be. But the angel said to her, "Do not be afraid, Mary, you have found favor with God. You will be with child and give birth to a son, and you are to give him the name Jesus."*

## Archangel Metatron

Archangel Metatron is not identified in the canonized books of the Bible but is mentioned in Jewish mystical texts and Islamic scripture. He is referred to as an archangel who was transformed from the man Enoch, a not-too-distant relative of Adam and Noah. I first learned of him through an interview with the musician Carlos Santana in *Rolling Stone* magazine. This story is presented in the next chapter and is a powerful example of how angels can interact in today's world to help people heal.

## Cherubim and Seraphim

Two other fascinating heavenly beings are the cherubim and seraphim. These are depicted as hybrid creatures with human and animal features. Descriptions of these creatures reveal that they appear in the form of a man with multiple wings, human faces, and the faces of lions, oxen, and eagles, in addition to bronze calves' feet. Their appearance also comes with loud noises like the "roar of rushing waters" in addition to bright lights.[10] According to the late Dr. Michael Heiser, a well-published Old Testament scholar and author, both of the Hebrew words for these creatures, *kerubim* (cherubim) and *serapim* (seraphim), describe the same function—to guard the presence of God. These guardians would serve as protection for those allowed in sacred places and as a terror to all others.[11] For example, in the biblical account of the fall of man from the Garden of Eden, after Adam and Eve were cast out, God placed cherubim at the entrance to keep others from the Tree of Life. But are they angels? That is an interesting question.

Dr. Heiser proposes that cherubim and seraphim are different beings than angels. His rationale is that the Hebrew word for angel, *mal'ak,* is never associated with these two names. Instead, their roles are related to providing protection, not delivering messages or instructing humans, which is a job for angels.

In addition, angels are never depicted in the Bible as having non-human features like multiple faces, animal parts, or wings. In Heiser's

It is important to note that angels are not just transparent, energetic beings floating about, providing gentle guidance through whispers in the wind. As mentioned in religious texts, they are involved with our earthly realm in tangible ways. For example, the two angels that visited Lot struck the men of Sodom with blindness. An angel freed the apostle Peter from his chains and opened an iron gate without touching it.

perspective, angels do not have wings like the cherubim and seraphim. However, as with many biblical topics, this is debated by some, who argue that the scripture describes flying angels.[12] The counterargument is that the texts state that the angels flew—they do not specify they had wings.

## Angels

I do not want to refer to this group as "regular" angels because it degrades them, and they certainly are extraordinary beings. As mentioned above, the word *angel,* in both Hebrew and Greek, means "messenger," and outside of the named archangels, cherubim, seraphim, and a few other entities, this term is more of a job description than anything else. The title of messenger implies a conveyer of information, but biblical accounts show us that angels do much more than that.

From a biblical perspective, angels, along with everything else, are created beings. There is little debate about that. However, there are some disagreements about precisely when they were created. Was it before creation, after, or at the same time? According to Dr. David Jones of the School of Theology, Philosophy, and History at St. Mary's University College, London, there is a consensus among Jewish, Christian, and Islamic theologians that angels were created before human beings.[13] As with just about every related topic in this discussion, we can find scholarly debates about whether angels are eternal, whether they were made from fire or light, what they look like, whether they can marry, if they exist outside of time and space, if people become angels when they die, and on and on. These are interesting questions, but to keep this book succinct, I can safely say that angels are energetic beings with intellect and will—they may or may not have wings. Still, they do interact with humans regularly and can also appear in human form.

It is important to note that angels are not just transparent, energetic beings floating about, providing gentle guidance through whispers in the wind. As mentioned in religious texts, they are involved with our earthly realm in tangible ways. For example, the two angels that visited Lot struck the men of Sodom with blindness.[14] An angel freed the apostle Peter from his chains[15] and opened an iron gate without touching it.[16] We can't forget that it was an angel that moved the stone from Jesus's tomb on the first Easter morning.[17] They have also been involved in our world in more serious ways. One example is when the Assyrians were planning to attack Jerusalem, and the night before the attack, an angel killed 185,000 soldiers.[18] A second example is in the New Testament, when an angel struck down King Herod after he neglected to give praise to God.[19]

## Angels in Catholicism

As the first and largest organized Christian church, Catholicism provides much information and direction related to angels. The fundamental book of Catholic beliefs, *The Catechism of the Catholic Church*, states that angels are pure spirits created by God; they are capable of thinking, loving, and serving as God's messengers. In addition, Catholics can pray to their guardian angel, the Virgin Mary (mother of Jesus), and saints. Saints are exceptional men and women who, after their deaths, hold a special place in heaven as spiritual guides and mentors.[20]

A notable Catholic philosopher and theologian, Saint Thomas Aquinas, spent considerable time studying angels—to the extent that he was known as "The Angel Doctor." Aquinas's contributions to our understanding of angels are said only to be surpassed by the earlier writings of Pseudo-Dionysius, a Greek author and Christian theologian in the late fifth to early sixth century.[21] A fascinating analysis of Aquinas's explanation of the nature of angels and their connection to quantum physics is reviewed in Chapter 6.

## Angels over Time

Society's view of angels has changed over time. C.S. Lewis, the famed Christian writer and Anglican lay theologian, points out that in the

Bible, the visitation of an angel is always alarming. However, in the Victorian period, the demeanors of angels were watered down, in a sense, from images depicting them having the power and authority of heaven to the soft, chubby infants and reassuring angels of nineteenth-century art.[22] It seems that Lewis has a point. Images of angels have changed over the centuries and can be seen in TV and movies as heavenly helpers (*It's a Wonderful Life, City of Angels,* and *Touched by an Angel*) or more sinister characters (*Constantine, Meet Joe Black,* and *Lucifer*).

There could be two explanations for this change in perspective. First, centuries ago, anything outside of everyday, natural occurrences invoked fear. For example, the sight of a bright comet in the Middle Ages was thought to foreshadow terrible natural phenomena, such as floods or earthquakes, as a result of the "heavy hand of God."[23] In our age of high-definition phones, TVs, and IMAX theaters, we see extraordinary images on a daily basis. Second, today humanity is more accepting of divine images and spiritual interactions than our predecessors. Also, in more recent years in the United States, the number of people who view themselves as "spiritual but not religious" and those not affiliated with religion has been increasing significantly. I review this subject in more detail in Chapter 6.

# Angels in Christianity

**John Patton and his wife** were pioneer missionaries to the New Hebrides Islands, now known as the Republic of Vanuatu in the South Pacific Ocean. Faithfully, they tried to live out the Christian gospel and model a Christian lifestyle. Even though the couple were met with hostility from the villagers, they returned insults with kindness, hatred with love.

It soon became apparent that even their lives were in danger. There were threats that their home would be burned and the missionary couple murdered, but the Pattons felt called by God. Praying for divine protection, they continued to minister in a spirit of love.

Then one night, they heard noises outside their small missionary compound. Looking out, they saw they were completely surrounded by the chief and his men with torches and spears. They were being true to their word. They had come to burn their home and kill the missionaries. The Pattons had no weapons. There was no earthly means of protection, but they could pray, and pray they did! Throughout the terror-filled night, they prayed for God to send his angels to protect them. They prayed that this war-like tribe would someday find peace with God.

When morning came, the tribe silently left. The Pattons were elated but very surprised. There seemed to be no reason for the war party to leave.

Others of fainter hearts would have sailed away from the island looking for more hospitable mission territory, but the Pattons felt called by God to stay. So fearlessly, yet gently and lovingly, they continued to tell members of the tribe about Christianity, but without any noticeable results.

A full year later, the chief became a Christian. Then, finally, John Patton was able to ask the question that had puzzled him for so long. "Chief, remember that night when you came and surrounded our house? Your men all had spears and torches. What had you planned to do?"

The chief replied, "We came to kill you and burn everything you have."

"What kept you from doing it?" the missionary asked.

"We were afraid of all those men who were guarding your house," the chief replied.

"But there were no men," Patton responded. "We were alone, my wife and I."

"No, no," the chief insisted. "There were many men around your house. Big men. Giants. They were awesome. They had no torches, but they glowed with a strange light, and each had a drawn sword in his hand. Who were they?"

"Let me explain what you saw," Patton said as he opened his Bible to 2 Kings, chapter 6. He read the biblical account of the time that the king of Aram sent his men to capture the prophet, Elisha. During the night, the army surrounded the place where Elisha was. In the morning, Elisha's helper saw that they were surrounded by an army with horses and chariots.

"'What shall we do?' the man asked in fear.

'Don't be afraid,' the prophet answered. 'Those who are with us are more than those who are with them.'

And Elisha prayed, 'O Lord, open his eyes so he may see.' Then the Lord opened the servant's eyes, and he looked and saw the hills full of horses and chariots of fire all around Elisha." (2 Kings 6:16-17)

—*Marilynn Carlson Webber and Dr. William D. Webber,*
*The Warrior Angels*[24]

*Chapter 2*

# More on
# Archangel Metatron

---

*"We've given you a tremendous experience, and we want something back."*

*—Archangel Metatron*

---

One archangel worth spending additional time on is Metatron. I first thought he sounded like one of the evil Decepticon robots in Michael Bay's *Transformers* movies, but this entity is much older. Archangel Metatron is not mentioned in the canonized books of the Bible, but rather in the Jewish Talmud, a book of Jewish law written in the second to fifth century AD. In addition, Metatron is mentioned in other Jewish mystical texts and Islamic scriptures. Metatron is referred to as the archangel who was transformed from the man Enoch, a not-too-distant relative of Adam and Noah.[1, 2]

Many descriptions from various sources describing Archangel Metatron's heavenly role are available—the information provided by the Jewish intertestamental books indicates he serves as a celestial scribe, guardian of divine secrets, and mediator between God and

It was through this connection that Archangel Metatron provided him with an important, somewhat cryptic message: "You will be inside the radio frequency, for the purpose of connecting the molecules with the light." Santana understood this meant that he would make a new album and be on the radio again.

man. Also, sources suggest this angel was the creator of the geometric pattern known as Metatron's Cube, a two-dimensional, flattened version of the five Platonic solids (tetrahedron, cube, octahedron, dodecahedron, or icosahedron). Considered one of the most sacred of all geometric patterns, Metatron's Cube is an ancient and perfect blueprint of Cosmic Creation, a design that also lies in us. It is Spirit's conceptual architecture of life.[3, 4]

I first learned about Archangel Metatron from an unusual source. As an avid fan of music, particularly classic rock, I followed Carlos Santana's career in the 1970s and 1980s. He is a Mexico-born American musician who combines a Latin sound with rock, jazz, and the blues. A Woodstock alumnus, his career flourished through the late 1980s. However, his music and popularity were waning; he had not produced any new albums in several years when I noticed that the song "Smooth" was being played on many pop-rock stations. This piece was a collaboration with Rob Thomas from a new group at the time, Matchbox Twenty. The album was titled *Supernatural* and included songs from notables such as Eric Clapton, Dave Matthews, CeeLo Green, and others. I loved "Smooth" and liked some of the other songs as well, and I was glad Santana was making a comeback. What knocked me off my feet was his interview with *Rolling Stone* magazine in March 2000, entitled "The Epic Life of Carlos Santana: A Tale of Angels, Devils, Gurus, Tijuana Whorehouses, Buried Secrets, and Redemption after Thirty Years of Rock & Roll" by Chris Heath.[5]

During the interview, Santana described what his life was like growing up and moving from Mexico to the United States, how important music has been in his life, and where his passion for it has taken him. However, the discussion did not start with music—it started with his strong and deeply embedded spiritual life and how this connection had a direct impact on his life and his musical revival.

What caught my eye was that in the first few moments of the interview, he stated he had been in regular contact with Archangel Metatron for the past six years. The communication included what is known as automatic writing. This is when a person transcribes conversations directly from a spiritual source, similar to dictation; in Santana's words, "It's kind of like a fax machine."[6] "Metatron is the architect of physical life." Santana explains, "Because of him, we can French kiss, we can hug, we can get a hot dog, wiggle our toe." Santana initially came in contact with the archangel in the early 1990s at a spiritual bookstore in Santa Cruz when some people invited him to participate in their meditation sessions. It was through this connection that Metatron provided him with an important, somewhat cryptic message: "You will be inside the radio frequency, for the purpose of connecting the molecules with the light." Santana understood this meant that he would make a new album and be on the radio again. This prophecy came true with the release of *Supernatural* in 1999, and the album subsequently saw tremendous success worldwide. It reached number one in eleven countries, including the United States, for twelve weeks and sold an estimated thirty million copies worldwide. In addition, the album won nine Grammy Awards and was voted Album of the Year. However, this is where the story went sideways.

In an interview with the *Chicago Tribune* in 2002, Santana explained that at the height of the *Supernatural* phenomenon, Archangel Metatron provided another message: "We've given you a tremendous experience, and we want something back. We want you to speak about your childhood molestation."[7] The archangel was referring to a very painful and private time in Santana's life, when a man who often bought him toys and gifts and brought him across the border from Tijuana, Mexico, abused him almost every other day for about two years when he was ten to twelve years old. Santana strongly resisted the request to share this deeply personal and painful part of his life and asked if there was another way. However, the archangel told him, "No, it's not for bargaining because many men are going to benefit from it." Subsequently, Santana scheduled interviews with several media channels—including *Rolling Stone, Chicago Tribune*, and CBS News—to share his life, his music, and for the first time, the painful story about his abuse. It appears that in addition to the bidding of Metatron, Santana understood why sharing his story was necessary. He said:

> *There are many people out there who have this kind of pain and anguish, and if you show your face and say, "I am healed. I can be healed." Whether you are a woman or man who has been raped or molested, you don't have to ruin the rest of your life and ruin your family's life by blaming yourself, feeling dirty, ashamed.*[8]

Not long after his story appeared in the media, Santana began receiving emails and messages from men from all over the world, saying it had also happened to them and thanking him for being so brave. Santana concluded, "As soon as I said that, like a domino effect, all of a sudden, all these men started coming out about all the molestations with priests."[9]

Around this same time, stories began to emerge about the sexual abuse of children by Catholic priests and cover-ups by their leadership. One of the first large cases that received attention in the United States was in Stockton, California, in 1998; it was determined that church leaders covered up the abusive behavior of one of their priests between 1978 and 1991.[10] In 2002 the *Boston Globe* published an article documenting stories of 130 people claiming a former priest allegedly sexually abused them for more than 3 decades.[11] Other cases surfaced in the United States and worldwide to the extent that, in January 2001, Pope John Paul II sent an apology by email for several injustices, including sexual abuse, committed by Roman Catholic clergy.[12]

This story of Santana and his connection with Archangel Metatron is fascinating. It shows that angels continue to interact with us to this day and did not stop at the end of biblical times. Also, it provides hope and encouragement that we, too, can receive spiritual guidance and assistance. As mentioned, our goal with this book is to provide information to you to help you make up your own mind and continue your journey in whatever way you would like. The next steps are up to you.

# Chapter 3

# Islam:
# A Reconfirmation

*"No one goes into prayer, except that an angel prays to their right and an angel prays to their left, and angels the size of mountains are praying behind them."*
—*Dr. Omar Suleiman*

There is a significant overlap between the Judeo-Christian tradition and Islamic tradition in regard to angels. The reason is that Muslims believe that Muhammad is the last in a series of prophets appearing in both the Old and New Testaments, and as a result, they share many of the Old and New Testament texts with Christians and Jews. Old Testament prophets identified within Islam are Adam, Noah, Abraham, and Moses. New Testament prophets include Zachariah, John the Baptist, and Jesus. The Archangel Gabriel conveyed the holy revelations through these prophets to form the two books of the Hebrew Bible for Jews and a New Testament for Christians (a different version from the canonized Christian New Testament), with the Qur'an as the final testament.

According to Dr. Musharraf Hussain, an Islamic scholar at the Karimia Institute, Nottingham, United Kingdom, the Qur'an is a reiteration of the previous revelations written in Arabic; it calls itself "the one that confirms what came before." Hussain added that Muhammad is the last prophet of God, and the Qur'an is the last revelation of God.[1]

Despite the acceptance of Old and New Testament prophets and scriptures within Islam, there are differences in how Judaism, Christianity, and Islam view angels and their roles. Similar to the Greek word *angelos,* the Arabic word for angel is *malak* (plural: *mala'ikah*), the root meaning of which is "messenger."

One important distinction between the three religions is that a belief in angels is one of Islam's articles of faith, meaning that one cannot be a complete Muslim if they do not believe in angels. Another significant difference compared to Judaism and Christianity is that the duties of the angels of Islam are explained in more detail in the Qur'an. For example, Dr. Omar Suleiman, founder and president of the Yaqeen Institute for Islamic Research in Irvington, Texas, explained that Muslims believe that one of the roles of angels is to offer protection during the night and ask for us to be forgiven. During the day, different angels guard and record all our actions. They change shifts in the morning, between the beginning of dawn and sunrise, called Fajr time, and in the evening at sunset, called Asr time. During these times, Allah gathers the angels around the faithful as they recite the Qur'an. In addition, other angels guard heaven and hell and perform various tasks, and angels are also involved in several ways on Judgment Day.[2, 3]

Similar to the apocryphal books in the Judeo-Christian tradition, Islam has the Hadith, which contains the words and actions of the Prophet Muhammad. These sayings include guidance to help Muslims in their day-to-day lives. From these texts, we learn that angels are generally invisible to humans, except in certain situations. For example, Archangel Gabriel appeared as a man to Adam, Moses, Mary, Jesus, and Muhammad. Angels also helped Muslims beat unbelievers in the pivotal battle of Badr in AD 624. In this fight, hundreds of angels were sent. Many Muslims saw their enemies thrown off their horses and heard the cracking of whips without seeing anyone.[4]

It is important to understand that in Islam, angels do not have free will. They do exactly what they are commanded to do and cannot disobey Allah. As a result, Muslims are required to pray to Allah directly, and if He wills, He can choose to provide assistance through His angels. As Dr. Hussain stated, "You might be able to equate them to Toyota's robots that make the cars. They are programmed to do a particular activity."

According to Islamic tradition, angels also play a critical role in the natural world—the clouds, mountains, wind, and rain. According to a renowned Islamic scholar, Ibn al-Qayyim, "Every movement in the universe is caused by angels."[5] In attempting to answer questions about how many angels exist, what they look like, and whether they have wings, Islamic scholars caution against making direct correlations between our physical world and experiences of the unseen spiritual realms. While we can glean meaning from descriptions conveyed about the unseen world, they contain images that we have never seen or imagined. As Dr. Zohair Abdul-Rahman from the Yaqeen Institute stated, "From the Islamic perspective, the reality of angels cannot be understood by imagining their descriptions based on our experiences in this world."[6]

It is important to understand that in Islam, angels do not have free will. They do exactly what they are commanded to do and cannot disobey Allah. As a result, Muslims are required to pray to Allah directly, and if He wills, He can choose to provide assistance through His angels. As Dr. Hussain stated, "You might be able to equate them to Toyota's robots that make the cars. They are programmed to do a particular activity."[7]

At a personal level, angels are involved in the lives of Muslims by providing love, support, protection, positive inspiration, and prayers. Dr. Suleiman provided a wonderful description of angels in his book and video series *Angels in Your Presence*. In them, he explained that all Muslims have five angels with them their entire lives: two that protect from the front and behind, called *mu'aqqibat*; two that record good and evil deeds, Al-Kiram and Al-Katibun; and one evil spirit, sheitan, that tempts them to sin by whispering to their hearts.[8]

The names and brief descriptions of notable angels of Islam are listed below. As mentioned, there are many sources and interpretations of their roles in our world, and I have included an overview of their duties. I encourage you to continue your search to find out more about these fascinating heavenly beings.

# Notable Angels in Islam

## Jibril (Gabriel)

Jibril, identified as Gabriel in the Hebrew and Christian Bibles, is viewed by both faiths as one of the greatest angels. In Islam they are described as conveying revelations from Allah to the prophets; they are mentioned in three places in the Qur'an. They appeared to the Prophet Muhammad as a person who could talk in addition to acting as the Prophet's guide on the night of His ascension.[9]

## Mika'il (Michael)

Mika'il (Michael in the Judeo-Christian tradition) is another one of the greatest angels and is responsible for the rain, the wind, and natural events, as well as managing what is planted on the field of the Earth. Mika'il is only mentioned in one place in the Qur'an. Mika'il is also believed to guard places of worship and reward people's good deeds. Serving also as an angel of mercy, he asks Allah to forgive people's sins.[10]

## Isra'il

Also identified as Azrael, Isra'il is referred to by his role as *malak al-maut* (which means "Angel of Death") in the Qur'an. His job is to collect the souls of people whose time of death has come. The Qur'an explains that the Angel of Death does not know the time of death for each person until God reveals that information. At God's command, the Angel of Death separates the soul from the body and returns it to God.[11]

## Isrāfīl

Although he is not mentioned in the Qur'an, insights about Isrāfīl are found in Islamic apocryphal sources. He is the Angel of Resurrection and Song and will blow the trumpet on Judgment Day. Isrāfīl also tutored Muhammad for three years in the duties of a prophet before he could receive the Qur'an. He has no clear counterpart in the Judeo-Christian religious texts, with some suggested links to Archangels Raphael, Uriel, and Seraphiel.[12]

## Munkar and Nakir

These are angels that question a person after death. They ask three questions and respond according to the answers: Who is your Lord? What is your religion? Who is your prophet? Allah then decides whether a person will reside in Jannah, an eternal afterlife of bliss, or in Jahannam, an ever-flaming pit of fire.[13]

## Al-Kiram and Al-Katibun

These angels sit on the right and left shoulders of humans. The angel on the right is responsible for recording the good deeds; the angel on the left is responsible for recording the bad deeds. Muslims believe the record book will be presented to Allah on Judgment Day.[14]

"Behold, two guardian angels appointed to learn a man's doings learn and note them, one sitting on the right and one on the left. Not a word does he utter, but there is a sentinel by him, ready to note it" (Qur'an 50:17–18).

# Angels in Islam

**In the Hadith of the prophet Muhammad,** he talks about three men's experiences with an angel—one was a bald man, another was a leper, and the third was a blind man. An angel approached the three of them, in human form, and asked, "What is it that you want? What is it that you want to change about yourself?" And the leper said, "I would like to have good skin because people feel an aversion towards me because of my leprosy." And the angel touched the man, and at once, his leprosy was cured. Then the angel asked, "What type of property is most beloved to you?" And the man said, "Camels." Then the angel brings him a pregnant camel and says, "May Allah bless you with this camel." (This shows that it's Allah that provides, not the angel.) So, now the man has the skin he wanted, and he also becomes wealthy as a result of a growing herd of camels.

The angel then approached the bald man and says, "What would you like to change about yourself?" And the bald man says, "I would love to have good hair. I feel like it would help me look good. I feel like it's what's missing in my life." So, the angel touches the man's head, and a full head of hair appears. And the angel then says to the man, "What type of property is most beloved to you?" And the man replied, "Cows." So, the same thing happens. A pregnant cow is provided, and the angel says, "May Allah bless you with it." And as a result, he has a growing herd of cows.

The angel goes to the person who is blind and asks, "What would you like?" He replied, "I would love to have my eyesight back." The angel wipes his eyes, and immediately, he can see again. And then he says to him, "What's the most beloved of property to you?" He replied, "Sheep." And he was given a pregnant ewe and a growing flock of sheep.

Each of the men had their cattle, were healed, and had the hair they wanted in addition to a bright financial future. The prophet said that the angel came back to each one of the men in a different human form, looking like each of them before they were healed. So, to the leper, the angel showed up with leprosy and poverty. To the one who was bald, the angel showed up looking like a poor bald person. The angel also showed up to the person who was blind in the form of a needy blind man.

When the angel approached each of them, the angel asked them for help and support—surprisingly, the leper and the bald man denied they used to be poor and told the angel, "We earned this." The angel responded, "Aren't you the person that used to be sick or bald? Weren't you once in need?" They denied they ever were poor or had issues and turned the angel away. Their arrogance caused them to forget the blessing of Allah. So, the angel gave them a chance to redeem themselves and said, "If you are lying, then may Allah return you to what you were before."

But the blind man passed the test. The prophet explained that the blind man, who had the greatest disability, as soon as he saw the angel appearing as he used to be, said, "Take from this property, whatever you want, for I was once like you, and Allah provided for me." Scholars point out that this man, out of the three, had the most difficulties and demonstrated great humility when he told the angel to take from what Allah had provided. Hearing this, the angel responded, "Keep your property with you because Allah is pleased with you and angry with your two companions." And so, the two companions lost everything that they had and were restored back to their former positions, and the blind person was able not just to keep the blessing of Allah in this life but also increased in their station in the hereafter.

Now back to us. The question is, when we see someone in need, are we actually encountering an angel? The answer is that we are never going to know for sure. Only Allah knows. Plus, an angel is not going to reveal themselves and say, "I am actually an angel." It would defeat the purpose if we were only honoring them because we thought they were an angel.

The point of this story, other than to provide an example of how angels interact with humans, is that it is good to honor the sick, the orphan, and those who are in need, and remember our own blessings and vulnerability.

We never know whom Allah has placed in front of us.

—*Omar Suleiman,* Angels in Your Presence[15]

*Chapter 4*

# Hinduism: Angel-Like Beings

---

*"Worshipers of the demigods go to the demigods, wor-shipers of the ancestors go to the ancestors, worshipers of the ghosts and spirits go to the ghosts and spirits, and my worshipers certainly come to me."*
—*Bhagavad Gita 9:25*

---

H induism is a polytheistic religion consisting of many gods, goddesses, and animal-like figures. Because there is no spe-cific Hindu founder or leader, the faith includes multiple traditions and philosophies. As a result, it is described as a family of religions.[1, 2] This description reminds me of a friend of mine who has such a large family that their annual reunions have to be held at a local high school football stadium. When I asked him what the reunions were like, he said it always feels like one big family. Many of the conversations center on who is related to whom and to which uncle, brother, father, or mother they are directly related. Much like a big family, Hinduism has many variations of teachings, and there are large numbers of sacred texts and scholars within Hinduism. Thousands of sources exist describing divine entities such as angels.

Hinduism does not present named angels in the same way as Judaism, Christianity, or Islam. As an alternative, it presents a variety of angel-like beings, including gods (Lord Krishna), saints (devas and devis—male and female deities), gurus (human spiritual teachers), and ancestors who have passed away.

The holy books of Hinduism are composed of Vedas, meaning "knowledge." They include four texts—Rig Veda, Sama Veda, Yajur Veda, and Atharva Veda. Also referred to as the Shruti ("that which is heard"), they are believed to consist of revelation and unquestionable truth and are considered eternal.[3] Another important collection of religious texts is called the Smriti ("that which has been remembered"). Smriti literature explains, interprets, and organizes Vedic texts. And, while considered less authoritative than the Vedic Shruti, the Smriti are consulted by Hindus more often because they present definite rules and laws to guide individuals and communities in their daily conduct.[4, 5] The Bhagavad Gita ("song of God" or "song of the Lord") is among the most important and popular Smriti texts, describing the relationship between the human warrior prince Arjuna and the god Krishna. The text discusses a variety of topics, including what constitutes right action, proper understanding, the meaning of life, and the nature of the Divine.[6]

Hinduism does not present named angels in the same way as Judaism, Christianity, or Islam. As an alternative, it presents a variety of angel-like beings, including gods (Lord Krishna), saints (devas and devis—male and female deities), gurus (human spiritual teachers), and ancestors who have passed away. The best-known Hindu gods are Brahma, the creator; Vishnu, the preserver; and Shiva, the destroyer. Some Hindu traditions believe in guardian angels. These beings can appear in human form but are less defined than in other faiths; they are a combination of two spiritual forces: devas and atman (the divine spark in each person).[7]

With such a large number of spiritual beings, many Hindus look to their favorite gods or goddesses in times of need. For example, author Shoba Narayan conveyed a time when she went to her mother when she was afraid of the dark:

> "Think of Hanuman," my mother always said. "He will protect you." (Hanuman is a Hinduism's Monkey-God, known for his strength and benevolence.) With that, she taught me a sloka (chant) that I could repeat whenever I was afraid.[8]

Ganesha (also known as Buddhi Vinayaka), an elephant-headed deity understood as "the remover of obstacles" and "the one who grants wisdom," is called upon at the start of any event to ensure success. By worshipping him, people receive the ability to distinguish the good from the bad and overcome difficulties. Lakshmi, the merciful goddess, is a deity who is always giving, and those who praise her and seek her blessings see affluence and fortune in their lives.

For Hindus, nature is also sacred. For example, rivers that provide water and nourishment are deemed goddesses, as are mountains. Deities can appear as humans but are typically shown to have multiple limbs, animal and human faces, multiple postures, and various objects, including weapons. These are understood to be symbolic of their roles. For example, the god Shiva (known as the destroyer and restorer) is pictured sitting in a lotus position with eyes half closed, depicting a meditative state, and a third eye depicting divine insight. On his body, human ashes show he has overcome death, and snakes wrapped around his neck indicate he has mastered ego and negativity.[9]

Sri Dilip (Jay) Lakhani, a theoretical physicist and founder of the popular Hindu Academy in England, stated that he personally had not seen an angel, so he could not confirm their existence. However, Lakhani admitted:

> There are higher realms of existence. People living in those realms are of a higher caliber, and perhaps they have the ability to interact with us, to help us, to protect us, to guide us. It is possible there are higher beings who are guiding you, holding your hand, and protecting you. So, we do agree with that concept.[10]

Regarding how God interacts with humans, prolific Hindu author Jayaram V provided an interesting statement:

> *According to Hinduism, God is indifferent under normal circumstances. He would not interfere in the lives of beings or their actions. However, when evil rises its head and begins to oppress people, He incarnates upon earth to fight with it and restore balance.*[11]

The Bhagavad Gita shows the somewhat passive relationship the gods have with humans and their ability to relate to each on their level: "However, one approaches me; I approach them in the same way" (4:11). Overall, the Hindu tradition presents a positive outlook and offers much freedom for a person finding their own way.

# Angels in Hinduism

**The importance of angels for the Hindu** lies not so much in the devas themselves but in the underlying Divinity and potency of which they are merely a manifestation. In India or Sri Lanka, Grandma may return home from the temple, telling of how she could not find her way in the dark as she walked to the temple for early puja. Suddenly, there before her was a being. It was not really walking, more floating in front of her, guiding her along the dim dirt path. It was, she will tell, the deity of the temple, come to grace and guide her in the hour of need, and to make assurance of His loving presence in her life. It was God Himself. Of this, she has no doubt.[12]

—*"New Angles on Angels,"* Hinduism Today

*Chapter 5*

# Buddhism: A Matter of Reality

---

*"Life is an illusion, a dream—a bubble—a shadow. ...
Nothing is permanent. Nothing is worthy of anger or
dispute. Nothing."*

—*The Buddha*

---

**M**y introduction to Buddhism came from a chance encounter with a Buddhist woman at work years ago; it jarred me from my grip on conservative Christian beliefs. She was a freelance writer hired to work on a few projects that day. When she mentioned she was a Buddhist, I was ready to pounce and point out all the holes in her faith, as I had learned to do in the groups and retreats I had attended. But this time, I listened more than I talked, amazed at how deeply she felt about her religion. She told me how she was raised as a Buddhist but was also taught about other religions, including Christianity. She described the altar she had in her home, where she went to read and meditate. She told me how she relied on her Buddhist scriptures throughout her life because they conveyed stories of how other believers overcame suffering and pain. Even though it was brief, the conversation had a huge impact on me. I was stunned that someone could feel as strongly about their religion and have as deep a personal connection as I did to mine.

I did not see that Buddhist woman again; I never got her name. No one at work knew anything about her, and most did not notice she was there that day. A few years later, when I was recovering from my long-held narrow beliefs about God, I remembered our conversation. I spent much time learning about this fascinating faith and immersed myself in the practice of meditation.

I learned that Buddhism was founded in India by Siddhartha Gautama (the Buddha) more than 2,500 years ago, in 500 BC. With nearly 500 million followers, Buddhism is one of the major world religions and/or philosophies.[1, 2] The reason for the "and/or" is that there is much debate about whether Buddhism is a religion, philosophy, thought tradition, or some combination.

On the philosophical side, Buddhism does not identify a deity, god, or ultimate supreme being to worship. Siddhartha was a man who left his home to find answers to profound questions related to the meaning of suffering and how we can eliminate it in our lives. After years of experimenting with various religious practices, he deserted his ideas about his spiritual journey and found his answers by obtaining enlightenment or nirvana.

Siddhartha taught that enlightenment means that a person is able to understand what is temporary in life, enabling them to see the true nature of things and then free themself from suffering. A good analogy would be the feeling experienced in meditation. With some practice, anyone can learn to quiet the mind, usually by observing one's breath. I have had the opportunity to be trained in a meditation technique that comes from the Buddha's original teachings, called Vipassana meditation. This practice is taught during ten-day silent retreats, and participants spend hours practicing how to quiet their minds and begin to look at the world without being affected by it. A key idea that comes up in this training is to "simply observe" everything in life and yourself. It took some time to start to experience this, but when I could, I found it forced me to view everything without judgment and accept

Buddhism holds a much different perspective of angels than the Judeo-Christian, Islamic, or Hindu faiths, mainly because, in Buddhist thinking, everything we see and experience is an illusion, a projection of our own consciousness.

all that is. Siddhartha and others achieving enlightenment are able to expand this perspective to a very deep level—beyond their lives, even past lives—to experience a transcendent freedom that is beyond anything we can imagine.

According to a widely respected teacher in the Vajrayana School of Buddhism, Dzogchen Ponlop Rinpoche, "Buddhism can be practiced as a religion, but that's not what the Buddha taught. The difference is in the investigation—as opposed to the faith—that you bring to it."[3] Rinpoche suggested that Buddhism is a science of the mind—exploring how we think, feel, and act leads us to understand who we are. It is a philosophy of life, a way to live to increase our chances for happiness.

On the religious side of the debate, Dr. Charles S. Prebish, associate professor of religious studies at Pennsylvania State University, explained that Buddhism offers an ultimate reality like nirvana or Buddhahood that prompts a personal transformation. According to his definition, "A religion is a philosophy that posits an ultimate reality, a path towards experiencing ultimate reality, and the potential for personal transformation. Buddhism checks all those boxes." Admittedly, Dr. Prebish stated that part of the disconnect in these discussions is that not everyone uses the same standards or criteria in their definitions.[4]

Joan Sutherland, a Zen Buddhist teacher in New Mexico, offered an interesting response to this debate. Her answer to the religion or philosophy question is a definitive "Yes-no-kind-of." She explained, "If there's a sacred text in Buddhism, it is the world itself. Your attachment to that text can be as religious as you like—but the resultant awakening may shake your faith."[5]

Buddhism holds a much different perspective of angels than the Judeo-Christian, Islamic, or Hindu faiths, mainly because, in Buddhist thinking, everything we see and experience is an illusion, a projection of our own consciousness. As the Buddha said, "Life is an illusion, a dream, a bubble, a shadow. ... Nothing is permanent. Nothing is worthy of anger or dispute. Nothing."[6] This is not to say that nothing is real; the illusions are what we project on reality and, as a result, are our source of suffering.

Buddhist scholar John Lee Pendall, co-owner of *The Tattooed Buddha* publication, described this illusion: it is like being in a dark room and, in the corner, you see a snake, coiled and ready to strike. You become frightened, thinking the snake may be venomous and may lunge at you at any moment. Then someone else enters the room, sees your concern, and tells you this is not a snake, but a rope coiled in the corner. They walk over and kick the rope to prove you were mistaken.

In that scenario, the fear was real enough when you thought the rope was a snake. To the mind, there was a snake in the room, and you reacted as if there was. So, by all standards, that snake was real to you. This is true for all the fear, fortitude, sorrow, joy, suffering, and pleasure we experience in life. A "mind-made world" means that the mind projects views and perspectives onto whatever it experiences.[7]

In other words, Buddhism teaches that the way things appear to us is not the way they truly are. Focusing only on what appears to us (our physical surroundings and time, composed of past, present, and future) is the cause of our suffering. The practices of contemplation and meditation taught by the Buddha help us question what we are experiencing and free us to gain insight into the way things really are. It's like being in the middle of a frightening nightmare and then awakening from your dream, or the relief that comes when you realize a snake is simply a rope.

Since the Buddhist concept of reality is based on how a person perceives the world, angels or angel-like entities fall firmly into a subjective category. As a result, there are no concrete definitions, descriptions, or stories of angels, as in the Judeo-Christian or Muslim traditions. Ajahn Sumedho, a senior Western representative of the Thai Forest Tradition of Theravada Buddhism, bluntly stated in a recent dharma talk that angels are portrayed to be beautiful, playing harps, living in heaven forever. But according to Sumedho, these ideas are thoughts that we create, stemming from religious traditions. When asked what Buddhist angels are like, Sumedho stated, "One is an old person, one is a sick person, one is a dead person, one is a monk meditating under a tree." This statement is interesting because it aligns exactly with the Four Signs that Siddhartha encountered, which motivated him to leave his life of luxury and pursue a path of enlightenment. Those four signs were an old man, a sick person, a corpse carried to cremation, and a monk in meditation beneath a tree.[8]

The word *angel* is rarely seen in Buddhist texts. However, nonhuman entities are identified as devas, which can be considered a close match. These beings are invisible to most humans and live in different realms of the universe. However, some people who have opened their divine eye (called *divyacaksu*) may be able to see them. In the Western world, some refer to this as the third eye or mind's eye. Devas have achieved their positions as a result of positive karma from lifetimes of acts of generosity, meditation, and asceticism. Once they have used up their positive karma, they return to lower levels of existence.[9, 10] From reading through numerous references, texts, blogs, websites, and lectures, I believe it is fair to say that, with few exceptions, traditional Buddhism teaches that whatever positions devas have or wherever they live, they have no role in human lives or Buddhist practice.

One other category worth noting is that of the bodhisattva. This is someone who has vowed to pursue awakening to become a buddha or is "bound for enlightenment." Descriptions of bodhisattvas range from "great mythical figures" to supernatural beings.[11] The Lotus Sutra, one of the most prominent and respected Buddhist Mahāyāna sacred texts, describes the bodies of bodhisattvas similarly to the way angels are described in other religious traditions, as "golden in hue, with thirty-two features and an immeasurable brightness. ... Such were they, then, immeasurable, boundless, beyond anything that can be known through calculation, simile, or parable."[12] These descriptions portray bodhisattvas as something more than humans, as further emphasized by Sheng Yen, a Taiwanese Buddhist monk and religious scholar, who stated that we must "transcend ourselves and transform ourselves from ordinary sentient beings to Bodhisattvas."[13] However, as with any ancient and vast tradition, there is much variability in definitions. Kosho Uchiyama, a Sōtō priest, abbot of Antai-ji, and author of more than twenty books on Zen Buddhism, wrote that a bodhisattva is an ordinary person who moves in the direction of the Buddha and that "you and I, actually, anyone who directs their attention, their life, to practicing the way of life of a Buddha is a bodhisattva."[14]

One common theme across all definitions and descriptions of bodhisattvas is that they have put their own spiritual path on hold to help all sentient beings achieve liberation, freedom, and enlightenment.

# Angels in Buddhism— Bodhisattvas

**A bodhisattva is someone who** has attained enlightenment or a depth of spiritual insight, and, instead of removing from the troubles of the world, remains in the thick of the hustle bustle of daily life in order to help and liberate others from suffering. Instead of retreating to an idyllic mountain to become a hermit, the bodhisattva is in the streets, the marketplace, the everyday world.

This quest to be of service to others influences all that a bodhisattva does. It influences their line of work, relationships, and interactions with others. This path of service is one that flows naturally from their ethos, their personal code, and life mission. This ethos has been forged by the discipline of inner contemplation and now spreads outward.

—*Michael Sunderland, "Zen Reflection of the Day: Modern Bodhisattvas," a Few Words*[15]

# Part Two

# Scientific and Psychological Perspectives

Scott Guerin, PhD

The most beautiful and most profound emotion we can experience is the sensation of the mystical. It is the sower of all true science. He to whom this emotion is a stranger, who can no longer wonder and stand rapt in awe, is as good as dead.

—*Albert Einstein*

# Chapter 6

# Where Did the Angels Go?

---

*"For those predisposed not to believe, no evidence is possible. But for those inclined to believe, no proof is necessary."*

—*Rex Hauck*

---

Ancient civilizations accepted the idea of angels. The first five chapters illustrated that angels have been a part of religious and cultural history throughout the world, with numerous stories and detailed descriptions of how angels interacted with humans. The next question is where they went.

The lack of visibility and awareness of angels in modern times does not mean they no longer exist. As noted earlier, the belief in angels is a fundamental requirement of Islam. Notable Islamic theologian Ibn Taymiyyah stated that while many scoff at the idea of angels, "All of humanity has generally affirmed the presence of [both] angels and demons except a few rare cases in different nations."[1] "You would not find an entire culture deny them outright, only particular individuals or groups from amongst them."[2]

While this may be true, most would agree that stories of angelic interventions are certainly not found in everyday society. So, what happened? Why do we not see or hear stories of angels in our society or culture as openly as in ancient times?

Rabbi Richard M. Baroff, former president of the Atlanta Rabbinical Association, wrote about this in the book *Angels: The Mysterious Messengers*. He suggested that the devaluation of angels, the transcendent, and the supernatural in modern times was a result of the Age of Enlightenment. Starting with the Scientific Revolution, in the 1600s, scientists and philosophers like Isaac Newton, John Locke, and others began "a movement away from the belief in this rich, almost medieval idea that angels and the afterlife [exist]."[3] As a result, people began seeing the world strictly through reason, rejecting and devaluing the transcendent and supernatural.

The Scientific Revolution initiated a shift in thinking that over-turned thousands of years of Greek and religious worldviews by replacing a qualitative with a quantitative view of nature, where the world behaves as a machine rather than an organism. In other words, Newtonian laws revealed that the physical world is made up of mechanical objects with predictable movements and motions that are able to be manipulated. As a result, spiritual and nonphysical real-ities, like angels, took a back seat to more "rational" and "scientifically grounded" theories. There is no room for angels in a machine.

Numerous studies and surveys show a growing resurgence of spirituality worldwide, and with that has come a revival of interest in angels.[4, 5] There are two main reasons for this shift in thinking.

## Quantum Physics Removes the Curtain to the Unseen World

A few hundred years after the Scientific Revolution, scientists started looking more closely at how objects worked at the subatomic level, specifically the behavior of atoms and their components. They found that the physical world at this level (under one micron, one-fiftieth of a human hair) did not operate exactly as Newton suggested in his classical theories. In the early 1900s, German physicists Max Planck and Werner Heisenberg, and theoretical physicist Albert Einstein challenged Newtonian theories at the subatomic level and ushered in the discipline of quantum physics.

A groundbreaking discovery confirming this new area of science was made in the famous double-slit experiment, first conducted by Clinton Davisson and Lester Germer in 1927. In this experiment, a beam of electrons was shown through a board containing two vertical slits and projected onto a screen. The classic physics model predicted that the light on the screen would be concentrated directly opposite each of the slits, showing just two lines of light on the screen. Instead, however, a series of several bright and dark bands appeared. The explanation for this was that the light coming through the slits did not move in a straight line as particles but changed to behave as waves that either joined or canceled waves from the neighboring slit. This produced several bands of light on the screen, just like two intersecting ripples in a pond. This meant that as the electron particles passed through the slits, they changed to act like waves. In scientific terms, electrons exist as a wave function, meaning they can act like a particle (discontinuous) and then convert to a wave (continuous) as a result of the "collapsing of the wave function."

So, what does quantum physics have to do with angels? One fascinating example is presented by Saint Thomas Aquinas, the Catholic priest mentioned in Chapter 1. In AD 1485, Aquinas published the *Summa Theologiae*, a compendium of theological teachings of the Catholic faith and the nature of God. In this work, he discussed how angels move through space and time:

> *The angelic movement, can be continuous. But it may, on the other hand, take place as an instantaneous transference of power from the whole of one place to the whole of another—and in this case, the angel's movement will be discontinuous.*[6]

The scientific breakthroughs
brought on through quantum
physics do not prove the existence
of angels or a spiritual world, but
they do provide a crack in the door
from the mechanistic Newtonian
world. Moreover, they start to shed
some light on the unseen world
by beginning to explain the
"para" in the paranormal and
the "super" in the supernatural.

In their book, *The Physics of Angels,* American theologian Matthew Fox and biologist Dr. Rupert Sheldrake pointed out that the discontinuous movement in which an angel "jumps from one place in which it was acting to another without needing to pass through all the places in between"[7] is "similar to the ideas about the movement of photons and other particles in quantum theory."[8] This means that angels can exist as a wave function, as both waves and particles that travel between distances instantaneously.

One last example of how quantum physics is blurring the mechanistic lines of the Newtonian world comes from research regarding the phenomenon known as quantum entanglement. In 2022 Alain Aspect, John Clauser, and Anton Zeilinger won the Nobel Prize for their experiments related to this theory, in which two particles can behave as one and affect each other, even though separated by enormous distances (on opposite sides of the planet or even a solar system). Einstein was also aware of this interconnection and described it as "spooky action at a distance."[9]

The scientific breakthroughs brought on through quantum physics do not prove the existence of angels or a spiritual world, but they do provide a crack in the door from the mechanistic Newtonian world. Moreover, they start to shed some light on the unseen world by beginning to explain the "para" in the paranormal and the "super" in the supernatural.

## The Rise of the "Nones"—Religiously Unaffiliated

The second reason for the revival of the interest in angels is the movement away from organized religion to more spiritual beliefs and practices. In 2017 a Pew Research study found that about one-quarter of US adults (27 percent) indicated they were spiritual but not religious, an increase of 8 percent over 5 years.[10] Other Pew Research surveys also showed trends among the religiously unaffiliated. These are people who, when asked about their religious affiliation, indicated that they did not have one. These results showed a 10 percent increase in the religiously unaffiliated over 12 years, from 2007 to 2019.[11] In addition, a recent follow-up study in 2021 showed a 13 percent increase in the unaffiliated over the last 14 years to almost 30 percent.[12] Worldwide, the number of unaffiliated was approximately 16 percent as of 2017.[13]

Why is this move from religion happening? Stephanie Kramer, a lead researcher at Pew Research, suggested that as societies develop and their basic needs are met, they have less need for religion. She also predicted that, based on a few population trend models, the religiously unaffiliated numbers would outpace the Christian population in the United States within a few decades.[14]

## New Age Beliefs

In thinking about this shift, a fundamental question emerges: where are people who were once religiously oriented moving? One answer could be that they are adopting more New Age beliefs and practices. The New Age movement includes an unstructured and wide range of spiritual and religious practices that began in the 1970s in the United States. While we cannot make any direct correlations to the above trends, a 2019 study found that approximately 60 percent of American adults accept at least 1 of these New Age beliefs—spiritual energy can be found in physical objects, psychics, reincarnation, or astrology.[15] A 2019 national Gallup poll of 1,025 Americans showed that 72 percent believed in angels.[16] This correlates with our international survey of 800 adults, which showed 75 percent (600) believed in angels, and of those that did, 36 percent (217) had had an angel encounter. Since some participants had multiple encounters, a total of 779 encounters were reported.[17] To see more survey results, visit *lookingforangelsbook.com*.

To summarize, the awareness of angels has waxed and waned over the centuries. However, we are seeing a resurgence in the belief in the involvement of angels, possibly due to a trend in people moving away from organized religion to spirituality and revolutionary discoveries in quantum physics. Furthermore, without a religious framework, people appear to be more open to connecting with divine entities directly and through psychic intuitive practitioners. A detailed guide on how to do this is presented in Part Three.

# Chapter 7

# Scientific Perspectives

---

*"To believe without questioning or to dismiss without investigation is to behave unscientifically."*
—*Margaret Mead, former president of the Association of the Advancement of Science*

---

As mentioned earlier, after my life crashed and burned despite my intense devotion to organized religion, I had a strong desire to continue my journey, but this time starting at zero, investigating spiritual topics. This took me to several areas where science and spirituality intersected.

One point that was obvious to me at the start was that science, as advanced as it is, is no more than our latest best guess of how our world works. This is abundantly true when considering the existence and nature of angels. This chapter reviews the scientific challenges related to investigating these divine creatures and offers healthy perspectives to consider as you progress on your journey.

## Measurable Phenomena

To begin, while many people across the globe believe in angels and have angel encounters, concrete scientific evidence of angels is hard to find.[1, 2, 3, 4] There are two main reasons for this. The first reason is that as a remnant of the Scientific Revolution, in our society, spiritual phenomena must be measurable and observable in order to be studied scientifically. As you know, numerous TV shows, movies, and YouTube channels present fascinating and compelling pictures, videos, and recordings of ghostly phenomena and other strange sightings occurring in places deemed haunted. However, many, if not all, of these can be characterized as rogue or transient phenomena, possibly because they relate to a particular geographical area or building. Research has been conducted for decades through organizations and educational institutions around the globe in paranormal and parapsychological disciplines with inconsistent findings. Parapsychology (also referred to as psi) investigates psychic phenomena and other paranormal experiences relating to near-death experiences, ghosts, spirits, and more. Organizations such as the Society for Psychical Research in London, the Koestler Parapsychology Unit of the University of Edinburgh, and the Rhine Research Center in Durham, North Carolina, conduct this type of research. I discuss more on how the mind can interact with the physical world in the next chapter.

Unfortunately, even though hundreds of recordings and images of supernatural events have been studied over the years, the evidence is still questioned. In 2021, in the presidential address at the Parapsychological Association and Society for Scientific Exploration annual conference, Dr. Renaud Evrard stated, "Despite over a hundred years of associated research efforts, the status of parapsychology as a scientific endeavor is disputed by a substantial section of the contemporary mainstream scientific community."[5] Dr. Evrard went on to say that this is based on skeptical public perceptions as well as publication bias, which occurs when studies are not published because people within the scientific and research communities do not like or agree with the findings.

It is also important to understand that lack of scientific proof does not mean something does not exist. For example, not too long ago, scientists would have fallen out of their chairs laughing if someone proposed the idea that life on Earth could thrive and reproduce using the toxic chemical arsenic, or that an ecosystem could flourish without light or oxygen—until they discovered both of these life-forms in a lake in California and in the Pacific Ocean.

The good news for those of us who believe in angels and look to interact with them is that this does not have to rock our world. This is because there is another generally accepted phenomenon with little to no confirming evidence, and that is prayer. I know this because my doctoral dissertation centered on the effects of prayer on a person's quality of life. In developing the study, I carefully reviewed 150 years of prayer research. Results across hundreds of studies showed that prayer had been demonstrated to be successful, with mixed results, to a barely significant degree. Throughout my research, I found a few scholars who stated that it might be impossible to study prayer in a laboratory setting because of numerous confounding variables, unknown influencers, the participants' disposition, and even God's will. Despite this, prayer remains embedded in our society as a way to seek comfort, help, and direction.

It is also important to understand that lack of scientific proof does not mean something does not exist. For example, not too long ago, scientists would have fallen out of their chairs laughing if someone proposed the idea that life on Earth could thrive and reproduce using the toxic chemical arsenic, or that an ecosystem could flourish without light or oxygen—until they discovered both of these life-forms in a lake in California and in the Pacific Ocean.[6, 7]

## Observable Phenomena

Not only must evidence of angels be measurable, but it must also be observable. Regarding angels and spirits, however, we must consider our physical limitations of sight and sound and how we can extend our capabilities.

From a strictly physical/biological perspective, our brains are encased in darkness and only receive information through five sensory inputs. In a way, this means we move through this world with a set of microphones, cameras, and other sensors that feed information to our brains, which, in turn, process the inputs and create what we perceive as reality. However, our sensory inputs are not unlimited.

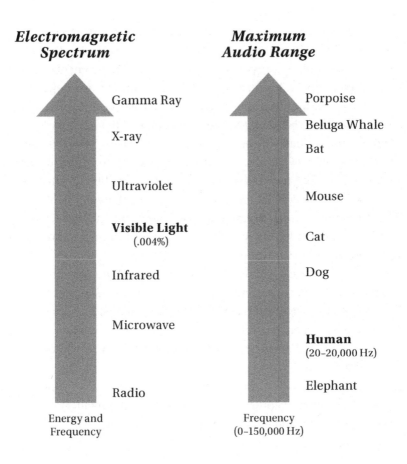

**Electromagnetic Spectrum**

Gamma Ray

X-ray

Ultraviolet

**Visible Light**
(.004%)

Infrared

Microwave

Radio

Energy and Frequency

**Maximum Audio Range**

Porpoise

Beluga Whale

Bat

Mouse

Cat

Dog

**Human**
(20–20,000 Hz)

Elephant

Frequency
(0–150,000 Hz)

For example, our eyes are limited to the frequency of physical light, which is 4.3 to 7.5 x 10 cycles per second or hertz (Hz). This is only .004 percent of the full electromagnetic energy spectrum bombarding us daily. In addition, we can only hear sounds within a frequency range from about 20 to 20,000 Hz.[8, 9] Outside of our visual, audio, and other senses, our brains have difficulty registering any physical sensations. The good news is that we have specialized equipment to help us expand our sensory capabilities just a little bit more.

Conventional cameras are designed to record the frequencies of visible light in the same way as the human eye, with significant differences. For example, an eye can resolve up to an equivalent of a fifty-two-megapixel camera. Modern digital cameras can capture images that are more than one hundred megapixels. Another aspect of vision is dynamic range, which is the ability to capture a range of light and dark images. While cameras have the advantage of being able to "see" the lighter or darker sections of images, the human eye is able to adjust to a greater degree and piece together a more accurate overall image. In addition, in dim and low-light situations, the light sensitivity of the human eye is comparable to digital cameras. However, cameras have the added ability to take long exposures lasting minutes to hours, enabling the camera to absorb very faint light sources.[10]

The human eye's most significant advantage over the standard camera and video equipment is the mind's ability to piece together elements of the scene to create a complete picture that cannot be replicated on a screen or printed page. This could be why some people see phenomena, like angels or spirits, that do not have any photographic or digital record.

There are some instances when spiritual entities can appear to the human eye and be captured on photographic equipment. However, this is not consistent, and many times the images are not clear.

## Nonvisual Frequencies of Energy

To help expand our sensory perception, specially designed equipment can capture broader wavelengths in the electromagnetic spectrum, outside of what the human eye can see. For example, some cameras are designed to record the next higher level of electromagnetic frequencies of ultraviolet light. In addition, X-ray machines record images from even higher frequencies and are commonly used in the medical and security industries, among others. Infrared (IR) energy is slower than visible light and can be recorded with IR cameras that are used in night vision applications. Some animals can see the IR spectrum, making them effective nighttime hunters. The next slowest levels of energy are microwave radiation, followed by radio waves, ultrasound waves, and finally, sound waves, starting at approximately 20,000 Hz.[11]

## Auras, Chakras, and Energy Fields

The human body also produces electricity with muscular activity radiating at 0–250 Hz. In the 1930s, the scientist Semyon Kirlian discovered how to record images of this energy, also called coronal discharges, using a special photographic process. The images showed an aura surrounding the body and other living things. This began many studies and images using his process, identified as Kirlian photography.

Decades later, Dr. Valerie Hunt, a diagnostic radiologist and former professor of physiological science at the University of California, conducted further investigations with more sensitive electromyography equipment and filtering devices. Hunt's work resulted in the discovery of another field of energy much higher than muscular activity, with frequencies of 500–20,000 Hz. The reason this high-frequency electrical energy had not been seen before, according to Hunt, was that scientists believed electrical energy was only expended during muscle contraction, heartbeats, or brain activity. Most interestingly, after further investigation, the researchers noted that these subtle fields of energy corresponded to areas of the body in the ancient Eastern concept of chakras. These energy fields are described as "wheel-like vortices of energy over nerve plexus and endocrine centers of the body" and correspond with specific areas and organs of the body.[12]

Currently, aura imaging cameras, which capture a person's auras and chakras to represent their energetic state visually, are available. They capture the person's aura at the time the image is taken; the aura may change over time. These readings can help the subject understand imbalances in their energy fields and make positive changes in their personal life. Subsequent readings can indicate the result of changes made in the subject's life. Trained operators of aura imaging cameras can be found at health fairs or other holistic health centers.

While aura imaging cameras do not capture images of angels and spirits, they show that real phenomena occur within our bodies that are unseen by the human eye. There is a connection between how energy moves throughout the body and how people interact with angels. We discuss this in the next chapter.

## Paranormal Investigations

The formal discipline of studying angels, ghosts, and other spiritual entities falls under the title of paranormal investigation, with *para* meaning above, beyond, or contrary to anything that is "normal." Some sources identify Charles Hoy Fort (1874–1932) as one of the first authors and researchers to scientifically investigate physical anomalies. Since then, many researchers and "ghost hunters" have been gathering information in an effort to verify, explain, or debunk paranormal phenomena. As mentioned above, numerous TV shows and movies report instances of supernatural events and amazing stories of spiritual forces interacting with our physical world. Some are extremely convincing; others are obviously dramatized to increase box office sales and viewership. It is outside of the scope of this book to delve into the images and recordings available. The purpose of reviewing this topic is to show how paranormal investigation is conducted in an attempt to extend the reach of human physical senses to record images of the unseen world.

Some investigators provoke spirits in order to capture activity. Some take a gentler approach. Some send ghosts to the light, and others don't. I can add that many law enforcement agencies use the services of paranormal investigators in solving crimes. While the information provided by the investigational psychic cannot be used in court, it can help to guide investigators in directions not previously considered. Going back to the scientific method, one ongoing issue is that paranormal phenomena need to be reproducible. And, of course, critics say all images are photoshopped and everything else is contrived.

We must keep in mind that even
the most pragmatic scientists will
agree that we do not understand
all types of energy and matter and
that there are many phenomena
occurring in the universe that we
have yet to explain.

The equipment used in paranormal investigations is chosen to capture and record images and sounds outside human capabilities. Devices like digital recorders, digital camcorders, and special microphones capture a wide range of sound, both near and at a distance. Electromagnetic field (EMF) detectors are used for frequencies in a specific area. Investigators may have a few different types of sensors, with some capable of recording very low frequencies (50–1,000 Hz) to very high frequencies (1,000–20,000 Hz). In addition, geophones can be used to sense vibrations, footsteps, and noises, and grid laser lights can be used to make it easier to detect movement or shadows.[13]

## Even the Most Brilliant Minds Are Comfortable with the Unknown

To summarize, if we restrict ourselves to accepting a phenomenon as real only if it is measurable and observable in a modern laboratory, the existence of angels, ghosts, and spirits will remain in question. We must keep in mind that even the most pragmatic scientists will agree that we do not understand all types of energy and matter and that there are many phenomena occurring in the universe that we have yet to explain. It is essential to be aware of the fundamental error of thinking that because science has advanced humankind to an incredible degree, science can explain all aspects of reality.

In addition, there are three philosophical challenges to consider, suggested by Dr. Zohair Abdul-Rahman from the Yaqeen Institute for Islamic Research. The first is the idea that angels and the supernatural world were initially superstitions invented to help humans cope with an uncertain future or natural phenomena, like the weather, comets, or shooting stars. This may have happened in the past but does not disprove their existence then or now.

The second philosophical challenge relates to something called the genetic fallacy. This is when an idea is dismissed because the source may be in question. For example, if someone says an angel visited them at night and told them their sister was going to have a baby, some may dismiss the statement because they do not believe in angels. But it does not change the fact that the sister received a positive pregnancy test the next day.

The third challenge is the idea that angels are not real because there is no scientific proof that they exist. The counterargument to this idea is that until there is scientific proof showing that it is impossible for them to exist, they cannot be ruled out as being real.[14]

Certainly, there is a lot to think about and continue to study. But, in the meantime, it is reasonable to make up our minds based on our own knowledge and experiences, as well as the considerations of those who have reported events that have been real to them.

*Chapter 8*

# Psychological Perspectives

---

*"Our brains filter out most of the unseen world; however, we can expand our view."*

—*Scott Guerin*

---

I f you put this book down and look around, you will see your surroundings and hear the sounds of nature, traffic, or a TV in the background. You might have thoughts about where you are, in addition to what you have to do by the end of the day, wondering if a storm is coming or what you will have for lunch.

Conventional thought is that everything comes down to how your mind perceives all available inputs, in addition to your memory, when piecing together your reality. I emphasize *your* reality because we all have different physical capabilities, experiences, and memories that will not exactly match anyone else's. The differences can be significant: the sky may not be the same shade of blue in another person's world. A mind-bending thought is that since our brains only recognize the physical world through our sensory receptors, what we perceive is not really reality. A video of a tree is not a tree—it is a recorded representation. In this sense, our view of the world is always one step away from reality.

Not only is our perception of reality constrained by our physical senses, but our nervous system also controls how we experience reality. One example is a section of the brain called the parietal lobe, located near the back and top of the head. Its purpose is to process sensory information, in addition to providing a sense of time and space. Neurologists conducted studies measuring the changes in cerebral blood flow to this area with experienced Tibetan Buddhist meditators. The results showed that the blood flow to the parietal lobe was significantly reduced during meditation, possibly providing the experience of endless time and space associated with deep meditation.[1] However, there is yet another aspect of how we experience and influence our reality.

## Parapsychology

Understanding how our mind can interact with and impact our physical world is known as parapsychology (psi). While it is not directly related to interacting with angels, psi research explores topics that are beyond what we know about how we perceive and influence our reality. I briefly discuss three related subtopics here. They relate to mind-matter interaction (MMI), distant healing intention, and other psi phenomena.

### *Mind-Matter Interaction*

One of the earliest study designs to determine if humans can manipulate physical objects with mental intentions used dice. Researchers conducted an analysis of 148 dice studies to determine if there was evidence of mental intentions influencing the outcome of tossed dice.[2] Random number generators (RNG) can be used in place of dice in studies. The focus of RNG studies is whether mental intentions can influence a circuit that produces a stream of approximately one thousand random ones and zeroes per second. This means that the chance of the circuit producing either one of these numbers is 50 percent. In a similar fashion to the analysis of dice studies, researchers conducted a review of 832 studies to determine if participants could influence the generator to output particular numbers or change a distribution solely based on their intention.[3] In both cases, the results showed a statistically significant change in the behavior of the dice and RNGs as a result of human intention.

Dr. Dean Radin, chief scientist at the Institute of Noetic Sciences in Novato, California, and a seminal researcher in consciousness development, stated:

> *After 60 years of experiments using tossed dice and their modern progeny, electronic RNGs, researchers have produced persuasive, consistent replicated evidence that mental intention is associated with the behavior of these physical systems. We know that the experimental results are not due to chance, selected reporting, poor experimental design, only a few individuals, or only a few experimenters.[4]*

## *Distant Healing Intention*

An area of study related to MMI is distant healing intention (DHI). DHI includes intentional healing activities claiming to transcend the usual constraints of distance. This can occur through prayer or other intentional practices such as remote reiki, spiritual healing, or remote energy healing. As mentioned in the previous chapter, I spent more than 2 years analyzing the impact of DHI through 150 years of prayer research, in addition to research regarding the influence of physical systems with paranormal manipulation, while developing my dissertation, "The Effects of Prayer on the Quality of Life in Older Adults" (Fielding Graduate University, Santa Barbara, California).

It is outside of the scope of this book to review decades of findings; however, it is safe to say that there are numerous studies that show the positive effects of intention in bacteria, plants, animals, and several human physiological conditions. The results are inconsistent and difficult to reproduce. Some researchers suggest this could be related to the many possible confounding variables when studying the impact of DHI, such as any hesitance on the part of the practitioner,

Angels seem to be able to move in and out of our typical physical and mental boundaries at specific times. In addition, they can even be selective by appearing to one person but not another in the same room at the same time. Can we expand our perception of information beyond our physical limitations and begin to experience things we have not been able to thus far? Can we develop psychic abilities just as we do physical abilities? Many people are saying we can.

the severity of the condition, or even the fact that a person's life path may not include perfect health. As Dr. Radin and colleagues stated in a recent review article of the evidence of DHI:

> *While some significant experimental effects have been observed, the evidence to date does not yet provide confidence in its clinical efficacy. The purported "nonlocal" nature of DHI raises significant methodological and theoretical challenges.*[5]

The authors went on to point out that in spite of the challenges, the practice of DHI is widespread, with more distant healers than therapists practicing any other form of complementary or alternative medicine in the United Kingdom. In addition, in the United States, DHI is the most common healing practice outside of conventional medicine.

## Other Psi Phenomena

In considering other psi phenomena—such as precognition, telepathy, remote viewing, and prediction of future events—research on this topic becomes even more intriguing. While some studies show fascinating results, others do not have the same findings. Also, there are variations in study designs and methods that make it difficult to compare studies. Another challenge with this area of research is that scientists have no hypothesis about how a person can predict such outcomes as which card will be shown a few seconds in advance or about how the activity of T cells changes during a remote healing session.

Because of these challenges, funding for robust studies is difficult to find. The good news is that there is some ongoing research in organizations around the world, as mentioned in the previous chapter. Another excellent source of psychical research is the Institute of Noetic Sciences (*noetic.org*). I encourage you to dig into the fascinating research being conducted at any of these organizations.

The reason why I took this slight detour into these psi phenomena is that it is important to understand that there is much to learn about how we piece together our world and how we create our reality. We know quite a bit about our physical senses and nervous system, but we have much to learn about the capabilities of our mind, and with that comes the ability to interact with the mostly unseen world of angels and spirit guides. Angels seem to be able to move in and out of our typical physical and mental boundaries at specific times. In addition, they can even be selective by appearing to one person but not another in the same room at the same time. Can we expand our perception of information beyond our physical limitations and begin to experience things we have not been able to thus far? Can we develop psychic abilities just as we do physical abilities? Many people say we can.

Moving on from looking at our physical and mental capabilities and how we interpret the world around us, an important distinction must be made between our physical selves and our mental selves—specifically, the difference between our brain and our mind. Is our mind a part of our brain, or does it exist on its own?

The reason why this is such an intriguing question is that if our mind is separate from our brain and nervous system, does that make at least part of us nonphysical? If so, we could very well be closer to angels and spirits than we ever knew. This is a huge step, but first let's take a look at some of the basic components of this idea.

### We Are Not Our Thoughts

In addition to our sensory inputs and our nervous system, where does our mind get its information from? We piece together these sensory inputs and make sense of them to create our reality. But what about our thoughts? Where do they come from? Attempts to answer these questions immediately place us in murky territory. Does our mind or consciousness reside within our physical nervous system and brain or somewhere else?

An important concept to understand is that you and your thoughts are two different things. This is easily observed when we are meditating—or trying to. For those of you who have little or no experience meditating, you can see what I mean by trying to quiet your mind. You can do this right now by closing your eyes and concentrating on your breath for one minute (not while driving, please). For most of us, thoughts will interrupt our concentration (like you have to pay a bill tomorrow, a good movie is on TV tonight, you have to go to the store, etc.).

Here is the key question: who is observing these thoughts by either addressing them or trying to ignore them in order to get back to concentrating on your breathing? The answer is that you are. It is you who is observing the thoughts bubbling up in your mind. Some say it is you that is your soul, the eternal being that is living in this temporary physical existence. The thoughts you are observing come from one of two places: from your brain or from outside you and your brain. This could be where information from the spirit world interacts with us.

We discuss this in greater detail later in the book, but let's take a few steps back to see how the ideas of our brain and mind have advanced over the years.

## A Short History of the Brain and Mind

Before the seventeenth century, a leading perspective was that the mind and the body were one unit. Because of this, diseases were thought to be the result of a person's transgressions, and some believed that for the soul to ascend to heaven, the body had to remain intact.[6] A dramatic shift in thinking occurred when the French philosopher and mathematician René Descartes proposed that the mind and body were two different substances, described as dualism. The mind was immaterial, and the body was material and unthinking. This concept opened the door for deeper analysis of human anatomy, and following the trends of the time, a mechanistic view of the body was adopted and the human mind was identified as a separate entity for the first time.

As you can imagine, numerous theories of the mind have been proposed, accepted, rejected, and revised over the centuries. Advancements in neurophysiology and neuropsychology have uncovered much about how the brain operates and illuminated concepts about the nature of the mind, generating almost continuous updates to established theories. One theory that has emerged over the years is that the parts of the brain, rather than operating as independent areas with specific functions, work more synergistically. One of these newer theories is the hierarchically mechanistic mind (HMM), which describes the mind as a complex adaptive system similar to a computer. Psychologist Dr. Gregg Henriques of James Madison University, Harrisonburg, Virginia, compared this system to a physical book with a cover, pages, size, weight, and more. The information contained in the book is the mind, and the experience of reviewing the information is consciousness.[7]

Without reviewing every theory and its iterations, we highlight two general schools of thought that are most prominent. One is called physicalism; it defines the mind as a result of the neurological connections within the brain that translate and interpret inputs from sensory receptors (sight, hearing, taste, touch, and smell) together with memory. The other perspective, called dualism, acknowledges that the mind and the associated phenomenon of consciousness are something beyond the brain. In this perspective, mental processes extend beyond the nervous system and reside somewhere "out there," suggesting a yet-to-be-understood physical explanation of how the mind works.[8]

The physicalist perspective is appealing to many researchers because neurological processes are (here are those words, again) observable and measurable. However, the famed Swiss psychiatrist and psychoanalyst Carl Jung believed in the existence of angels and a nonphysical aspect of our reality. He focused much of his work on the spiritual aspects of life and understood the dangers of viewing the world solely as material or mechanistic. He wrote:

> *Under the influence of scientific materialism, everything that could not be seen with the eyes or touched with the hands was held in doubt. Such things were even laughed at for their supposed affinity with metaphysics. Nothing was considered to be scientific or admitted to be true unless it could be perceived by the sense or traced back to a physical being.*[9]

106

The challenging aspect of dualism and the idea that the mind is beyond the brain is that it is difficult, if not impossible, to measure. In considering the nature of the mind and whether it resides within a complex neurological system or outside of it, Jung believed the human psyche, composed of conscious and unconscious thoughts, was not bound to the physical brain. He wrote:

> *We must completely give up the idea of the psyche's being somehow connected with the brain and remember instead the "meaningful" or "intelligent" behavior of the lower organisms, which are without a brain. Here we find ourselves much closer to the formal factor, which, as I have said, has nothing to do with brain activity.*[10]

Jung also interviewed a woman who had had an out-of-body experience giving birth to her child. The woman slipped into a coma for about half an hour after a significant loss of blood and was able to verify several details of the room and who was present during the time she was unconscious. Jung commented:

> *Then we must ask ourselves whether there is some other nervous substrate in us, apart from the cerebrum, that can think and perceive, or whether the psychic processes that go on in us during loss of consciousness are synchronistic phenomena, i.e., events which have no causal connection with organic processes. This last possibility cannot be rejected out of hand in view of the existence of ESP, i.e., of perceptions independent of space and time, which cannot be explained as processes in the biological substrate.*[11]

One of Jung's more notable and controversial contributions is the idea of collective unconsciousness. This theory is based on the idea that the mind is more than the brain, with all humans connected

In psychological terms, we cannot verify what a person saw or heard to determine if an angelic encounter was physically real, occurring only in the mind, or taking place due to something immaterial, spiritual, or otherwise "out there." Jung knew we are both spiritual and material beings and live in a world where we experience both.

through the unconscious mind, with access to the history of thoughts and behaviors of all humankind. It is easy to apply a metaphysical perspective to this term; however, if you read through Jung's writings, he viewed this as inherited instincts rather than common spiritual connections.

In psychological terms, we cannot verify what a person saw or heard to determine if an angelic encounter was physically real, occurring only in the mind, or taking place due to something immaterial, spiritual, or otherwise "out there." Jung knew we are both spiritual and material beings and live in a world where we experience both. He suggested we keep an eye on both realities:

> *If I recognize only naturalistic values and explain everything in physical terms, I shall depreciate, hinder, or even destroy the spiritual development of my patients, and if I hold exclusively to a spiritual interpretation, then I will misunderstand and do violence to the natural man in his right to exist as a physical being.*[12]

## We Can Train Ourselves to Interact with Angels

If you accept the reality of angels and the spirit world, while science catches up, and would like to interact with angels or spirit teams, there are two ways to begin to make these connections. Nichole goes into detail about how you can do this in the next chapters, but to prep yourself to begin this journey, you can train yourself to see the evidence and signs of them around you. You can also shift your vibrational levels to be able to experience these celestial beings.

One common theme of the conversations and research I have completed with psychics, intuitives, and healers is that they all say connecting with angels and our spirit team is a skill that can be learned and developed by anyone. Still, it can be intimidating when we meet someone who seems gifted with psychic or intuitive abilities that came naturally to them, even as children. Even so, I have never heard or read of a psychic, intuitive, or healer of any kind who says that you either have it or you don't.

As a psychologist and educator, I can understand what psychics have been saying about learning to connect with the spirit world. I have been experiencing a greater awareness of spirits and spirit guides in the last few years. Initially, I asked to slowly learn about this rather than have a dramatic event shake me to my soul. However, in recent months, I have been asking to up the pace.

## Increasing Our Awareness

One of the key things to keep in mind in becoming aware of and interacting with angels is to trust our feelings, thoughts, and intuitions. We must also think less about how or why we may feel this way or that and simply believe that we have an inner guidance system that receives input from sources outside of ourselves.

This could be viewed as a new category of human intelligence waiting to be identified. To date, human development psychologists have identified eight intelligences: mathematical, language, body/physical, spatial, musical, intra- and interpersonal, and naturalistic. People who have exceptional natural skills in math, music, sports, and so on are identified as having intelligences in these areas. It's important to note that not only people with these strengths can be good at them; others can also achieve a high level of success, just not as easily. As you will see, psychic abilities can also be learned, just like riding a bike, playing an instrument, or playing a new video game.

Here is an excellent example of how we can increase our awareness and sensitivity. In college, I bought a used sound system with excellent components that included a high-end receiver, huge speakers, and a vinyl record turntable. (Turntables are making a comeback now; then, they were state-of-the-art!) I would blast my favorite Elton John or Fleetwood Mac albums at deafening levels in my dorm room. It was great.

One day a friend who lived in my dorm came pounding on my door. He was tall and thin, with neatly kept, wavy black hair, and always dressed well. He was also a computer engineering major who had an even better sound system in his room a few doors down from me.

"What the hell are you doing?" he screamed over the music.

"I know it's loud, but everyone outside is enjoying the music," I said sarcastically, as I turned down the volume. "You play your music just as loud. So what's your problem?"

"I don't care about the sound," he shot back. "It's just that you have played those two albums a dozen times over the last two weeks and are ruining them."

"Ugh, that's why I got them, so I could play them," I replied.

"Yes, but you are ruining them. You can only play a vinyl album about five times before the needle starts wearing down the highs and roughing up the lows. After you buy a new album, you make a high-end recording on another medium and keep the record as a master. Now, your records sound like crap, they're all midrange, and you can't hear the sound of each instrument like you can in a good-quality recording," he explained, talking to me as if I were in kindergarten.

Knowing that I needed further education, he invited me to his room to hear a few of his jazz pieces recorded from albums on his system. He stopped and replayed parts to highlight what he was talking about.

"Can you hear the flute section, wind instruments, the baritones, and how you can easily distinguish them from one another?" He asked in a way that begged me to confirm that I understood and appreciated music at this high level.

"Yes, I see what you mean," I replied.

With time, I was sure I could get to his level of awareness, but I was not interested in going that far. Elton John's songs seemed just fine, even after playing them twenty or thirty times on my turntable.

In the same way we learn to identify sounds on a record, we can learn to see the many signs the spirit world sends, letting us know they are with us. In our research on angel encounters, 75 percent of study participants indicated they believed in angels, and of those, 36 percent said they had had angel encounters. We defined several types of angel encounters, such as seeing repeating number patterns or sequences, seeing items like coins or feathers, or seeing specific animals or insects repeatedly. Visit *lookingforangelsbook.com* for full study results.

## Shifting Our Vibration

Another perspective is that as we shift our vibrational levels, we gain the ability to experience the sights and sounds of the spiritual realm. As mentioned in the previous chapter, Dr. Valerie Hunt identified energy levels in the human body that were not generated by muscular activity and showed that energy changes depending on what we are doing. For example, in further research with a woman dancing in a meditative state, Dr. Hunt was able to record diminished energy levels in the dancer's upper and lower arm and back and increased levels at the top of her head as she danced.[13] This change in the distribution of the energy in the dancer's body corresponds with the energy of the chakras and how energy is channeled from outer parts of the body through the crown chakra (top of the head) during heightened states of meditation.

An excellent example of the impact of increasing our vibrational levels is provided by award-winning harpist Peter Sterling. Peter began to play the harp after a series of life-changing angelic encounters in the canyons of Sedona, Arizona, in the early 1990s. He discovered how to interact with the spirit world and how to facilitate a vibrant connection with Spirit as he explored Sedona's Red Rock outback canyons. It was through these interactions that he developed the divine music of the angels in his work. You can learn more about Peter and his music on his website, *harpmagic.com*, or listen to Nichole's fascinating interview with him on the *A Psychic's Story* podcast, episode 121: "The Song of the Angels."

A big takeaway from Peter's work for me was his suggestions about how to begin to see angelic beings. He explained that you should get into a calm, meditative place in a room with low levels of light and begin to ask for your angels to show themselves to you. Slowly and subtly, you will see small flashes and sparks of light, mostly in your peripheral vision. After you spend time in this state of mind in several sessions and ask for your angels to show themselves, they will become more and more apparent. Your journey from there will be your own and will be different for everyone. I am at the very beginning of mine.

Another example of the impact of increasing our vibrational levels can be found in the life of Anna Gannon. During a meditation retreat in India, she began to experience what felt like an electric charge shooting up her spine. Eventually, she started hearing people's thoughts and feelings as her psychic and intuitive abilities opened. She described her experience as follows: "I awoke an electrical force within my body. This electricity opened my intuitive abilities and allowed me to understand and remember the energy that resides within and around us all." You can learn more about Anna and her journey on her website, *annagannon.com*, or listen to her interview with Nichole on the *A Psychic's Story* podcast, episode 115: "Trust."

For those of you who are just learning about the spirit world and taking the first small steps to make spiritual connections, like me, these ideas will help. It is a process that you have total control over and that you can proceed with at your own pace. It's all a matter of having an open mind and heart and trusting that you are surrounded by love and support beyond your imagination.

## Why Do Imaginary Friends Go Away?

When considering our brains possibly changing to perceive information beyond our current physical capabilities, I thought of imaginary friends. It is estimated that by the age of 7, approximately 37 percent of children have an imaginary friend. These can appear as humans, animals, or fantasy figures and can be a part of the child's life for years. Children with these friends tend to be less shy, laugh more with friends, and be better at imagining how someone else might think.[14]

Just like with many other things a child experiences from age two to age seven, the brain strengthens if certain neural connections are used consistently, and these are extinguished if not used at all. For example, if a four-year-old starts practicing the piano, their abilities will develop. If they stop at age eight, their skills will diminish. Perhaps, it is the same way with a child's perception of an imaginary friend. As they grow, if other friends accept and share their experiences with their imaginary friends, these relationships will grow. However, if a child is laughed at or not supported by their parents when they mention their friend, the friend goes away. Perhaps these imaginary friends could be angels. Living in a society that does not fully accept them, they go away as a child matures.

As you will learn in Part Three, understanding the presence and interaction of angels in your life can be a great first step in establishing a strong relationship with your guides.

## Angels in the Clinical Setting

Psychologists and psychiatrists generally follow the scientific method, meaning everything must be measurable and observable to be real. In a clinical context, this can play out in two considerably different ways: The first is through psychiatry, the behavioral branch of medicine with a focus on drug therapy. The second is the psychological approach, in which a therapist helps the client by communicating and interacting with them to assess, diagnose, and treat troubling emotional reactions, ways of thinking, and/or behaviors.

The practice of psychiatry is based on the idea that the root of mental and emotional problems is biological. The patient's reports of communication with angels or spiritual beings may be seen as a symptom of a psychosis-related disorder, often schizophrenia or bipolar disorder, as a form of visual and auditory hallucinations.

From this perspective, the images and sounds the patient "sees" and "hears" are not real and are caused by adverse chemical reactions and/or abnormalities in the brain.[15] If the symptoms are severe, treatment would usually be antipsychotic drug therapy or hospitalization if needed.

A common psychological approach is person-centered therapy, also known as Rogerian or client-based therapy. This means that the therapist conveys unconditional positive regard to the client by being empathetic, not judgmental, and not making any assessment regarding whether the voices or images are real or not. Instead, the focus is on how the images and voices impact the client. If the relationship is positive, they listen and treat the angel as of central importance to the client and support the interactions. Areas to explore are whether it is a fantasy, real, or concrete for the patient. Or could it be a defense mechanism—"I can't make any connections with people, but I can with my angel"? From a client-centered perspective, it does not matter if the angel is real or not if it is real to the patient.

Dr. Cassandra Vieten of the University of California and Dr. David Lukoff of the Spiritual Competency Academy believe that a robust body of evidence shows that one's spiritual and religious background, beliefs, and practices (SRBBPs) play a role in psychological well-being for most people. While not specifically pertaining to angels, SRBBPs have been shown to elevate mood, lessen distress, and improve coping processes. The authors point out that research shows most clients would like their therapists to discuss SRBBPs in their sessions, and those whose therapists did rated their care at the highest levels. Nonetheless, 75 percent of psychology training programs do not provide any courses in religion or spirituality, underscoring the need for further training and awareness programs. The authors believe that attention to people's spiritual and religious domains should result in greater client satisfaction, better outcomes, and a more complete approach to clinical care.[16]

From my perspective, most therapists would not quickly diagnose angel communications as a psychotic symptom. The only time a client-centered therapist would challenge a client's thinking about a relationship or communication with a spiritual being would be the following:

- The client was troubled as a result of the interactions.

- The client was directed to inflict harm on themselves or others.

- The client was encouraged to invoke any type of violence.

- The client was directed to do something extremely disruptive for themselves or their family (leave their family and move away, run away, quit their job with no other way to support themselves, and so on).

To summarize, considering the reality of angels from scientific and psychological perspectives is challenging and at the same time reassuring, depending on how you decide to look at the topic. Many questions relate to what the mind is and how it interacts with the nervous system and brain. For example, do angels operate at such a high frequency that we have yet to discover how to record their actions? Or, is there another form of energy surrounding us that we presently are not aware of that other beings have learned to access? As Jung stated, we are both spiritual and material beings, and we should keep in mind that we live in a world where we experience both.

The question of the reality of angels and our interactions with them can only be answered by you, through your knowledge and experiences. Our hope is that this book will assist you in exploring your relationship with angels and help you feel comfortable connecting with them and your spirit guides.

# Part Three

# Understanding Modern-Day Angels

Nichole Bigley

There are those who have reached God directly, retaining no trace of worldly limits, and remembering their own identity perfectly. These might be called the teachers of teachers because, although they're no longer visible, their image can still be called upon. And they will appear when and where it is most helpful for them to do so. No one can call on them in vain. Nor is there anyone of whom they're unaware. All needs are known to them, and all mistakes are recognized and overlooked by them. The time will come when this is understood. Meanwhile, they give all their gifts to the teachers of God who look to them for help.

—*Helen Schucman and William Thetford,*
A Course in Miracles

# Chapter 9

# Your Spirit Team
## (aka Modern-Day Angels)

---

*"If you wish to not love, keep your heart sealed. If you prefer not to see, keep your eyes shut. If you don't want to hear, keep your ears closed. If you wish to fully live, then open your mind, heart, and soul to all the possibilities the Universe has to offer. Everything is waiting there for you, at this very moment. All you have to do is believe and ask, and we will assist."*

*—Your Spirit Team*

---

My memories of and connection to Spirit occurred very early in life. One night, when I was about four years old, my father was putting me to bed. He told me that before we come here to Earth, we pick who our parents are. Imagine his surprise when I replied, "I know."

I immediately recalled what I would describe now as the galaxy or space. I was looking down at Earth and saw a little girl playing outside. She had beautiful dark curls and a sweet smile. I said, "She's the one. I want her to be my mother." As I started to move forward, a voice told me, "Not now." I felt disappointed, but before I could turn around, I heard, "It's time."

The next thing I knew, I was zipping down toward Earth. I don't have many memories of being in the womb, but I do clearly remember what it was like to be born. As soon as the light hit my eyes, I felt the dense heaviness of having a physical body and the overwhelming sensation of being cold. Yes, I was crying, as babies do. However, it was because my next thought was "No! Not this. Not this again."

Even though I was only four years old, I did my best to explain all this to my dad. I can still recall the look on his face. The next day, my mom asked me to share with her what I had told my dad, and I shared the same story with the same details. This time, however, I remembered more things, like how the hospital room was set up, how many people (doctors and nurses) were there, where I was taken to get cleaned up, and more. I can't speak on behalf of my parents, but I can only imagine that it was at this point that they knew they had a different type of child on their hands.

Remembering what it was like on the other side helped me connect with Universal Energy and Source, including my own spirit team in this life. Recalling how my communication with them was telepathic, through thoughts and emotions, before I was born is helpful because that's primarily how they communicate with me and send me messages to this day.

As mentioned in "Our Stories" at the beginning of the book, we all have a spirit team. It is composed of a variety of enlightened spiritual beings, or what might also be considered modern-day angels (which I often refer to using the collective terms *angels*, *guides*, and *team*). This universal team includes archangels, ascended masters, deities, guardian angels, spirit guides, and departed loved ones. Some even have elemental beings like fairies or dragons by their side. (But that is a book for another day.)

In the upcoming chapters, you will learn how these spiritual beings differ and how to distinguish between them. But regardless of their differences, they are all here for the same reason: to help us stay connected to the Divine and navigate our life on Earth. Our angels and guides work behind the scenes to guide and help us, to reawaken our gifts and align our spirit with our higher self in order to achieve the mission we set for ourselves before we came here to this planet.

Most people think they have one guardian angel or spirit guide, but we are not limited to just one team member. We have anywhere from five to upwards of one hundred or more around us at any given time. It has been my experience that, depending on the person and the particular needs or situations they are experiencing, different members of their spirit team step forward. You may have a stronger connection to one—as I do with Archangel Michael—but you still have many standing by and ready to assist at a moment's notice.

Our spirit team is a rather eager and ambitious group because their *soul* purpose is to inspire and motivate us, reassure and console us in times of need, and even steer us away from danger when they can. In order to do this, they will send us messages and signs, remove obstacles, open doors, create opportunities, and offer solutions. Their job throughout all of this is to love and guide us during our life in order to embody the frequency of love. Being in the frequency of love helps you remember and return to your soul's innate intuitive abilities and basic instincts.

Believing in, trusting, and acting on your spirit team's guidance can make the difference between living a spiritual life and existence that is in flow and living a life in which you feel stuck and not in alignment. If you seek growth or change and rely primarily on positive intentions and thoughts, the Universe can only do so much on your behalf. Your team is engaged but can't move things forward or even manifest all the possibilities the Universe has to offer. If you give them permission to interact with you and ask them for messages and signs— ask them to open those doors, to create opportunities, and to bring you solutions—you are removing yourself from trying to control the outcome and trusting in the Divine, which in turn generates results in ways that are in alignment with your higher self. There is a missing step in the saying "ask and you shall receive." It should actually be "ask and be guided in order to receive."

The more you are open to your angels and guides and communicating with them, the more you begin to see synchronicities throughout your daily life. You begin to see how they use your own intuitive senses—mentally, emotionally, physically, and spiritually—to communicate with you. Your universal team members are assigned to you for a reason; they know what you signed up to do in this lifetime and even other lifetimes. They know the optimal path for you to get there. And they only have the best intentions in mind for you to achieve your heart's desires.

As beings with free will, our choices allow the energy around us to flow. Tuning into your angels and guides gives you the opportunity for the greater happiness that is in divine flow. Engaging them will enable your life to move at a purposeful pace. Understanding who these beings are and how your universal team is composed is the first step to becoming more consciously aware. And remember, no matter who is on your spirit team, they will only support and assist you, not do the work for you. It is up to you, and you alone, to act on your team's advice in a way that feels right for you.

## Spirit Team Basics

As mentioned earlier in this chapter, our universal teams are composed of enlightened beings, including archangels, certain religious figures (also known as ascended masters), guardian angels, deities, spirit guides, and loved ones from the other side. They also include the higher power or creator source that we all came from and All That Is. Call It God, Yahweh, Allah, the Divine, Universe, Universal Source, Source, Spirit, of I Am, of God, or something else: Spirit says it doesn't have a preferred name.

Like that of all energetic beings, God's energy doesn't have a gender. Some angels and guides do energetically feel more masculine, feminine, or androgynous at times, depending on how they portray themselves and how someone interprets them. For example, nurturing might feel "feminine," while directness might feel "masculine." In regard to your loved ones, they will present themselves with human traits, such as gender and age, in order for you to recognize or relate to them.

God, or Universal Source, is definitely part of your spirit team and can be called upon at any time. The energy is magnificent and unlimited. Because that energy source can sometimes be difficult for human beings to comprehend, it is often easier for us to connect with our spirit team instead.

Because we all come from Source and will return to it when we depart our physical bodies, we are all one and connected. The concept that God created us in His image is indeed true. But in reality, we are a piece of Universal Source that split off in order for the Creator to experience any and all levels of existence through us. We are a living extension and embodiment of All That Is; a part of God exists in each of our souls.

Source is everywhere. It spreads across all time, space, and dimensions. It emanates around and through every living soul, including plants and animals. When God channels through people using their intuitive abilities, miracles can happen.

Spirit says that God's plan is for us to work with Source to create a living heaven on Earth. This doesn't require that we worship God. Rather, when we have an understanding about how the Universe and our spirit team work together on our behalf, we can embrace and live with love. It goes back to our life's purpose: to experience, give, and receive love. It is through this that we vibrate at a frequency that creates healing environments and harmonious connections with All That Is. When we find love and peace within ourselves, we, in turn, can be in gratitude and in service to others.

I believe in God because it was God I felt when I was in "space" looking down at Earth. It was through Source's love and guidance that I felt and heard the answers when I was about to incarnate again in this lifetime. When I was a child, I could still feel that connection, and I intuitively knew that while I was no longer on the other side, I was still part of Source. Our souls can never be separate from God—we are but a drop of water in one ocean. It was also because of this experience and sense of knowing that my relationship with my angels and guides blossomed. As I got older, whenever I would question what was "real," I would close my eyes, take deep breaths, and ask to be reunited with that feeling of oneness, the energy of God that is so clear, peaceful, and safe. This is what I wish for all of you reading this book—for you to feel this omnipresence within and around you.

Another member of your spirit team, or family of beings, is your higher self. Your higher self is an intelligent being who is your eternal consciousness. It is an inseparable ray of the Universe and, therefore, "one-self." Some people also refer to the higher self as an oversoul. (As humans, we certainly like to name and define things.) An oversoul is the same concept as the higher self, in that we each have an over-encompassing aspect of our being that is eternal and oversees all we (as human beings and souls) do.

Our higher self is not held back by one lifetime. Rather, it oversees and is connected to all our lifetimes simultaneously in this Earth plane and other places and times of existence. This enables our higher self to give us access to our innate spiritual connection to Source Energy and all that there is. Within this connection is the ability to receive information without our ego, subconscious mind, or perceived "logic" getting in the way. We can tap into our higher self by quieting and stilling our logical mind. When we are truly connected, it is a way to release the ego's need to be in control and have a say in what is coming through to us.

Communications from our higher self are very subtle, and this is why quieting the mind is essential. Otherwise, it can be easy to ignore or discount the messages from our higher self altogether. Intention is key in order to be open to communication and input from the higher self. One way I can distinguish if I am connecting with my higher self is that it feels like a part of myself that is crystal clear—clear in how it feels and what it wants. There is no questioning what I am thinking or feeling; it just *is*. If the message is really strong, I refer to it as my *gut* intuition, a sense of knowing that is so big I can't shake it.

It is important to connect to this aspect of ourselves not only because we receive messages and information more clearly, but also because we come into alignment with the deepest part of our souls and what we are here to do. Doing so also makes it easier for us to be in touch with God and our spirit team.

Because our higher self, or oversoul, can be incarnate in the past, present, and future in other lifetimes, timelines, and realities, we can connect with the other parts of ourselves that share a soul signature with us. These beings are not only a part of ourselves, but also a part of our soul lineage and are just one of many reasons we might be drawn to certain cultures, places, or times. Communicating and being in alignment with your higher self helps you make choices in your day-to-day life based on your higher purpose. I review how to connect with your higher self later in this chapter.

Doubt, fear, disbelief, hopelessness, and lack of faith are what shut down our connection to God and our higher self. Believe in yourself. Trust that the connection will get stronger. Release the fear that is holding you back and making you feel stuck. Your intention must also be pure. If you are seeking to communicate and be in alignment with Source or your higher self for someone else or to feed your ego, or for any reason other than being in a state of oneness, then it won't work.

## What Is Oneness?

Before I came back to Earth while I was on the other side, I experienced being in a state of BE-ing or oneness. It was a divine union with Universal Source, our Creator, God. This energy is love, and within that, love exists, along with peace, joy, and happiness. Oneness, or God's energy, is palpable and meant to be felt. It is innate within each of us, and it is our spiritual right to be in a state of BE-ing and connected to oneness. This is the vibration at which our angels and guides operate, and when our own vibration matches it, we are able to tune into the frequency (like a radio signal) that allows us to connect to one another and spiritual beings in that same state or on the same channel.

Some people may think of this state as "high vibes" or "high vibration." However, a few years ago, when communicating with Spirit, I was told that it is a myth and misconception that we need to "raise our vibration" in order to connect with that which is within us, the Divine Source, or our spirit team. The terms *high* and *low* denote a hierarchy. In actuality, being in oneness is a state of BE-ing present and tapping or tuning into the vibrations of love, bliss, and peace. (Note: For now, I use the term *higher self* not because of hierarchy, but because it helps me visualize and picture the part of my soul that oversees this life and my other lives and souls.) Therefore, being in a state of oneness is the best way to strengthen your connection to God, your angels, guides, and departed loved ones.

### Becoming Present with Oneness

There are many ways to get into the state of oneness. One way is through meditation. I prefer to use an intention, which is similar to meditation but, to me, is much easier. In simple terms, the purpose of meditation is to clear your mind and help you be present. As humans, we can get hung up on what that means. I often hear, "I feel like I am doing it wrong." That is because our minds can wander, and it can be hard to stop thinking about what we should be doing while we're meditating. With an intention, you have a clear focus. As you have a clear goal in mind, visualize the intention, listen to the words, and feel your breath; in and out, we are able to more easily get into that state of BE-ing. Neither way, meditation or intention, is right or wrong. It is merely a matter of preference. In many ways, intentions are also like prayer. (If you look at how some people place their hands in prayer—clasped together pointing up—that formation acts as a physical antenna from our body pointing up to Source and heaven.)

The following intention to become present with oneness takes only a few minutes a day. If possible, it is best to practice this daily until it becomes a part of your routine. It doesn't matter when or how you do this intention—before bed, in the shower, while you're walking outside. The possibilities are endless. The steps are as follows:

- Get in a comfortable and relaxed position.

- If you are sitting or lying down, close your eyes. If you are walking outside in nature, taking a shower, or doing something similar, please keep your eyes open.

- Breathe in deeply.

- Breathe out deeply.

- With each breath, feel each inhale and exhale with your entire body.

- You are present. You are calm. You are peaceful.

- As you feel more and more relaxed with each breath, take a moment to release—either mentally, physically, or emotionally—anything that might be weighing on you.

- If you'd like, you can visualize handing whatever that thought, physical sensation, or emotion is over to your guides and angels. Ask your spirit team to take it from you and transmute it into love and light.

- As you breathe in and out and release, ask your higher self, guides, and angels to bring forth and integrate within you whatever is needed for your best and highest good. (The phrase "best and highest good" is a filter that removes your ego from the situation and from the desire to control the outcome.) Love. Peace. Bliss. Joy. Happiness. Hope.

- When you're ready, imagine that your feet are anchored and rooted to the ground. From your feet, an energetic grounding cord begins to grow, moving down slowly toward the center of Mother Earth.

- As this grounding cord travels down in a column of golden white light, it anchors to the center of the Earth.

- The divine love of Mother Earth radiates from Earth's core back up the column of light until it reaches the tips of your toes and the bottom of your feet, sweeping up your legs, thighs, tailbone, and hips, clearing out any stagnant energy it comes across.

- As this energy pulsates through you, it continues to move up your spine, nourishing your entire body, physically, mentally, emotionally, and spiritually.

- Breathe in and out.

- This golden white light is Universal Source, the I Am presence, and spreads along the energetic neurological branches that are the Tree of Life within you.

- Breathe in and out.

- This light and energy expand in love through your stomach, all the way up until they reach the center of your chest and sacred heart.

- Your entire heart fills with love, and as it does, you allow any further resistances in your physical, mental, emotional, and spiritual bodies to fully release.

- Breathe in and out.

- You are now in a total state of peace and ease—past, present, future, now.

- Breathe in further and continue to receive the increasing flow of Earth's energy as it regenerates every cell of your body and BE-ing.

- Let go of any thought that you are separate from Earth or God.

- As your breath softens, the golden white light works its way toward your shoulders and neck, moving up your face and to the front and back of your head.

- Resting a moment on your forehead and third eye, the Source Energy pulsates and tingles, clearing anything out that no longer serves you.

- Your breath feels even lighter as the energy moves to the top of your head and out in a beam of golden white light upward to the sky, universe, and Source.

- This golden white light is connecting you to God, to oneness.

- A gentle waterfall of love and light beams back down toward you, filling up your whole self.

- Breathe into the welcoming embrace of both God and Mother Earth. As above, so below.

- You rest in perfect communion.

- As you continue to breathe in and out deeply, notice the power of oneness, Earth, and your higher self and how it completely fills your energetic body, mind, heart, and soul. The circle of light expands within and around you.

- Release the illusion that you are alone or that you must do anything alone.

- Notice how your heart is one with your energetic body.

- Recognize how the air you are breathing is part of NO-thing and everything at the same time.

- Notice how you are one with All That Is, a perfect state of oneness and BE-ing.

*Additional exercises and intentions, such as ground, clear, and protect, are shared in Part Five.*

In addition to meditation, practicing intention, and prayer, you can get into a state of oneness with All That Is with other tools and resources:

- Connecting with your spirit team (This is most likely why you picked up this book!)

- Using energy healing modalities:

    o *Acupuncture:* A practice that uses energy pathways, called meridians, to restore balance and harmony. The concept is that by inserting needles into specific points along the body's meridians, stagnant energy can be unblocked and released, and the flow of wellness restored.

    o *Craniosacral therapy:* A light touch treatment that uses gentle hands-on techniques to examine the movement of fluids in and around the central nervous system. This therapy is said to relieve stress, tension headaches, and neck pain. It is also used to restore balance and wellness after traumatic injuries.

    o *Ecstatic dance:* A form of energy healing, ecstatic dance uses movement and music to open the body, mind, and spirit. During an ecstatic dance session, people move freely to express their emotions and connect with their inner power. This type of dance is thought to release blocked energy, clear the mind, and boost self-confidence.

    o *Massage:* This is one of the oldest and most common forms of energy healing. Massage therapists use their hands to move energy around your body. This can help promote relaxation and improve blood flow and lymphatic circulation.

o   *Pranic healing:* This holistic approach uses prana (Sanskrit for "life force energy") to balance, harmonize, and transform the body's energy processes.

o   *Qigong:* This system of energy healing uses movement, breathwork, and visualization to open and balance the energy pathways of the body. It is thought to improve health and help relieve stress, anxiety, and pain.

o   *Reflexology:* This is a type of massage that uses pressure points on the feet, hands, and ears to promote healing. Reflexologists believe that these pressure points correspond to different parts of the body. Massaging or applying pressure to these points can encourage energy to flow freely and restore balance.

o   *Reiki:* This energy healing technique uses Universal Energy to restore balance and harmony. Before being able to work on oneself or others, a person becomes attuned through a process that opens energetic pathways. The practitioner then works as a healing vessel for Universal Source, which directs energy to where it is needed, mostly by placing hands near or on the body. However, long-distance reiki can also be performed without being present or in person. Recipients of reiki may feel relaxed and peaceful during the session, as well as experience the release of stuck emotions.

It is also important to note that there are many different types of reiki available. Usui (from Mikao Usui) reiki is the Western method and one of the most widely used versions available today. Other core types of reiki are Jikiden (Eastern method), Karuna, Lighterian, and Sekhem or Seichem. In addition to these principal types of reiki, other practitioners have branded their own versions, including Holy Fire, Blue Star, Rainbow, and many more. People have asked me if one type is "better" than another. Healing energy is healing energy from Source, no matter what it is called. If you feel drawn to one style or another and it resonates with you, go with it. Also, remember that just because something is more expensive doesn't make it the "best."

○ *Shamanic healing:* This method uses plant medicines and intentional ceremonies to restore balance to the body, mind, and spirit. Shamanic healers use tools like the drum, prayers, and rituals to help shift energy and restore health.

○ *Sound healing:* This modality uses sound and vibration to restore balance and harmony in the body. The concept is that sound is the only energy that can easily move through both physical and energetic space. By listening to certain sounds or music, you can stimulate certain parts of the body to promote relaxation and improve mental clarity.

○ *Tapping or Emotional Freedom Technique (EFT):* This alternative to acupressure therapy treatment draws on the ancient Chinese practice of acupuncture and modern (or energy) psychology. Practitioners restore balance to disrupted energy flow by lightly tapping on acupoints on the hands, face, and body, while focusing on an issue or emotion someone is experiencing.

○ *Therapeutic touch:* Also known by some as healing touch or noncontact therapeutic touch, this is a form of energy therapy in which practitioners sense your energy through their hands and then send positive energy back to you. It is similar to reiki as an alternative medicine in that blocked energies can be released. However, unlike reiki, therapeutic touch does not require the practitioner to receive an attunement.

o   *Yoga:* This ancient healing modality uses movement, meditation, and the chakra system to support healing and well-being. Some popular styles of yoga that focus on energy healing are Iyengar, Kundalini, and Vinyasa.

Additional ways to connect with your spirit team include the following:

- Being in gratitude

- Being present

- Clearing, balancing, and aligning your chakras

- Earthing or forest bathing

- Journaling or doing automatic writing (Automatic writing, also called psychography, is when a person produces written words without consciously writing. It can be used as an exercise to increase your creativity or improve your writing, but it also can be used as an exercise to channel more subconscious thoughts with or without your higher self or Source.)

- Listening to calming music or sounds

- Practicing being still—mentally or physically

- Sitting in silence

- Spending time in nature

- Using crystals

- Using essential oils

- Using breathwork (Breathwork is a term for various breathing practices in which the conscious control of breathing is said to influence a person's mental, emotional, or physical state with a therapeutic effect. It is helpful for relaxation and stress in a similar way to meditation.) The following are both useful breathing exercises:

○ **One to Ten and Ten to One:**

> Breathe in for one second, hold, and breathe out for one second.

> Breathe in for two seconds, hold, and breathe out for two seconds.

> Breathe in for three seconds, hold, and breathe out for three seconds.

> Breathe in for four seconds, hold, and breathe out for four seconds.

> Breathe in for five seconds, hold, and breathe out for five seconds.

> Breathe in for six seconds, hold, and breathe out for six seconds.

> Breathe in for seven seconds, hold, and breathe out for seven seconds.

> Breathe in for eight seconds, hold, and breathe out for eight seconds.

> Breathe in for nine seconds, hold, and breathe out for nine seconds.

> Breathe in for ten seconds, hold, and breathe out for ten seconds.

> *(Then repeat this backwards from ten to one.)*

○   *Box:*

Breathe out slowly, releasing all the air from your lungs.

Breathe in through your nose as you slowly count to four in your head.

Hold your breath for a count of four.

Exhale for another count of four.

Hold your breath again for a count of four.

(*Repeat for three to four rounds.*)

How do you know you are in a state of BE-ing or oneness? It takes practice and time. Be sure to dedicate time in your daily routine for at least a month or longer. As you do, you will begin to feel yourself shift.

# Ways to Connect with Your Higher Self

There are many ways you can connect with your higher self. The easiest way I have found is to get into a state of BE-ing and oneness, have a pure and clear intention, and make a request such as, "I ask to connect with and be in alignment with my higher self, to receive information and messages clearly and succinctly that are for my best and highest good." (The phrase "best and highest good" is a filter that removes your ego from the situation and from the desire to control the outcome.) Then be open to how and what comes through.

If you want to practice and have a more detailed approach, you can do the following:

- Get in a comfortable position.

- Relax your shoulders, close your eyes, and take some deep breaths.

- As you breathe in and out each time, contract and relax all the muscles in your body, getting into a deeper state of rest.

- Once you've done this a few times, become aware of your breath, allowing it to flow in and out effortlessly.

- Allow further relaxation and presence as you continue to breathe.

- Begin to focus on your heart space and imagine a moment when you experienced unconditional love. Hold onto this feeling.

- Ask your guides and angels to envelop you in love and light, bringing in healing and protective energy that surrounds you on all levels.

- Feel that state of safety and protection.

- Call upon your higher self, your oversoul, to be present and come closer. Say, "I call in my higher self. I ask to connect with and be in alignment with you, to receive information and messages clearly and succinctly for my best and highest good."

- Imagine a part of yourself is coming closer and closer toward your body and energetic space.

- Continue to be as present as possible and use all of your awareness and senses—physical, mental, emotional, and spiritual—to pick up sensations, messages, or information.

- Ask to be given a signal of what it feels like when your higher self is present or communicating with you.

- When you feel your higher self is present, you can begin to ask questions.

- As the energy flows through you, do not doubt or judge what you receive.

- Tune back in with your heart and feel what resonates.

- When you feel like your time with your higher self is complete, imagine releasing it back to Source.

- Come back to your body through your breath.

- Place your hands wherever you feel led—your heart, forehead, stomach area, or elsewhere.

- Thank your higher self and your spirit team for this amazing experience.

The above can be a good intention to do before you go to sleep because you can continue to receive information while you sleep. But you can also do it at any time of the day. Having a regular routine and practice will get you in the energetic space to be quiet, present, and consciously aware of what the connection to your higher self and Source feels like to you.

# Nichole's Higher Self Story

**More often than not,** when I connect with my higher self, it is subtle. I receive information and messages primarily in the form of thoughts. These "ideas" are like an inner voice and can be as simple as when to do something during the day, like reading a passage in a book at a specific time, or they can be deeper and feel more urgent. If you're wondering why this sounds like intuition, that's because it is! When we are connected with our higher self, the direction and guidance we receive flow through us through our various senses, including our psychic/intuitive abilities. The way I can distinguish if it is mine is that it feels like my voice and like me. It isn't ego, which questions what it is I am feeling, thinking, or doing. It just is.

I will never forget the first time I heard Spirit speak. It was a bright, sunny day. I was ten and was playing at the park near my home with a friend and my one-year-old sister. I remember feeling at peace and grateful for what a gorgeous day it was. All of a sudden, I heard a voice that was all around me boom, "Get out! Get out *now*!" It was nowhere and yet everywhere at once and rang with such urgency that it startled me. Bewildered, I looked at my friend, who was pushing my sister on the swing. No one else was around. The park was completely empty. This feeling of dread washed over me. Because the feeling and the voice were so clear and urgent, I picked up my sister and headed toward the park exit. Right then, a car pulled up and stopped at the park entrance. A woman was driving the car, and a man got out of the passenger seat. He headed toward us, blocking our exit. As he did, I instinctually placed my sister on my hip, as much out of his reach as possible. The man began to ask us questions: "What are your names?" "What color eyes does the baby have?" "How old is she?" As he stepped closer to "get a good look," my mom suddenly shouted from the house, "Girls! It is time to come home!" The man took one look at my mom, ran to the waiting car, and jumped in as the car sped away.

It wasn't until I was older that my mom told me that she had received two visions of my sister crying and screaming and had an overwhelming urge to check on us. When she looked outside, she saw the man standing before us and immediately called out.

Over the years, I wondered if the voice was a guardian angel or even Archangel Michael protecting me. The voice wasn't distinct, meaning it wasn't high or low, female or male. Yet it sounded familiar. I have since determined that it was all of it—God, Archangel Michael, my spirit team—but more importantly, it was my higher self, watching over and informing me that I had a choice to make at that moment. We are all one, and the Divine works with and through us in all ways.

# Chakras and Subtle Energy

Every physical manifestation—such as the body, objects, or other entities—has a "subtle" component. For instance, our physical body is an
extension of our emotional body, which is part of our mental body,
which is part of our psychic body, which is part of our spiritual body,
and so on to increasingly more subtle bodies, which have faster or
higher rates of vibration.

Much like the physical body, each of these subtler bodies is a whole
system that is joined together energetically by a subtle energy nervous
system. Just as the physical nervous system channels energy and life
force to our physical body, the subtle energy nervous system channels
life force to the subtle bodies.

The central part of the subtle energy nervous system is a central
"cord" of energy that resembles and roughly follows the spinal cord
in our physical body. Made up of chakras (a Sanskrit word that means
"wheel"), it channels the energy from the Earth below our feet, up the
central energetic cord, and then through the top of our head into the
sky or ethers above us. In this way, we are connected to both the Earth
and the sky, from the core of the planet to the heavens. This central
energetic cord channels the energy of oneness to empower us. If it is
blocked, we will lack vitality in our energetic bodies.

Along the central energetic cord are seven main chakras, also
referred to as energy wheels. These spinning disks of energy help
energize, regulate, and stimulate elements of our physical, mental,
emotional, and spiritual bodies and are meant to spin at a regular,
even speed. Each subtle energy chakra corresponds to and influences
parts of our physical body and our emotions. The chakras need to stay
clear, aligned, and activated to remain functional. If they are closed or
blocked, that may cause issues, including dis-EASE and illness, in the
associated areas of the body.

Our subtle energy bodies extend well beyond our physical bodies.
Above our heads are sky chakras that connect us to Source. Below
our feet are Earth chakras that ground us to the planet. Surrounding
our physical body is an invisible (to the naked eye) energy field, also
known as an aura. Our aura is an increasingly fine vibration that also

corresponds to our physical body, emotions, thoughts, and subtle bodies. An aura may present as a single color or several layers of color. The color of an aura can represent our physical health as well as our emotional, mental, psychic, and spiritual states. When an aura is strong, it is protective and keeps away harmful energies and influences, including others' negative thoughts or emotions.

There are also other minor chakras in our subtle energy system, such as chakras in the center of your palms and the bottom of your feet. The hand chakras can send and receive energy, while the chakras in your feet provide additional grounding and create a connection between you and the Earth. Foot chakras can send and receive energy from the Earth and channel it into your energetic and physical bodies.

Although chakras are often shown on diagrams on top of or in front of the body, they are actually centered within the body. They extend from the front to the back, and you can work with them on either side of the body.

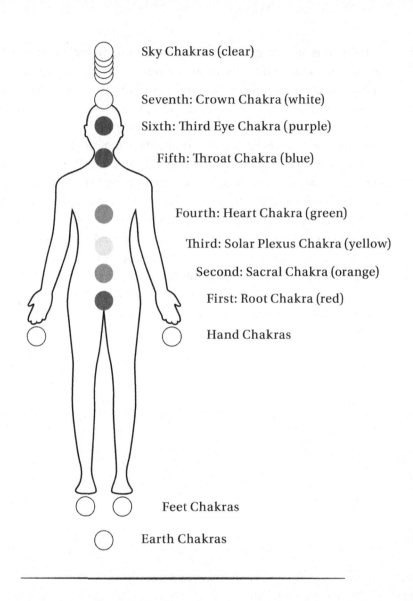

Sky Chakras (clear)

Seventh: Crown Chakra (white)

Sixth: Third Eye Chakra (purple)

Fifth: Throat Chakra (blue)

Fourth: Heart Chakra (green)

Third: Solar Plexus Chakra (yellow)

Second: Sacral Chakra (orange)

First: Root Chakra (red)

Hand Chakras

Feet Chakras

Earth Chakras

As we go through life experiences, our chakras can become blocked. We might physically experience blockages as sensations, vibrations, sounds, or other sensory input. When you perceive that you are blocked, trust it and work to remove the blockage.

The more you work with the chakras and your aura, the more you will understand them. Here is an overview of each of the seven main chakras, as well as the Earth and sky chakras.

| | |
|---|---|
| *Sky Chakras* | There are five clear chakras stacked vertically above the crown of our head, each one larger than the last. Each successive chakra connects us to a higher realm of spiritual reality, supporting embodied spiritual wisdom, love, bliss, joy, and the Divine. |
| *Crown (Seventh) Chakra* | Located at or just above the crown of the head, the crown chakra can be white or violet. It relates to spirituality, expanded consciousness, and enlightenment. When open, energy from the crown chakra is channeled into the other chakras, and they become energized. When this chakra is blocked, you may feel a lack of overall energy, feel stubborn or narrow-minded, lack a sense of purpose, or ignore spiritual guidance. |
| *Third Eye (Sixth) Chakra* | Located in the middle of the forehead, between the eyebrows, the third eye chakra is purple, or sometimes indigo or royal blue, in color. Physically, it relates to the pituitary gland and glandular system, forehead, eyes, ears, and head. When open, it brings psychic awareness and intuition. It also increases imagination and creativity. When blocked, intuition decreases, and knowledge is limited to intellectual reasoning. A blocked third eye chakra may also manifest through headaches, migraines, and issues with the eyes, ears, and brain. |

| | |
|---|---|
| **Throat (Fifth) Chakra** | Located in the middle of the throat and light blue in color, this chakra is connected to verbal communication. Physically, this chakra is related to the thyroid and glands, throat and neck, and surrounding bones and musculature. When the throat chakra is open, we can find words for and express our deepest truths; we are true to our word and can speak with confidence. A blocked throat chakra can make us afraid to speak up, or we may speak without thinking or dominate conversations. Physically, a blockage may bring throat and neck issues, thyroid problems, and health trouble relating to teeth, mouth, ears, shoulders, and the upper back. |
| **Heart (Fourth) Chakra** | This chakra is located in the middle of the chest, between the pectorals. The heart chakra is green, and when open, this chakra is the center of love, compassion, empathy, truthfulness, happiness, acceptance, and one's sense of connection with others. Physically, it is associated with the heart, chest muscles, middle spine, and lungs. A blocked heart chakra can manifest as selfishness, greed, loneliness, isolation, or insecurity. Physically, a blockage can result in heart or blood issues, poor circulation, and difficulty with respiration. The heart chakra is also the bridge between our upper and lower chakras. |

| | |
|---|---|
| **Solar Plexus (Third) Chakra** | Also called the naval point, this chakra is located in the abdomen, roughly around the naval, and is yellow in color. Physically, it is related to our nervous system, digestion, upper bowels, kidneys, adrenal glands, pancreas, lower back, and surrounding organs. Emotionally, it is related to self-confidence, strong emotional boundaries, and personal power. When open, the solar plexus chakra brings vitality to our physical body, strengthens our nervous system, gives us willpower, and allows us to concentrate. When blocked, it can contribute to stomach problems and ulcers, fatigue, stress, poor resistance to disease, and eating or digestive problems. |
| **Sacral (Second) Chakra** | Located four to five inches above the pelvic bone, the sacral chakra is orange. This chakra relates to the female sexual organs, reproductive system, uterus, bladder, urinary tract, and lower back. It is also related to masculine and feminine sensuality, creativity, and pleasure. When the sacral chakra is open, it alleviates guilt and shame about personal sensuality, supports creativity, and helps strengthen the pelvic muscles. A blocked sacral chakra can bring infection, impotency, and problems associated with other physical areas in that part of the body. |

| | |
|---|---|
| **Root (First) Chakra** | Located near the back of the spine, the root chakra is red. It relates to the male reproductive system, male sexuality and virility, the lower spine, the tailbone, the muscles of the perineum, the legs, and the feet. An open root chakra can bring physical strength, energy, a sense of stability, physical and emotional security, and one's sense of competence and protection. Physically, a blockage in this chakra may lead to problems with the lower spine, colon, and elimination system (such as constipation), as well as issues with sexuality or impotence. Emotionally, there may be issues with rage, sexual dysfunction, greed, panic, fear, or anxiety. |
| **Earth Chakras** | The Earth chakras are located twelve to eighteen inches below the feet. These chakras help ground you to the magnetic core of the Earth, energizing your physical, mental, emotional, and spiritual bodies to support health and vitality. Through these chakras, we connect to the fundamental nature of our being and our relationship with the planet. It is also where we can discharge our excess energy. Grounding into the Earth chakras gives us access to the "root" energy and stability to help our upper chakras. It can also bring us into relationship with the Earth beings or elements. If you are not connected to the Earth chakras, you may feel dizzy, disconnected, or disoriented. |

The more you work

with the chakras

and your aura,

the more you

*will understand them.*

To clear, align, and activate your chakras, do the ground, clear, and protect intention (see page 296 or 351).

Every living thing has an aura around it. Each color represents something different. There are twelve primary aura colors. Seven of those colors relate to the seven main chakras.

However, there are shades of the primary colors that bring the total number to over twenty. The primary aura colors are red, orange, yellow, green, blue, indigo, purple, pink, silver, brown, black, and white. Below are brief meanings of the primary aura colors.

*Red:* Red in an aura represents emotional and psychic balance or grounding.

*Orange:* Orange in an aura signifies one's happiness with family, friends, and/or environment.

*Yellow:* Yellow in an aura means inner happiness and balance with one's self.

*Green:* Green in an aura indicates that one has either a kind, loving heart or is in love with someone who balances them out. (Green is the color of self-love, not pink.)

*Blue:* Blue in an aura represents someone who is in a calm state.

*Indigo:* Indigo in an aura signifies someone who is in tune with their higher self.

*Purple:* Purple in an aura means the person is intuitive and/or using their intuition.

*Pink:* Pink in an aura indicates someone who is happy and in harmony with those who are around them. (Pink and green vibrate on the same frequency level.)

*Silver:* Silver in an aura represents abundance (spiritual or material wealth).

*Brown:* Brown in an aura signifies selfishness.

*Black:* Black in an aura means there is anger, grief, or sadness built up. It can also indicate illness.

*White:* White in an aura is the rarest color. It indicates the person is concerned with spiritual matters and does not care about material possessions or needs. It can also symbolize that the person is healthy.

# A Room Filled with Angels

### A Story from April B.

**The following happened when I was pregnant** with my first child. I was about four or five months pregnant when we visited my father-in-law's mother in the hospital. She had been there for about a week, and we knew she wouldn't make it much longer.

My husband and I visited her in the hospital; she touched my belly and said she could feel the baby moving. I had not felt the baby yet, but I encouraged her anyway.

We settled in a corner of the room as many other family members came in to be with her. I felt led to bow my head and pray, but I somehow knew I was talking directly to the lady on her deathbed to tell her (in my head) that she had so many people that loved her there and how I could see she was having trouble breathing and that it was okay to go.

I felt her say (telepathically), "All my children are not here." She wouldn't leave until they were all there. I told her that they were on the way, but we would make sure they were being taken care of. I told her, "It's okay. I'll take care of them."

I felt her struggle with that decision, but then she released it. Her brother was standing right next to her. My head was still bowed, and I could hear him speaking in tongues; he was a retired Evangelist preacher. I looked up to watch him as he spoke, but his mouth was not moving.

I bowed my head again, and I was still hearing him speak in tongues in my head. When he finished, I saw in my third eye a portal open up behind him. As it opened, the room became *completely filled* with angels. It was *packed* in there. They were rejoicing and singing her favorite old Baptist hymn.

I kick myself now because I intuitively knew it was her favorite song but never wrote it down and have since forgotten the exact hymn. The energy was pure joy, love, and excitement! They were worshipping.

As soon as the portal closed and the angels left, a nurse confirmed she was dead.

Everyone started crying, but I got mad. It was like they were ruining my spiritual high. I wanted to get up and dance and rejoice and clap and sing! How could they be so sad?

She was now in the most amazing place! But, of course, no one else saw or felt it. My husband, who was right beside me, had no idea that any of this happened. It was one of the most beautiful experiences of my life. Six years later, I had a reading with an angel communicator, and the first person that came through was Marge, also known as Margie.

I didn't know who it was at the time. It took me a few weeks to realize that's the name of my father-in-law's mother. I'm so grateful to know she remembers me and she's close by!

# Chapter 10

# Archangels

> *"Divine life is the spirit in everything that exists—from the atom to the archangel. Angels are but a spark from the eternal fire that is Source—the immanence of the universe, the solidarity of humankind—we are all but one."*
>
> *—Nichole Bigley*

Archangels are energetic spiritual beings. Except for Archangels Metatron and Sandalphon, twins who began as human, archangels have never been incarnated on Earth or any other planet or dimension. They are extremely powerful and one of the closest sources of energy to the Divine. As human beings in the physical, we can experience life and the emotions that come with it, as well as take action in ways that they can't. (See "Part One: Angels in Religion" for a review of archangels in religion.)

When people come to me for a session, they often ask what their *soul* purpose is. Our *only* true purpose while here on Earth is to remember where we came from, the Divine Source, and to try as much as possible to stay connected to and align with it in our human form. When we channel that, we are in a state of true BE-ing and unconditional love. That love is a form of energy that vibrates out. If we all

In addition to helping us to remember and reconnect to a state of love, archangels, like other members of our spirit team, assist us in navigating life and in achieving additional spiritual goals we set for ourselves during our journey here.

were to focus on ourselves and connect to this state of oneness, then we'd all be in the energy of love. There would be what we think is unattainable—peace on Earth or, better yet, a living heaven on Earth. The meaning of life, therefore, is love—to give love and to receive love as much and as often as possible.

In addition to helping us to remember and reconnect to a state of love, archangels, like other members of our spirit team, assist us in navigating life and in achieving additional spiritual goals we set for ourselves during our journey here. They often oversee our other angels and guides, depending on the situation or circumstances, and their role should not be confused with the role our guardian angel(s) play. Think of archangels like bouncers, allowing certain energies to come into your space and interact with you. However, because we are beings of free will and choice, we do need to give them permission to engage with us and interact on our behalf. (Our guardian angels, by the way, do not need our permission to engage with us—more on that later.)

I've found that knowing the names of the archangels and understanding who they are and how they show up is helpful to be able to connect with and work with them. The following section of the book lists each of the archangels and what they represent. This list includes the qualities associated with each of the archangels, along with the colors, elements, crystals, planets, zodiac signs, and chakras typically connected with their presence. In later sections of the book, you will find ways to connect and communicate with them. Please also note that when reading about associations or correspondences with the archangels, or any other energetic beings, they may or may not resonate with you, which is totally fine. This is meant to be general information to help you in your discovery of modern-day angels and your spiritual journey. Feel free to do your own research. As you tap into and communicate with your spirit team, you will uncover your own way of connecting and communicating with the Divine.

## Archangel Ariel

(Also known as Arael, Ariael, "Earth's great Lord, "lion or lioness of God," and "Spirit of air")

*"I am here to help manifest unlimited abundance and divine providence. I can help you awaken your spirit, see the beauty of today, and bring abundance into the world."*

—*Archangel Ariel*

Archangel Ariel's name means "lion or lioness of God," and when she is near, you may see lions or feel lion energy around you. Because of this, some artwork portrays Ariel as having a lion's head.

Archangel Ariel is found primarily in Christian and Judaic mysticism and kabbalistic magic, including the Testament of Solomon, the Greater Key of Solomon, and *The Hierarchy of the Blessed Angels*. In *The Hierarchy of the Blessed Angels* by Thomas Heywood, Ariel is said to rule the waters as "Earth's great Lord." Other writings mention her with other elemental titles, such as "Spirit of air." Therefore, you may also feel or hear the wind when Ariel is around, as she is associated with it.

Archangel Ariel works closely with King Solomon to conduct manifestation, spirit releasement, and divine magic, and oversees nature angels called sprites. Sprites are similar to fairies, and their purpose is to keep the environment healthy near bodies of water such as oceans, lakes, rivers, creeks, streams, and ponds. Given this, Ariel is heavily involved with healing and protecting nature, including wild and domestic animals. She often brings animals and pets to you to help manifest and tap into the energy of unconditional love. When our pets cross over the rainbow bridge, Ariel is there to greet them. She also often works with Archangel Raphael in healing capacities. When Ariel is around, you may experience or see pale pink or rainbows.

Archangel Ariel helps with the following:

- Animal communication

- Divine magic

- Healing—environment, people, and animals

- Manifestation

- Protection

Archangel Ariel is associated with the following:

- Color/aura: pale pink and/or rainbow

- Elements: all four elements—earth, wind, water, fire (but especially wind and water)

- Crystal: rose quartz

- Planet: Venus

- Zodiac: Aries

- Chakra: root

*Note: Archangel Ariel is one of the few angels, along with Archangels Haniel and Jophiel, portrayed as female. However, archangels and angels technically have no canonical gender.*

# Archangel Azrael

(Also known as Azrail, Ashriel, Azriel, Azaril, "Angel of Death," Isra'il, and "whom God helps")

*"Call on me in times of need, when the grieving process is too much. I, along with other angels, your loved ones, and God, will support you with dynamic love."*
—*Archangel Azrael*

Because Archangel Azrael is a tower of strength, his role is primarily to help people cross over to heaven at the time of physical death. He is often seen with a sword or scythe or wearing a hood. Azrael not only comforts people prior to their physical passing to ease suffering and to help them assimilate on the other side, but he also surrounds grieving family members with healing energy and divine light to help them cope with the loss of a loved one.

Because of his role in helping people with grief, Archangel Azrael can be found working with grief counselors and therapists to help shield them from their clients' emotions and pain. He is also a transformer of mental and emotional anxieties who assists people with depression and other illnesses that affect our mental and emotional systems. When Azrael shows up, a state of calm tends to wash over people. It isn't a euphoric feeling, but rather one of stability and inner stillness.

Call upon Archangel Azrael to bring comfort to a dying loved one, to assist someone at the time of transition, or if you've recently lost someone and need help with the grieving process. When Azrael is around, you may smell myrrh or see creamy or white light. (Other sources note that Azrael uses/has the color indigo when he is around as well.)

Archangel Azrael helps with the following:

- Comfort during stressful times and situations

- Connection to heaven

- Healing—grief, sadness, depression, and mental or emotional issues

- Prevention of negative thoughts

- Soul transitions from life on Earth to the other side

Archangel Azrael is associated with the following:

- Color/aura: creamy white/pearl and white

- Element: cosmos

- Crystals: calcite, yellow calcite, muscovite, and obsidian

- Planet: Pluto

- Zodiac: Capricorn

- Chakra: heart

# *Archangel Chamuel*

(Also known as "he who sees God," "he who seeks God," Camiel, Camiul, Camniel, Cancel, Jahoel, Kermuel, Khamael, Samael, Seraphiel, and Shemuel)

*"Life is meant to be shared with family and friends. Relationships are the biggest gift life has to offer because they allow you to see yourself in order to grow as an individual."*

*—Archangel Chamuel*

Archangel Chamuel's name means "he who sees God" or "he who seeks God." Chamuel is one of the seven core archangels and is the powerful angelic leader of the powers, angels who oversee and protect the world from lower energies.

Archangel Chamuel also protects us on a personal level. Considered an angel of love, he helps not only to expand and develop love within ourselves, but also to enhance our love for others and build strong and lasting relationships. Chamuel says that our expectations of ourselves and others often cause the most pain. When we learn to question and release these expectations, we begin to understand who we really are at our core, in order to tap into unconditional love.

You'll know Archangel Chamuel is working with you if you feel flutters in the pit of your stomach or tingles up and down your body. His energy is very kind, loving, and sweet, helping us seek out important aspects of our lives, like careers, relationships, and life purpose. Chamuel is often depicted with a heart of armor because he represents love and focuses on peaceful relationships. When Chamuel is around, you may experience or see the colors pink or pale green.

Archangel Chamuel helps with the following:

- Careers
- Life purpose
- Love—self-love and love for others
- Relationships
- World peace

Archangel Chamuel is associated with the following:

- Color/aura: pink and pale green
- Element: fire
- Crystals: carnelian, fluorite, green fluorite, red jasper, and pink/rose quartz
- Planets: Earth, Mars, and Venus
- Zodiac: Taurus
- Chakra: heart

# Archangel Gabriel

(Also known as Abruel, Gabrielle, "God is my strength," Jibril, Jiburili, and Serafili)

*"Feel at peace knowing that you are powerful, have purpose, and your dreams are attainable."*
—*Archangel Gabriel*

Archangel Gabriel's name means "God is my strength." Sometimes depicted as female and sometimes as male, Gabriel is one of the seven core archangels and is the famous angel who told Mary about the impending birth of her son Jesus of Nazareth and Elizabeth about the impending birth of her son, John the Baptist. Gabriel also dictated the Qur'an, the spiritual text of Islam, to Muhammad. As a result of these foretellings, Gabriel is known as the "messenger angel." A powerful and strong archangel, Gabriel helps bring forth messages of all kinds and also helps us find our voices and speak up. Those who work with Gabriel will find themselves pushed into action that often leads to positive results.

Archangel Gabriel is usually depicted clothed in blue or white garments, carrying a lily, a trumpet, a shining lantern, a branch from paradise, a scroll, and a scepter. When Gabriel appears, the color most often associated with them is white.

Archangel Gabriel loves to help hopeful parents through conception or the process of adopting a child. They create bliss and provide strength and courage when, at times, it may feel impossible. Gabriel also helps to open doors for anyone whose life purpose involves communication or the arts.

Archangel Gabriel helps with the following:

- Angel communication via intuition

- Artistic endeavors

- Careers in communications such as marketing, writing, journalism, and more

- Courage and confidence to speak up

- Mediumship (communicating with those who have passed)

Archangel Gabriel is associated with the following:

- Color/aura: white and copper

- Element: water

- Crystals: amber, carnelian, citrine, and clear quartz

- Planet: moon (technically not a planet)

- Zodiac: Cancer

- Chakra: sacral

*Note: Like our souls, angels are genderless. Further, some see Archangel Gabriel as female and others as male, and representations of Gabriel in religion and art differ, with either masculine or feminine features. For this reason, Gabriel is referred to as "they/them."*

# Archangel Haniel

(Also known as Anael, Aniel, "Angel of Joy," "glory of God," "grace of God," "joy of God," Hamiel, and Onoel)

*"Trust that I can help elevate you to the level of which you have come—God's grace, love, and eternal beauty."*

—*Archangel Haniel*

Archangel Haniel's name means "glory of God," "grace of God," or "joy of God." As a result, Haniel is viewed as the Angel of Joy. She is also seen as the Archangel of Intuition and helps us bring more happiness, ease, grace, and patience into our lives. To enjoy the company of loved ones and friends or to add beauty and harmony to your life, call upon Haniel. When she shows up, her moon goddess energy feels etheric and mystical. The color often associated with Haniel's presence is turquoise or blue.

Archangel Haniel also helps us recover and tap into the lost secrets of natural healing remedies, including the moon's energy and crystals. It is said that she assisted a group of men known as "priests-astronomers" in ancient Babylon; they did divination and healing work through astrology and astronomy. She is mentioned in some kabbalistic texts as escorting Enoch to the spirit world. Enoch was one of only two humans who was transformed into an archangel (Elijah was the other). Because of this, she often works with lightworkers and healers to develop their intuitive gifts and abilities.

Because of her calmness and steadiness, Archangel Haniel will also enable you to be poised and centered before or during an important event like a performance, speech, or job interview.

Archangel Haniel helps with the following:

- Happiness and joy
- Healing abilities
- Moon energy
- Poise and grace
- Psychic and intuitive abilities

Archangel Haniel is associated with the following:

- Color/aura: bluish white and turquoise—a blended blue green
- Element: earth
- Crystals: angelite, azurite-malachite, blue lace agate, charoite, fluorite, garnet, and moonstone
- Planets: Venus, Saturn, and the moon (technically not a planet)
- Zodiac: Taurus and Libra
- Chakra: throat

*Note: Archangel Haniel is one of the few angels, along with Archangels Ariel and Jophiel, portrayed as female. However, archangels and angels technically have no canonical gender.*

# Archangel Jeremiel

(Also known as "mercy of God," Ramiel, and Remiel)

*"Strength comes from adventure of the journey and eternal being. I am here to assure you that everything is moving forward in perfect timing."*
—*Archangel Jeremiel*

Archangel Jeremiel's name means "mercy of God." He is associated with helping Baruch, an author of Judaic texts in the first century AD, with his prophetic visions, such as the coming of the Messiah. In another vision, Jeremiel took Baruch on a tour of the different levels of heaven.

While Archangel Azrael helps souls release their energy from this world, Archangel Jeremiel meets the soul as soon as their energy lifts from the body. They both help souls cross over, but Jeremiel is there to help newly crossed-over souls review their lives. A life review is a service Jeremiel offers the living as well. If you'd like to take inventory of your life up until now and make positive adjustments, call upon Jeremiel. He will help you assess your life and address the things to learn from your experiences. Doing so will make you stronger and more centered moving forward. When Jeremiel is near, you may experience or see dark purple and instantly feel comforted, safe, and at ease.

Archangel Jeremiel helps with the following:

- Concerns about the future
- Life reviews and making life changes
- Psychic dreams, visions, and interpretations
- Release of fear and worry
- Soul transitions from life on Earth to the other side

Archangel Jeremiel is associated with the following:

- Color/aura: dark purple
- Element: earth
- Crystals: amethyst and selenite
- Planet: Earth
- Zodiac: Scorpio
- Chakra: third eye

## *Archangel Jophiel*

(Also known as "beauty of God," Dina, Iofiel, Iophiel, Jofiel, "patron of artists and illumination," Yofiel, Youfiel, Zophiel, and Zuriel)

---

*"Beauty is all around us. You only have to look around and within to see, embrace, and feel it on all levels."*
—*Archangel Jophiel*

Archangel Jophiel's name means "beauty of God." Jophiel is one of the seven core archangels who are in charge of the cherubim. She is known as the patron of artists and illumination and is often depicted in iconography holding a flaming sword, as it is said that she was the archangel who drove Adam and Eve out of the Garden of Eden and guarded the gate to prevent their reentry.

As the Archangel of Art and Beauty, Jophiel assists us in both the metaphysical and physical worlds. First, she helps us have beautiful, positive thoughts and see and appreciate the splendor around us. She doesn't just get us to think positively for a certain period of time, but works with us to shift our perspectives and perceptions in order to rewire the mind. This allows us to become more confident and resilient, as well as to create, manifest, and attract more goodness into our lives.

Archangel Jophiel also ignites our creative spark and helps with artistic projects, giving us ideas and energy to carry out creative aspirations. Jophiel is known to bring inspiration and beauty to the home, work, and relationships. When Jophiel is around, you may experience or see the color yellow.

Archangel Jophiel helps with the following:

- Beautiful, positive thoughts
- Creative endeavors and inspiration
- Feng shui and interior decorating
- Manifestation
- Prioritization

Archangel Jophiel is associated with the following:

- Color/aura: yellow and dark pink
- Element: fire
- Crystals: calcite, citrine, pink tourmaline, rubellite, smoky quartz, and tiger's eye
- Planet: Saturn
- Zodiac: Libra
- Chakra: solar plexus

*Note: Due to the association with beauty, Archangel Jophiel is one of the few angels, along with Archangels Ariel and Haniel, sometimes portrayed as female. However, archangels and angels technically have no canonical gender.*

# Archangel Metatron
(Also known as Metatetron, Merraton, Metaraon, and Mittron)

*"Life isn't meant to be as hard as humans make it out to be. Lean on me to help prioritize and get things done on all levels. I can even bend time to ensure productivity."*
—*Archangel Metatron*

The meaning of Archangel Metatron's name is an enigma, since his name doesn't end in the *el* ("of God") suffix like the names of other archangels. Scholars, researchers, and the like have debated Metatron's name over time, but there is no consensus, and its precise origin is unknown. Some experts believe that the name originated from ancient texts and may have been a magic word or a derivation of the name Yahweh, the Hebrew term for the unspoken sacred name of God. Others suggest Metatron came from either the word *mattara* ("keeper of the watch") or the word *memater* ("to guard or protect"). Another theory is that the name is a combination of two Greek words meaning "after" and "throne," suggesting the idea of "one who serves behind the throne."

Regardless of the meaning of his unusual name, Archangel Metatron was one of only two archangels (the other being his twin brother, Archangel Sandalphon) who were once mortal men who walked upon Earth. Since his creation occurred after that of the other archangels, it makes Metatron the youngest of the group.

Before transforming into an archangel, Metatron was once Enoch, a prophet and scribe. It is said in the book of Genesis that Enoch "walked with God" and retained his God-given purity in his mortal life, during which he was also an honest and skilled scholar of heavenly secrets, having received the Book of the Angel Raziel or the Sepher Raziel. Because of this, God escorted Enoch to the highest level of heaven (seventh heaven), gave him wings, and transformed him into Archangel Metatron. His job is to record everything that happens on Earth. These vibrational recordings are kept in the Book of Life, also known as the Akashic records.

174

In sacred geometry, Archangel Metatron oversees the flow of energy in a mystical cube known as Metatron's Cube, which contains all of the geometric shapes in God's creation and represents the patterns that make up everything God has made. These duties tie in with Metatron's work overseeing the Tree of Life, where he sends creative energy down from the top (the crown) of the tree toward all the parts of creation.

Archangel Metatron's energy is highly focused, fiery, and strong. He is motivated and will encourage you to take action and move forward in life. Given his experience as both a human and an angel, Metatron often acts as an intermediary between Earth and heaven. He helps us understand our connection to the Divine and helps us learn how to work with the angelic realm. Metatron will bring the vibration of ease into your life. He says that life doesn't have to be as difficult as we make it out to be. According to him, when we follow our hearts and what resonates with us, we are in alignment with our higher selves and that much closer to fulfilling our purpose here on Earth. More about Metatron was shared earlier in this book (see Chapter 2).

Archangel Metatron helps with the following:

- Accomplishments and goals
- Alignment with the higher self, purpose, and God's will
- Organization and recordkeeping
- Prioritization
- Time management

Archangel Metatron is associated with the following:

- Color/aura: seafoam green and violet
- Element: fire
- Crystals: trolleite quartz and watermelon tourmaline
- Planets: Earth and the sun (technically not a planet)
- Zodiac: Virgo
- Chakra: crown

# *Archangel Michael*

(Also known as Beshter, "he who is like God," "he who looks like God," "leader of the heavenly hosts," Mika'il, Mikal, "patron of police officers," Sabbathiel, and Saint Michael)

*"Fear is not a part of who you are—only love. When you experience fear, remember that you are connected to the Divine at all times and that I am here to help. I will instantly be by your side whenever you need me."*
—*Archangel Michael*

Archangel Michael's name means "he who is like God" or "he who looks like God." Michael is the leader of the archangels (or leader of the heavenly hosts) and is one of the seven core archangels. He's also in charge of the order of angels called the virtues. The virtues are angels who rid the Earth and people of fear; they are great defenders of all that is good. Michael enlists and works with humans he calls lightworkers (people who work within the light of God), asking them to conduct spiritual teachings and energy healings to serve humankind.

Throughout time, Archangel Michael has brought courage to leaders and inspired lightworkers worldwide. It was Michael who taught Adam how to farm in the Garden of Eden. Joan of Arc said she was motivated by Michael to lead France during the Hundred Years' War. He was canonized as Saint Michael, the patron of police officers, in 1950 because he helps to protect with bravery.

Archangel Michael is extremely tall and usually carries a sword that he uses to cut out and remove fear or the things that cause it. In addition to carrying a sword, he often has a banner or scales with him and is depicted treading on a dragon.

When Archangel Michael is around, you may see sparkles or flashes of blue or purplish-blue light. Michael's presence is reassuring and powerful. You feel safe, secure, and filled with pure love at all times when he is around. With his fiery energy, people sometimes feel physically hot, or even sweat, due to the heat Michael brings with him. This is also why lightworkers often experience heat emanating from their hands when conducting energy healings.

Archangel Michael helps with the following:

- Alignment with life and soul purpose and plan

- Bravery, courage, and strength

- Commitment and dedication

- Healing—all aspects of the mind, body, and soul—mentally, physically, emotionally, and spiritually

- Protection against all things

Archangel Michael is associated with the following:

- Color/aura: royal blue

- Element: fire

- Crystals: clear quartz, lapis lazuli, sodalite, sugilite, and obsidian

- Planet: sun (technically not a planet)

- Zodiac: Leo

- Chakras: all chakras, but primarily the throat

# Archangel Raguel

(Also known as "Archangel of Justice and Fairness," Akrasiel, "friend of God," Raguil, Rufael, and Suryan)

*"We angels open the hearts of everyone involved. Harmony and calm are brought to the situation. Arguments and conflicts are resolved now through peaceful resolution."*

—*Archangel Raguel*

Archangel Raguel's name means "friend of God." His main role in heaven is to oversee all of the other archangels and angels to ensure that they are working together in divine order. Because of this, Raguel is often referred to as the Archangel of Justice and Fairness. He is the angel to call on if a legal situation or mediation is needed. Raguel is also a champion for the underdog, stepping in to help them feel more empowered and respected.

Archangel Raguel works to uncover traumas and what triggers them. (If you've had major physical or emotional trauma, please work in conjunction with a professional, licensed therapist.) Enthusiastic, friendly, and loving, Raguel steps in when peace, comfort, or an energetic boost is needed. He also helps people to see a situation from another's perspective and to create healthy, energetic boundaries in life.

Archangel Raguel is often depicted holding a judge's gavel, which represents his work fighting injustice in the world so that good will triumph over evil. When Raguel is around, you may experience or see the colors light or pale blue or aquamarine.

Archangel Raguel helps with the following:

- Empowerment

- Harmony and order

- Healthy, energetic boundaries

- Justice

- Resolution and mediation of conflict and disputes

Archangel Raguel is associated with the following:

- Color/aura: light or pale blue or aquamarine

- Element: wood

- Crystal: aquamarine

- Planet: Mercury

- Zodiac: Sagittarius

- Chakra: throat

## *Archangel Raphael*

(Also known as "God heals," "God has healed," Isrāfīl, Labbiel, "patron of the sick," and "patron of travelers")

> *"I will work with you to create long-lasting change within your life, one step at a time, and to keep your energy clear and your body healthy."*
> —*Archangel Raphael*

Archangel Raphael's name means "God heals" or "God has healed." Raphael is one of the seven core archangels and is first mentioned in the book of Tobit and in 1 Enoch from the third and second century BC. In the book of Tobit, Raphael travels with Tobit's son, Tobias, and keeps him safe from harm, earning Raphael the role as the patron of travelers. Raphael not only supports people when it comes to safe travel, but also helps those on spiritual journeys, assisting them in their search for the truth and giving them guidance along the way.

In later Jewish tradition, Archangel Raphael became identified as one of the three heavenly visitors entertained by Abraham at the Oak of Mamre. And in Islam, where his name is Isrāfīl, he became known as the unnamed angel of Qur'an 6:73, standing with a trumpet to his lips to announce the Day of Judgment when it arrives.

Christian tradition later identifies Archangel Raphael (in John 5:2–4) with healing and as the angel who stirred waters in the pool of Bethesda, where Jesus miraculously healed a paralyzed man. Because of this, as well as Raphael showing Tobias how to use things in medicinal ways for healing treatments and healing Tobit's blindness, Raphael is considered the patron of healing—a healer of the mind, body, and spirit. Lightworkers and energy healers can ask Raphael to open third eyes or for guidance before or during healing sessions. He even assists with establishing energy healing practices by bringing in clients. Raphael is also a healer for all animals and will assist in finding lost pets.

Archangel Raphael is sweet, loving, kind, and gentle. When Raphael is around, you instantly feel calm and may see sparkles or flashes of light purple or emerald-green light. He often works with Archangel Ariel in healing capacities and with Archangel Michael to remove lower energies or spirits from people, places, or things. Raphael is often depicted holding a staff or standing on a fish, which alludes to his healing of Tobias with the fish's gall.

Archangel Raphael helps with the following:

- Guidance and support for healers

- Healing—humans and animals on all levels—mentally, physically, spiritually, and emotionally (including the auric field, chakras, and the physical body)

- Psychic abilities

- Space clearing

- Spirit releasement

Archangel Raphael is associated with the following:

- Color/aura: emerald green and/or light purple

- Element: air

- Crystals: emerald, jade, malachite, and rose quartz

- Planet: Mercury

- Zodiac: Virgo

- Chakras: all chakras, but primarily the heart

# Archangel Raziel

(Also known as "Angel of Mysteries," "Angel of Secrets," "Keeper of All Magic," Gallitsur, "God is my Mystery," Ratziel, Rezial, "secret of God," Saraqael, and Suriel)

*"Use your universal right and power to claim blessings in your life. You can also work with me to bring esoteric information and understand spiritual truths."*

*—Archangel Raziel*

Archangel Raziel's name means "secret of God." In the Kabbalah of Judaism, Raziel is known as Gallitsur, an angel within the teachings of Jewish mysticism, and is the Angel of Secrets and the Angel of Mysteries. Because Raziel works closely with the Creator, he knows the secrets of the universe and how it operates. He wrote down these secrets in code in the Book of the Angel Raziel or Sepher Raziel. (Some believe the book was written by a Jewish scholar during the Middle Ages.) It is difficult to decipher, and it is said that readers must ask Raziel to assist in decoding it.

Archangel Raziel gave the book to Adam for guidance about manifestation and God's grace. The prophet Enoch later received it before he ascended and transformed into Archangel Metatron. Noah also used this information to build his ark before the flood, as well as for help afterward.

When present, Archangel Raziel's wisdom and love can feel subtle; you may also experience or see prisms or rainbows. He helps with understanding the esoteric, conscious connection, sacred geometry, and other deeper principles. Given his knowledge of the secrets of the universe, Raziel assists with manifestation and can open people up to higher levels of psychic abilities and information. Doing so increases the ability to see, hear, feel, and know the Divine.

Archangel Raziel helps with the following:

- Conscious connection

- Divine magic

- Esoteric knowledge and higher levels of information

- Manifestation

- Psychic abilities

Archangel Raziel is associated with the following:

- Color/aura: all the colors of the rainbow (rather than a single color)

- Element: fire

- Crystal: clear quartz

- Planet: Neptune

- Zodiac: Leo

- Chakras: throat and crown

# Archangel Sandalphon

**(Also known as "Angel of Music," Sandolphon, and Sandolfon)**

*"Your prayers have been heard and answered.
Have faith."*

*—Archangel Sandalphon*

Archangel Sandalphon is only one of two archangels whose names don't end in the *el* ("of God") suffix like those of the others. In Greek, Sandalphon means "brother" or "co-brother," a reference to his twin brother, Archangel Metatron. As mentioned before, Sandalphon and Metatron are the only two archangels who were originally mortal men. Both are described as the twin cherubs in the Ark of the Covenant in the book known as the Greater Key of Solomon.

Before he became an archangel, Sandalphon was the prophet Elijah. God gave him sacred assignments as a mortal while on Earth. In order to reward Elijah for a job well done, God transformed him into Archangel Sandalphon, allowing him to continue his sacred service in heaven. Elijah's ascension was recorded in the second chapter of the book of 2 Kings, in which he was lifted up to heaven in a whirlwind by a fiery chariot pulled by two horses of fire.

It is widely known that Archangel Sandalphon is the tallest of the archangels, stretching from Earth all the way to heaven with his feet still planted on the ground. His height is described as taking five hundred years to travel by foot. Because of this, his chief role is to carry human prayers to God so they can be answered. The saying "from your lips to God's ears" certainly applies here. Due to his connection to Earth, most people associate the colors and sounds of nature with Sandalphon's presence. His work and energy can also be seen whenever the life energy of creation is around, whether through the vibrant colors of trees and flowers, the clear blue sky, or the golden sunlight.

Archangel Sandalphon brings messages through gentle whispers and connects deeply with people through music. He is often depicted in art playing music to illustrate his role as the Angel of Music. He provides mental and emotional healing through music. If you hear repeated songs or lyrics, it is often Sandalphon answering your prayers. As a once earthly being, Sandalphon is known as Earth's guardian and the protector of the unborn. Some say he can even help determine the gender of an unborn child. During pregnancy, he offers protection while babies are still in the womb and helps bring safety to the mother and child during childbirth.

Archangel Sandalphon helps with the following:

- Awakening and ascension

- Music—sending messages and healing through it

- Prayers and signs—delivering and answering

- Safety—unborn babies and mothers

- Service—being in service to others

Archangel Sandalphon is associated with the following:

- Color/aura: turquoise

- Elements: all nature elements

- Crystals: turquoise and smoky quartz

- Planet: Earth

- Zodiac: Pisces

- Chakra: throat

## Archangel Uriel

(Also known as Auriel, "Archangel of the North," "fire of God," "God is light," and "God's light")

*"If you have lost your spark—never fear. For I will show you the brilliant glow within, guide you to your truth, and infuse you with strength and determination to see things through."*

—Archangel Uriel

Archangel Uriel's name means "God is light," "God's light," or "fire of God." He is one of the seven core archangels and is regarded as the Archangel of the North and of the element of earth. As a result, Uriel is often associated with the vegetation of Earth and is often shown holding stems of wheat.

Archangel Uriel is also considered one of the wisest angels and is known to give prophecies and to illuminate situations. It is Uriel who warned Noah of the impending flood; he helped the prophet Ezra interpret mystical predictions about the Messiah and delivered Kabbalah to the world. It is said that Uriel also gave humankind the knowledge of alchemy and the practice of manifestation.

Archangel Uriel assists people who need creative insight, knowledge of any kind (including intellectual information), and realistic solutions. For this reason, he patronizes everyone involved in science and education.

Unlike that of other archangels, Uriel's presence is often more subtle. For example, after asking for assistance, an idea or solution will suddenly enter your mind. Know that it is Archangel Uriel.

Given his association with Noah and the flood, Archangel Uriel is also tied to the weather, including rain, thunder, lightning, and natural disasters. Ask Uriel to avert tragedy in these circumstances or to recover afterward.

Archangel Uriel is often depicted carrying a book or a papyrus scroll, representing wisdom. When Uriel is around, you may experience or see the color red.

Archangel Uriel helps with the following:

- Alchemy and divine magic
- Creative insights, problem-solving, and solutions
- Manifestation
- Spiritual understanding
- Weather

Archangel Uriel is associated with the following:

- Color/aura: yellow and red
- Elements: earth and fire
- Crystal: amber
- Planet: Mars
- Zodiac: Aquarius
- Chakra: solar plexus

## *Archangel Zadkiel*

(Also known as "Angel of Mercy and Benevolence," "patron of all who forgive," "the righteousness of God," Satqiel, Tzadkiel, Zadakiel, and Zidekiel)

> *"If there's something you're not seeing, I will help you to see clearly. If you need more compassion, I will fill your heart with mercy. If you are holding onto unforgiveness, I will release it fully. Trust that every detail is taken care of with divine grace, harmony, and wisdom."*
>
> *—Archangel Zadkiel*

Archangel Zadkiel's name means "the righteousness of God." He is one of the seven core archangels and is considered to be the Angel of Mercy and Benevolence and the patron of all who forgive.

Archangel Zadkiel stopped Abraham from sacrificing his son Isaac as an offering to God. As such, Zadkiel can help others feel mercy and compassion and help them let go of judgment in order to forgive. Zadkiel is often depicted holding a knife or dagger. He works alongside Archangel Michael to replace negative thoughts and emotions with love and compassion. Zadkiel assists in removing egoic thoughts and helping people see the divine light within themselves and others.

Archangel Zadkiel assists with memory functions, helping people develop memory in general, memorize things, or remember information. When Zadkiel is around, you may experience or see the color purple.

Archangel Zadkiel helps with the following:

- Compassion and mercy
- Forgiveness of self and others
- Healing
- Memory enhancement and recall
- Removal of egoic thoughts

Archangel Zadkiel is associated with the following:

- Color/aura: dark indigo blue
- Element: metal
- Crystal: lapis lazuli
- Planet: Jupiter
- Zodiac: Gemini
- Chakra: third eye

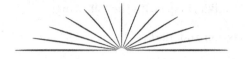

# Channeling an Archangel

## A Story from Barbara L.

**I have always known** that I was sensitive to energies but chose instead to connect through mediums, even after they would tell me I could do it on my own, especially with the angels. As time went on, the angels' persistence in connecting with me grew harder to deny.

Two years ago, I slipped on black ice and got a pretty good concussion. For the first time as an adult, I was forced to slow down and stop. I began a daily meditation practice, and it was life-changing and beautiful. But I still didn't believe that I could communicate with angels, so I searched for the right class, read tons of books, and tried to find a mentor.

One day while cleaning, I walked down the upstairs hallway, and a black feather flew in front of me. (I had left a window open just a little as I was doing laundry.) I immediately panicked, thinking it must mean death or something terrible, so I picked it up and threw it back out the window and continued on.

About fifteen minutes later, I came back down the hall and there was the black feather right there in the middle of the floor. I picked it up and thought, Okay, you have my full attention now; let's see what this is about.

As I sat in meditation, I saw this beautiful angelic being who I could only describe as looking like Aladdin. Curious, I searched online for an angel who looks like Aladdin, and this picture of Archangel Raziel came up. I almost dropped the tablet I was holding.

It was the angel in the vision I had seen. I had never heard of him before and felt embarrassed. So, I sat again and asked if this was Archangel Raziel, and my left hand started trembling and my index finger started intensely tapping the tablet.

I couldn't make my finger stop tapping or slow my mind. I thought I was going crazy. I had to get up, walk away, and recenter myself. I sat down again later that night, and as the connection was building, my finger started tapping again. This time I just let it happen. It started moving as if I were writing with my left hand (I am right-handed).

At the same time, words were coming through me that didn't feel like my own. I grabbed a pen and paper, and my left hand began writing the most beautiful words about love and light. The words just flowed and flowed through me over the pages.

When it slowed down and I read what I wrote, it was as if I was seeing these words for the first time. This started a lovely relationship with the beautiful Archangel Raziel.

*Chapter 11*

# Ascended Masters

---

*"If we are serious about dreaming our awakening into being and creating a peaceful, loving Earth in which the heart, spirit and soul are the only true leaders, we must continue to keep our focus on thoughts of unity and all that truly brings us together."*

*—Diane Hall*

---

In the 1870s, Helena P. Blavatsky, a Russian mystic and author who cofounded the Theosophical Society, presented the idea of Masters of the Ancient Wisdom or "enlightened beings." However, the term *ascended master* was first introduced and used by Baird T. Spalding in 1924 in his multivolume book series *Life and Teachings of the Masters of the Far East.* Godfre Ray King (also known as Guy Ballard) further popularized the concept of ascended masters through his book *Unveiled Mysteries,* in which he stated that the ascended master Saint Germain gave him the information to write it.

An ascended master is a notable spiritual teacher, healer, or prophet who previously walked the Earth on a journey of self-mastery, just as you are now. During their life experiences and ascension process, they gained mastery over the physical limitations of this dimension, balanced their negative karma, and fulfilled their divine plan. Throughout many incarnations, these souls chose to live in their greatest potential, accomplishing many lifetimes of purposeful service here on Earth—and in some instances, on other planets or in other solar systems as well.

As they get closer to becoming an ascended master, a soul consciously opens to the realization that all of their incarnations are happening simultaneously. It is this conscious awareness that gives them a deeper understanding of their connection to the Divine and alignment with their higher self.

Upon graduating from the physical Earth plane, all souls ascend and contain within them a living "library" of wisdom (also known as the Akashic records) gained from all of their physical embodiments.

Souls that are in the process of becoming an ascended master have the choice to share their embodied wisdom by serving other souls on a similar journey as an ascended master, teacher, mentor, or guide. These spiritually enlightened beings consciously decide to be in service to humankind and Earth by helping us to attain our own ascension and move forward in spiritual evolution beyond this planet. They remain attentive to the spiritual needs of humanity by inspiring and motivating us in our spiritual growth. By helping us each individually, they are, in turn, helping the collective world.

Ascended masters come from all cultures, religions, and civilizations. In many traditions and organizations worldwide, they are known as the Spiritual Hierarchy of Earth or the Great Brotherhood of Light. Some examples of ascended masters you might be familiar with include Jesus and Buddha.

I've worked with several ascended masters during my life, including Jesus. But it took some time to get there. Unlike Archangel Michael, I couldn't feel and sense the ascended masters so easily.

As I grew up, I trusted my inner knowing that certain things—call it God, Universe, and Source (GUS)—were "real." It wasn't blind faith, but rather a deep sense that something existed beyond me and outside of the everyday. I was able to completely trust this feeling because I remembered my connection to the Divine before I came to Earth. But when it came to spiritual beings like Jesus, I didn't know what to think, feel, or believe. I didn't doubt that someone named Jesus had been here on Earth, nor that his life and teachings had launched an entire worldwide religion and inspired the masses. It was the narrative we had been told that I doubted. He lived—yes. However, was he merely a man who once walked the Earth or the true son of God who once walked on water?

To answer questions like these, where the answers don't easily come to me intuitively, I've always taken the approach of employing a healthy dose of curiosity. I told myself early on that I would be open to possibilities but let the Universe show me situations and/or things I needed to experience. All the things I believe in today—the Universe, God connection, archangels—I have experienced, and therefore 100 percent believe to be true.

A few weeks after my reiki master certification, my then-boyfriend shared some medical news. He worked at a hospital and, during his shifts, had been having some heart issues. They ran tests and, based on the results, found that his heart was failing. At such a young age, he understandably was upset. However, he worked out, ate right, and took care of himself. While he could have surgery and take other medical steps to help his heart, it would always be weak and would progressively get worse as he got older. In that moment of despair, I received a message for him to try a reiki session.

Before then, I hadn't even told him I had gotten my reiki master certification, let alone shared with him that I talked to angels. The reason was that he was a hardcore medical practitioner; logic ruled and the supernatural just didn't fit in his world. I remember calmly telling him everything would be all right and asking him if he would be open to trying a holistic practice like reiki. At the very least, I urged that it would relax him. Since I was so new in my certification, I asked my mentor if she would work on him. She agreed but with a caveat—we had to work on him together.

And that's how, a few days later, I found myself in a room with my boyfriend on a massage table as my mentor began to send him reiki energy. She was standing at his head, and I was standing at his feet. I recall praying to God and asking the angels for a miracle. I tapped into the love that I felt for my boyfriend and just let that flow from me into him. Typically, when working on something, whether it is an energy healing or an intuitive session, I like to keep my eyes closed so that I can pay attention to the information and visuals I receive with my mind's eye. But I felt led to open my eyes at one point. At that moment, with the candlelight flickering, I looked at him lying on the table. There was a blanket over him. On the blanket, a shadow began to take form. My eyes grew wide, but I wasn't afraid. I was curious. We were in the presence of angelic energy, and I felt loved and protected. As I was trying to make out what the shape of the form was, my mentor sensed something and opened her eyes too. She looked around and saw nothing. She mouthed, "What is going on?" I didn't want to interrupt the session, so I just waved her on. As she closed her eyes, I focused again on the form on the blanket. It had taken the shape of the Shroud of Turin. I instantly knew that it was Jesus Christ. The next message I received was "All will be well." With his eyes still closed, my boyfriend began to weep.

As he relaxed in another room, my mentor and I washed our hands. She asked me what I had seen, and I described it to her. I was in a state of both disbelief and immense gratitude. I didn't want her to share with him what I had experienced in that room. Up until a few days before, he hadn't even known that I had gotten my reiki certification. Now, I was supposed to tell him that I had seen Jesus Christ? That we had experienced a miracle? My ego feared that he wouldn't believe me or, worse, that he would think I was insane and break up with me. But she told me that, as lightworkers, we need to stand in our truth. So, I told him. He didn't say much. I think he was overwhelmed by the entire experience, let alone that tidbit of information.

Several days after the energy healing, he went in for another round of his tests and a second opinion. A few days later, the results came back. There were absolutely no signs of a heart condition. His heart was healthy. He was in total disbelief. To add to his utter amazement, when the doctors went to compare the second results to the first test results, they couldn't find the paperwork. They looked high and low, but it had gone missing. I told him that Spirit was saying that it was a chapter in his life that was now closed. There was no reason to dig it back up or try and understand why it happened, other than to acknowledge and embrace that he had experienced a miracle and it was a gift from the Universe. Sometime soon after that, he broke up with me. I wasn't sad because I had experienced a miracle too. And my path was clear to me now.

That was the first experience I had with Jesus Christ, whom I consider an ascended master. It was also the first time outside of Archangel Michael that I had become acutely aware of other spiritual beings on my team and by my side. For the purpose of this book, I have asked them who would like to be featured in this chapter. The following is what they shared.

# Buddha

(Also known as Buddha Gautama, Lord Goutama, Siddhartha Buddha, and Siddhartha Gautama)

*"The root of suffering is attachment."*
*—Buddha*

Born on May 8 on a full moon around 500 BC, Prince Gautama Siddhartha grew up wealthy, behind palace walls. However, as he grew older and saw life outside the palace, he noticed the extreme poverty and illness others experienced. Wanting to alleviate the suffering he witnessed, he renounced his title and wealth and left where he grew up.

When he felt that wasn't enough, Siddhartha sat underneath a fig tree and vowed not to get up until he became fully enlightened. For forty-nine days, he ignored bodily needs like hunger and sleep. Once these were overcome, he saw that he had lived and died many times over. He saw what he had done during his past lives, the good as well as the bad. It was with this awareness that Siddhartha was able to understand negative emotions, pain, and death—and more importantly, how to overcome them. When he finally stood, he was Buddha, "the Enlightened or Awakened One." And the fig tree became known as the bodhi- or bo-tree.

Buddha's teachings help us understand detachment from suffering for inner peace. This is what became the basis for Buddhism. He proposed that the key to a happy life was "the Middle Way"—moderation in all things.

Buddha helps with the following:

- Balance in all things

- Detachment from suffering

- Inner peace

- Joy and happiness

- Spiritual growth and understanding

# Mary

(Also known as "beloved mother," Maryam, Mother Mary, Our Lady, Our Lady of Guadalupe, "Queen of the Angels," and Virgin Mary)

---

*"All people, regardless of culture or beliefs, are one. We embody the very source that created us. When we live more fully and are conscious of our presence, we align with our higher selves and purpose here on Earth."*

—*Mary*

Mary was born in 18 BC, on September 8, and lived in Nazareth, a small working-class village. She was a first-century Jewish woman of Nazareth, the wife of Joseph, and the mother of Jesus Christ. Because Joseph worked as a carpenter outside the home, it is said that Mary spent her time tending to family and household needs. Historians speculate that she led a difficult life trying to raise money for food and avoiding the dangers of religious, political, and military uprisings. It is also believed that Mary may have taken baby Jesus to Qumran and lived there temporarily among the Essenes to learn the mystical secrets of the Dead Sea Scrolls.

In Christianity, Mary is commonly referred to as the Virgin Mary, in accordance with the belief that the Holy Spirit impregnated her, thereby allowing her to conceive her firstborn son, Jesus, miraculously, without having sexual relations with her husband, Joseph.

The Eastern and Oriental Orthodox Church of the East and the Catholic, Anglican, and Lutheran Churches believe that Mary, as the mother of Jesus, is the Mother of God. Other Protestant views on Mary vary, with some holding her to have considerably less status.

In Islam, Mary is known as Maryam, the mother of Isa. She is often referred to by the title Sayyidatuna, meaning "Our Lady." This title parallels to Sayyiduna ("Our Lord"), used for the prophets. She is also called Tahira, meaning "one who has been purified," representing her status as one who must be protected at all times.

Mary has been called the Queen of Angels, given her interaction with Archangel Gabriel on the announcement of Jesus's incarnation. She loves to work with children and guides us to use our intelligence, wisdom, and love when dealing with them. When she shows up, her energetic presence is loving, patient, and kind. She is often felt by a sweet, loving warmth in the heart area.

Mary helps with the following:

- Children

- Communication with angels

- Healing power

- Love

- Understanding and mercy

# Mary Magdalene

(Also known as Mary of Madala, Mary of Madgala, "the Magdalene," "the Madeleine," and "she of a thousand angels")

*"Think of and embrace me as a mentor for your spiritual evolution."*

—*Mary Magdalene*

In both the Catholic and Protestant traditions, as well as the popular culture of the Western world, Mary Magdalene is portrayed by the Church as a prostitute who was redeemed by her love for Jesus Christ. However, neither the Eastern Orthodox traditions nor the Gnostic traditions portray her in this way. The labeling of Mary Magdalene as a prostitute originated with Pope Gregory the Great, when he issued Homily 33 in AD 591. Gregory claimed that the seven devils that Jesus cast out of Mary Magdalene were the seven deadly sins, and he reinterpreted her act of washing Jesus's feet with her tears and drying them with her hair.

Gregory asserted that Mary Magdalene, Mary (sister of Martha and Lazarus of Bethany), and the unnamed sinner in Luke who anoints Christ's feet were all the same person. And although the Catholic Church officially redacted this decree in 1969, Gregory's depiction of Mary Magdalene is still believed by many to be true.

In reality, little is known for certain about Mary Magdalene. Indeed, even the origin of her name is unclear. Her epithet, "the Magdalene," indicates that she came from Magdala, a fishing village in Israel on the western shore of the Sea of Galilee. Others believe that Magdala means "tower," "magnificent," or "great" and that calling her Mary Magdalene is like calling her "Mary the Great."

What is known is that she was an independent woman who finan-
cially aided and traveled with Jesus as one of his followers. It is said
that when Jesus's men abandoned him at the hour of mortal danger,
Mary Magdalene was one of the only people who stayed with him,
witnessing both his crucifixion and his resurrection. She was present
at Jesus's tomb, was the first person to whom Jesus appeared after his
resurrection, and was the first to share news of the miracle. Further,
in the Gospel of Mary, which isn't officially recognized by the Church,
Mary Magdalene is framed as the only disciple who truly understands
Jesus's spiritual message, which puts her in direct conflict with other
apostles. This all demonstrates Mary Magdalene's strength, power,
and uniqueness.

Mary Magdalene helps with the following:

- Devotion

- Grace

- Mercy

- Spiritual awakenings and evolution

- Understanding eternal life

# Melchizedek

(Also known as "king of righteousness" and "genuine or rightful king")

*"There is one great truth on this planet, and that is whoever you are, or whatever it is that you do when you're called to do something, it's because that desire originated in the soul of the universe. It's your mission on Earth. To realize one's destiny is a person's only obligation."*

—*Melchizedek*

Melchizedek's history differs according to sources. In the Dead Sea Scrolls, he is named Michael, and there is a reference to Melchizedek being the same energetic being as Archangel Michael and Jesus. In letters to the Hebrews from the apostle Paul, he shares that Melchizedek and Jesus are both high priests. Further, the Eastern spiritual text Nag Hammadi discusses Melchizedek being a past incarnation of Jesus Christ. Additionally, ancient mystical texts describe him as conducting spiritual releasement on a large scale and working alongside Archangel Michael. According to the book of Enoch, Melchizedek was the son of Noah's brother Nir. Nir's wife died before giving birth, and Melchizedek was delivered posthumously. However, there is other speculation that he is actually Noah's son Shem.

Despite this conflicting history, Melchizedek means "king of righteousness" or "genuine or rightful king." He was a Canaanite priest-king of Salem (now known as Jerusalem) and was a teacher of Abraham. It is said that Melchizedek made the first offering of bread and wine to Abraham for his military victory and is even depicted in a stone sculpture holding a cup at the Chartres Cathedral in France.

Today, Melchizedek is believed to be the leader of a group of high spiritual beings who are custodians and teachers of ancient secrets and who operate on the Law of No Interference, meaning they don't interfere and only assist when called upon.

Melchizedek helps with the following:

- Energy clearing and purification

- Esoteric understanding

- Manifestation

- Protection from psychic attacks

- Spirit releasement

# Merlin
## (Also known as Emrys, Merddin, Merlyn, and Myrddin)

*"Pain is what you get through in order to find the truth."*

—Merlin

Much myth and lore surround Merlin. Did he really live, or is he merely a legend? Merlin represents the magical wizard archetype. A sage and wise advisor to King Arthur during the fifth century in Wales, Merlin is said to be a powerful magician, spiritual teacher, and psychic visionary. He is also associated with Guinevere (wife of King Arthur), the Lady of the Lake (aka the fairy Viviane), and the goddesses of Avalon and Glastonbury.

Some spiritual practitioners believe that Merlin is an incarnation of Saint Germain. Merlin loves to work with people, help them tap into the magical side of energy, and guide them to be in service and not for self-gain.

Merlin helps with the following:

- Alchemy or divine magic

- Crystal work

- Energy healing work

- Prophecy or divination

- Psychic abilities

*Much myth*

*and lore*

surround Merlin.

Did he really live,

or is he merely

*a legend?*

# Saint Francis

(Also known as Francis Bernardone, Giovanni di Pietro di Bernardone, Saint Francis of Assisi, and Poverello)

*"Start by doing what is necessary, then what is possible, and suddenly you are doing the impossible."*
—*Saint Francis*

Born in 1181 in Assisi, Italy, to a wealthy cloth merchant and noblewoman, Giovanni di Pietro di Bernardone, also known as Francesco or Francis for short, grew up carefree and well loved. Like many of his class in Italy, Francis learned the military arts and engaged in the rivalries among local towns. During one such war between Assisi and neighboring Perugia, he was wounded and imprisoned for a year. After his release, Francis suffered a long illness, most likely caused by his imprisonment.

When he recovered, he resumed his military career and set out to fight the war on the side of the pope. It was at this point that Francis had a dream in which he saw his father's house glorified with signs of military and religious items. A voice then told him to end his journey in order "to serve the Master rather than the man." This experience profoundly changed him; from then on, he followed a path of spiritual devotion.

When Francis returned home, he searched for a new direction in his life. After another vision in which Jesus called upon him to fix the roof of a church, he sold some of his father's goods to pay for the repairs. While the priest did not take his money, he did allow Francis to stay in the church to pray and fast. His father came looking for Francis and ended up imprisoning him and asking the Bishop of Assisi to support him in having Francis change his ways. Francis instead returned the money he had taken, took off his clothes, and handed them to his father as a sign of separation from worldly ways.

He stated, "From now on, I say only 'Our Father who art in heaven.'" At this, the bishop covered Francis with his own robe.

Gradually, Francis's reputation for simplicity and selflessness began to attract followers as he took a vow of poverty and devoted his life to doing compassionate work and preaching to others. He said that he felt commanded to do so by Jesus himself. Legend has it that he would also preach to birds, animals, and reptiles about God's love and that they would seemingly be enthralled. Birds would become quiet. Rabbits would hop in his lap. And during one visit to the Italian town of Gubbio, Francis was even able to tame a wolf with his love.

Francis passed away on October 4, 1226. Two years later, he was canonized as Saint Francis of Assisi and is known as the patron saint of the environment and animals because he loved all creatures. While in the spirit world, Saint Francis tends to be around people who are animal lovers or whose life purpose involves helping these angels on Earth and the planet.

Saint Francis helps with the following:

- Animal communication

- Healing—animals and environment

- Life purpose and direction

- Need for detachment from people, places, or things

- Peace—personal and global

# Saint Germain

(Also known as Comte de Saint Germain, Count of Saint Germain, "der Wundermann/the Wonderman of Europe," and Saint Germaine)

*"Attention is the key—for where man's attention goes, there goes his energy, and he himself can only follow."*
—*Saint Germain*

Saint Germain was a royal count and lived in the French region called Saint-Germain in the eighteenth century. His real name is unknown, and his birth and background are relatively obscure. An adventurer with an interest in science, alchemy, and the arts, he achieved prominence in European high society and has been considered by some to be one of the world's greatest philosophers.

Saint Germain is believed to have been born between 1690 and 1710. Later in life, he claimed to be the son of Prince Francis II Rákóczi of Transylvania, which would explain his great wealth and extensive education. However, others believe he *was* Prince Rákóczi. Some report that his father was Comte Adanero and his mother was Marie de Neubourg, the widow of Charles II of Spain.

Regardless of his origin, Saint Germain went to great lengths to deliberately confuse people and conceal his actual name, using different pseudonyms wherever he traveled. He'd even make outlandish claims, like being five hundred years old, in order to deflect inquiries about his background. This led Voltaire, the famous French writer, to call him "the Wonderman," stating that "he is a man who does not die and who knows everything."

As Saint Germain rubbed elbows with European royalty and high society, he'd regale them with his multiple talents (that he allegedly acquired under the tutelage of the last of the Medicis in Italy), including speaking numerous languages, playing the violin flawlessly, painting exquisite artwork (often with gems and crystals in strong, bold colors), and even giving accurate psychic readings. He also spent time studying and teaching the occult and alchemy, and was involved in founding several secret societies, including the Freemasons. Thus, it isn't surprising that he gave friends elixirs that supposedly would restore youth and boasted that he could turn lead into gold. He'd often talk about his multiple past lives, claiming that he was with Nero in Rome in one of them.

As a visionary, Saint Germain was deeply involved in politics, and it is believed that he was partially responsible for Catherine the Great taking the throne. Furthermore, he'd often offer his psychic visions freely. Fifteen years before it happened, he foretold the French Revolution to Marie Antoinette.

Saint Germain helps with the following:

- Clarity about one's life purpose or calling

- Clear direction

- Energy or space clearings

- Manifestation

- Psychic information and psychic protection

*Note: Saint Germain is not a Catholic saint and is not to be confused with Saint Germaine Cousin or Saint Germanus, who are two actual Catholic saints. In addition, his name has occasionally caused him to be confused for Claude Louis, Comte de Saint-Germain, a noted French general.*

# Saint Padre Pio

(Also known as Francisco Forgione, Padre Pio, and Saint Pius of Pietrelcina)

*"Prayer is the oxygen of the soul."*
*—Saint Padre Pio*

Francisco Forgione was born in Naples, Italy, on May 25, 1887. At age sixteen, he changed his name to Pio, meaning "pious," when he entered the Capuchin monastery. At age seventeen, he fell ill, complaining of loss of appetite, insomnia, exhaustion, fainting spells, and migraines. Religious devotees point to this as the time when the inexplicable phenomena began to occur. During prayers, for example, Pio appeared to others to be in a stupor, as if he were absent. A fellow friar later claimed to have seen him levitating above the ground. Soon after, Padre Pio began to experience stigmata—wounds on his hands and feet where Jesus had been impaled with nails. This lasted for fifty years, until his death.

Padre Pio is said to have had the gift of reading souls and the ability to bilocate and accurately predict the future, among other supernatural phenomena. He communicated with angels, worked miracles, and conducted healings, including helping the blind to see. During his healings, Padre Pio asked people to admit the true underlying source of their ailment or pain out loud. In doing so, the root cause (e.g., trauma, deep-seated emotions, or other) of the illness was identified, and the person became healed.

When Padre Pio shows up, he is very spirited and brings forth a lot of enthusiasm, optimism, and faith. You will likely feel uplifted and light.

Padre Pio helps with the following:

- Ability to heal on all levels—personal and global

- Communication with angels

- Forgiveness

- Passion for oneself or others

- Spiritual growth

# The Virgin Mary and a White Rose

### *A Story from Denise T.*

**In my early twenties** (I'm forty-one now), I was introduced to Sylvia Browne. In her books, she talks a lot about Mother God (another name for the Virgin Mary). Sylvia wrote that you can ask the Virgin Mary for a sign to show you that she is with you. All you have to do is ask for a rose within seven days. I thought that was so cool and said, "I'm going to try it." So, I asked for a white rose.

Every day I was anxiously waiting for my white rose to arrive. Day seven came and no rose. I came home from work that day sad, thinking about why my rose hadn't come. My brother was home and asked me to watch a movie with him. I agreed and thought maybe it would distract me from my disappointment. We were watching the movie, and in it, someone died and the main character was going to the funeral. All of a sudden, the camera zooms in to what he is holding in his hand—a white rose and, attached to the rose, a note.

The camera focuses on the note, and it reads, "God works in mysterious ways!" OMG, the joy that shot through my body at that moment! I had the biggest smile on my face. Every time I think of that day, a huge smile always appears, and I can still feel the love and joy from knowing that Mother God is always with me.

# Chapter 12

# Deities

---

*"The heavens are too immense, too beautiful and varied, to fit into the mind of any one deity."*

—*John Pipkin*

---

A deity or god is a supernatural being who is considered to be divine or sacred. *The Oxford English Dictionary* defines a deity as "a god or goddess and anything revered as divine." I believe many of the deities that people believe in today were likely people who once lived on Earth and, after becoming a legend over time, began to be worshipped. As you can imagine, the origin stories and nature of specific deities vary greatly and can sometimes present a blurred picture of who and what they are. However, as I did with the ascended masters, I asked which deities should be featured in this book, and the following is what they shared.

# *Apollo*

(Also known as Apollo the Sun God, Apollon, Apolo, and "God of the Sun and the Light")

*"Myths can't be translated or understood as they once did in ancient times. We alone can find our own meaning in time."*

—*Apollo*

Apollo is one of the Olympian deities in classical Greek and Roman religion and mythology. The national divinity of the Greeks, Apollo has been recognized as a god of archery, dance, music, poetry, truth, prophecy, healing and diseases, the sun (and light), and more. Considered the most beautiful god and Zeus's favorite son, Apollo is one of the most important and complex of the Greek gods. He and his twin sister, Artemis, goddess of the hunt, were born to a Titan goddess named Leto.

As the patron deity of Delphi, Apollo is a prophetic deity of the Delphic Oracle. He wards off evil and is called the averter of evil. Medicine and healing, also associated with mythology, tell that Apollo delivered people from (and also created) epidemics and protected animals from diseases and predators. As a guardian of the young, Apollo helps with the health and education of children.

The invention of archery is credited to Apollo and Artemis, and he is usually depicted as carrying a bow and arrows. His other symbols are the lyre, python, sword, laurel, laurel wreath, and cypress. Poet and author Homer and philosopher Porphyry both wrote that Apollo had a hawk as a messenger, and in many myths, Apollo transformed into a hawk, which was sacred to the gods.

Apollo helps with the following:

- Arts—music, dance, and poetry
- Children—health and education
- Healing—animals and people
- Prophecy
- Protection against evil

# Artemis

(Also known as Artemis Calliste, Delia, "Huntress of Souls," Luna, Mother Artemis, and Phoebe)

*"Your only goal—as is mine—should be to bring light to this world."*

—*Artemis*

Artemis was born to the Greek god Zeus and the Titan goddess Leto. Her twin brother is Apollo. In Greek religion, Artemis is the goddess of nature, wild animals, the hunt, and vegetation, as well as childbirth, care of children, and chastity. She was regarded as one of the most prominent lunar deities in mythology, alongside two moon goddesses—Selene and Hecate. The goddess Diana is her Roman equivalent. Her symbols are the bow and arrow, crescent moon, spear, torch and cypress, and palm and walnut trees. Animals associated with her are the deer, serpent, dog, boar, goat, bear, quail, and buzzard.

Known as the Huntress of Souls, Artemis spends most of her time in nature with the wood nymphs, carrying a bow and arrow. She fiercely protects anyone who calls upon her through her wisdom and mainly defends animals, children, and single women. A powerful manifestor, Artemis teaches the importance of spending time in nature and becoming more authentic by aligning with our higher selves.

Artemis helps with the following:

- Children
- Environmentalism
- Feminine power
- Intuition
- Wildlife

A powerful manifestor,

Artemis teaches the

importance of spending

time in nature and

*becoming more authentic*

by aligning with

our higher selves.

# Ganesh

(Also known as Buddhi Vinayaka, Ganesha, Ganapataya, Pillaiyar, and Vinayaka)

*"Obstacles are either self-imposed, representing your fear to move forward, or detours in the right direction. I can help you move through or around them with unwavering love."*

—*Ganesh*

Ganesh is one of the most well-known deities in the Hindu religion and culture. His image, usually identified by his elephant head, is found throughout India, and Hindu denominations worship him regardless of affiliation. There are many different stories as to why Ganesh has an elephant head. In most tales, Ganesh lost his head due to his father's anger, and his mother took the first head she could find—a baby elephant's—and placed it on her son's neck. In Hinduism, Ganesh is the first deity contacted during prayers.

Ganesh is known to remove obstacles and bring good luck to anyone who asks for his help. As the Hindu god of prosperity, intellect, and wisdom, he also assists with writing, science, and art projects. When he shows up, his energy is extremely loving, gentle, and sweet. It is also very strong in presence. Similar to Archangel Michael, Ganesh is a loving, loyal, and protective force.

He is called the Remover of All Obstacles because he knocks out anything that stands in your way that isn't for your best and highest good. Imagine an elephant as the gentle giant that it is. As it moves forward, it clears a path to make the way easier for you to navigate. That is how Ganesh works.

The mantra "Om Gam Ganapataye Namaha" is used to call in the energy of Ganesh and inspire transformation. The meaning of each element of the mantra is as follows:

- **Om:** This is the sound that represents the birth of the universe and the connection between all living beings.

- **Gam:** This is the sound of the root chakra that awakens the energy at the base of the spine, where Ganesh is thought to reside.

- **Ganapataye:** This is another name for Ganesh.

- **Namaha:** This is a salutation similar to namaste.

Ganesh helps with the following:

- Artistic, creative, science, or writing projects

- Intellect or wisdom

- Prosperity and abundance

- Removal of obstacles or blockages

- Transcendence and enhanced awareness

# Hecate

(Also known as Artemis, Brimo Crataeis, Persephone, Selene, and the Triple Goddess)

*"I am she that is the natural mother of all things, governess of all the elements, the initial progeny of worlds, chief of powers divine, queen of heaven, the principal of the gods celestial, the light of the goddesses."*

—*Hecate*

The name Hecate means "worker from afar" (from the Greek word *hekatos*). She was an important figure in Greek mythology and religion, and was often associated with other gods and goddesses, such as Artemis, Persephone, and Hermes. Her scope of divine duties was extensive in Greek religion, and she was most notably the goddess of magic, witchcraft, the night, and the moon. Further, she was the goddess and protector of the *oikos* (meaning "house and household" in Greek) and entranceways. Hecate also supported and protected athletes, children, hunters, farmers, fishermen, and warriors.

Hecate was commonly depicted in Greek poetry wearing a long robe and holding burning torches in her hands, given her connection with the night. Later, Hecate's most prevalent and iconic representation was as a triple-formed goddess, with each form standing back-to-back looking at each direction of the crossroads. The three bodies represent her triple aspect as goddess of the underworld, Earth, and sky. Most often these are in human form, but sometimes she was depicted having the head of a dog, a lion, and a horse, representing different constellations and time periods. Hecate's most sacred animal was the dog, with her presence accompanied by the sound of dogs' barks from the underworld.

Hecate symbolizes the dualities of "good" and "bad." Her powers are believed to transcend the boundaries of the sky, Earth, seas, and underworld. It is because of this that she is often called upon to bestow prosperity, wealth, fertility, and wisdom, as well as for protection or guidance in difficult times. Due to her dualistic nature, she can bestow these blessings on people, but also withhold them. She is also believed to help with mental illness and to oversee magic of all kinds, including spells.

Hecate helps with the following:

- Agriculture

- Crossroads and travel

- Households

- Magic

- Nighttime (and the moon)

# Ida-Ten

(Also known as Idaten, Hufa Weituo Zuntian Pusa or "Wei Tuo," and Skanda)

*"Go in peace and be of light."*
*—Ida-Ten*

When alive, Ida-Ten was a Mahāyāna bodhisattva and devoted guardian of Buddhist monasteries designed to protect and preserve the teachings of Buddhism. He is now considered a Japanese god of protection and is also known as Skanda, a Chinese god of protection. He is sometimes referred to in the Chinese tradition as Hufa Weituo Zuntian Pusa (or "Wei Tuo" for short), meaning "Honored Dharma Protector Skanda Bodhisattva." Because of this, Ida-Ten is also held in high regard for purity, truth, justice, and the law.

When Ida-Ten shows up, there is often a subtle shift of energy that occurs. He is quiet yet powerful, often sending advice around ethical or legal situations, and works at miraculous speed.

Ida-Ten helps with the following:

- Justice

- Persecution due to religious and/or spiritual beliefs

- Positive energy

- Protection

- Truth

*Note: Ida-Ten technically could be considered an ascended master, but because little is known about his early life, he is placed here as a deity.*

*When Ida-Ten shows up,*

there is often a subtle shift of

energy that occurs.

*He is quiet yet powerful.*

# Isis

(Also known as Divine Mother, "Goddess of the Mysteries," "Goddess of Nature," Isis Myrionymos, "Lady of Magic," and "Mistress of Hermetic Wisdom")

*"Stand in strength and power through loving confidence."*

—*Isis*

Isis is an ancient Egyptian goddess of fertility, motherhood, magic, death, healing, and rebirth. She was the first daughter of Geb (the god of Earth) and Nut (the goddess of the sky). She married her brother Osiris. While she was away, her other brother Seth murdered Osiris. When she returned and discovered the murder, she was able to revive Osiris, and they conceived a son, Horus.

Scholars regard Isis as the original high priestess of magic due to the legend that she convinced Ra to reveal his secret name to her. It is said that as soon as she heard the secret name, Isis automatically received the understanding of high magic. As a result, Isis is believed to use magical rods to heal and rattles to remove negative energies. Her reputed magical power was greater than that of all other gods, protecting the kingdom from its enemies, governing the skies and the natural world, and even having power over fate itself.

Isis is also considered a queen of the underworld because she resurrected her slain brother and husband and was believed to help the dead enter the afterlife. Her protective wings are engraved around Egyptian sarcophaguses, as they symbolize Isis's ability to renew the souls of the dead.

Isis helps with the following:

- Communication with people who have passed over

- Divine magic

- Energetic healing on all levels—emotionally, physically, mentally, and spiritually

- Fertility and/or feminine energy and strength

- Protection

# *Jesus*

(Also known as Acharya, Christ, Immanuel, Isa ibn Maryam, Jesus Christ, Jesus of Nazareth, "Lamb of God," Messiah, Rabbi, "Son of Man," "Good Shepherd," and Yeshua)

> *"I will take your pain. I will carry your burden. I will give you rest. My peace I give you."*
>
> *—Jesus*

Jesus was born to Mary and Joseph in Bethlehem, which is in the hill country of the Holy Land just south of Jerusalem. His actual date of birth is not stated in the Gospels or in any historical sources, but most scholars assume it occurred between 6 BC ("before Christ") and 4 BC. The common traditional dating of the birth date of Jesus is December 25, a date first given by Pope Julius in AD 350 (or anno Domini, meaning "in the year of the lord" in Latin), although the claim is unfounded.

Virtually all modern scholars agree that Jesus existed historically. Accounts of his life are contained in the Gospels, especially the four canonical Gospels in the New Testament. Academic research has resulted in uncertainty of how historically reliable the Gospels are and how accurately they reflect the historical Jesus. What is known is that Jesus was a first-century Galilean Jew, preacher, and religious leader. He was baptized by John the Baptist and began his own ministry, in which he discussed how to best follow God, engaged in healings, taught in parables, and gathered followers.

Jesus is the central figure of Christianity, currently the world's largest religion. Most Christians believe Jesus to be the incarnation of God the Son and the awaited Messiah—the Christ that is prophesied in the Hebrew Bible. Jesus is associated with the Godhead that acknowledges him as part of the Holy Trinity—God the Father, Son, and Holy Spirit. Christianity views Jesus as God's son and equal to the Father and the Holy Spirit.

The precise identity of Jesus has been debated for thousands of years. Ascribing Jesus as equal to God the Father is the core of Christianity, and many believe that is the reason why he was crucified. Other religions, such as Judaism and Islam, view Jesus not as God himself but as a rabbi, priest, and prophet. Still others identify Jesus as an ascended master, a category not mentioned in sacred texts.

Jesus was arrested in Jerusalem shortly after the Last Supper and tried by the authorities, who turned him over to the Roman government, which had him crucified. His followers, including Mary Magdalene, stated he rose from the dead three days after his death, before ascending to heaven. The community that formed in the aftermath eventually became the early Chrisitan Church, and accounts of his life and teachings resulted in the written Gospels.

Jesus helps with the following:

- Faith

- Forgiveness—of self and others

- Healing (on all levels)

- Hope and peace

- Miracles

# Kwan Yin

(Also known as Guanyin, Kanin, Kannon, Kwannon, Kuan Yin, "Mother Mary of the East," and Quan Yin)

*"I always hear and answer your prayers, but also help you to uncover and understand what your true needs are through compassion."*

—*Kwan Yin*

The embodiment of compassion, Kwan Yin is said to be "she who hears the cries of the world." One of Buddhism's most beloved bodhisattvas, she also holds a special place in the hearts of people of other faiths, including Daoists and Confucianists.

Kwan Yin is the protector of women, children, sailors, fishermen, anyone in trouble, and the sick, disabled, and poor. Some Buddhist schools present her as male and female interchangeably. The idea is that a bodhisattva, a being of great realization who vows to forego enlightenment until all sentient beings are liberated, can manifest in whatever form will most effectively free beings from suffering.

According to legend, when trying to alleviate the suffering of human beings, Kwan Yin's head split into eleven pieces. Wanting to help her, Amitabha Buddha awarded Kwan Yin eleven heads with which to hear the cries of the world. But when she heard all the cries and reached out to address the needs of so many, her two arms shattered. This time, Amitabha gave Kwan Yin a thousand arms, and it's said that even now she's still using those arms to offer her compassion to all.

When Kwan Yin is around, she may try and get your attention through the use of flowers, or you may feel a heart-centered connection.

Kwan Yin helps with the following:

- Compassion
- Kindness to self and others
- Mercy
- Protection
- Spiritual enlightenment

# Serapis Bey

**(Also known as Apis, Asar-Apis, Serapis, and Osiris-Apis)**

*"Once you have made a serious commitment to your ascension, all of heaven is yours, and it will assist you in wonderous ways."*

*—Serapis Bey*

Serapis Bey was originally known as an Egyptian god of the underworld named Serapis, who was in charge of the ascension at Luxor, Egypt. He is thought to have incarnated as a high priest in one of the Temples of Sacred Fire on Atlantis and migrated to Egypt at the time of the destruction of Atlantis. He is believed to have many other incarnations on Earth, including the Egyptian Pharaoh Amenhotep III, who constructed the Temple of Luxor to the god Amun; Leonidas, the king of Sparta; and the philosophers Confucius and Plato.

Serapis Bey is considered part of the Spiritual Hierarchy of Earth, also known as the Great Brotherhood of Light, and helps people work toward ascension through spiritual enlightenment and understand the process of change. An extremely loving ascended master, he is actively involved in bringing peace to Earth. He also loves to motivate people toward healthy lifestyles, including fitness, self-care, and spiritual wellness. Consider him a spiritual fitness guru who inspires, motivates, and provides hope for the future.


Serapis Bey helps with the following:

- Communication with the Divine

- Motivation for a healthy lifestyle

- Overcoming unhealthy situations—people, places, or things

- Peace—personal and global

- Spiritual growth and ascension

*An extremely loving*

ascended master,

Serapis Bey

is actively involved in

*bringing peace to Earth.*

# *Tara*

### (Also known as Green Tara and White Tara)

*"Allow me to fill you with overflowing love, joy, and compassion."*

—*Tara*

Although she is formally associated with Buddhism in Tibet, Mongolia, and Nepal, Tara is an iconic Buddhist goddess of many colors and has become one of the most familiar figures of Buddhism around the world. According to an Indian text called *Homage to the Twenty-One Taras* that reached Tibet in the twelfth century, there are twenty-one Taras. The Taras come in many colors, but the two most popular are White Tara and Green Tara.

It is said that Avalokitesvara, the bodhisattva (enlightened one) of compassion and protection, shed tears that formed a lake. From that lake, a lotus flower came to the top of the water, and when it opened, the goddess Tara stepped out. In a variation of the original legend, White Tara was born from the tears from Avalokitesvara's left eye, and Green Tara was born from the tears of his right eye. She is the female counterpart of Avalokitesvara.

In many ways, these two Taras complement each other. Green Tara often is depicted with a half-open lotus, representing night. White Tara holds a fully blooming lotus, representing the day. Green Tara embodies activity. White Tara embodies grace and serenity and the love of a mother for her child. Together, they represent the boundless compassion that is active in the world both day and night. In her Yellow, Blue, and Red personas, Tara is temperamental, but as White and Green Tara, she is loving and helpful.

The name Tara means "star," and she provides guidance and direction for people, whether it is to help us find our way on our spiritual journey, in our daily life, or in travel.

Green Tara helps with the following:

- Compassion

- Emergency help—physical or spiritual

- Insight and guidance

- Overcoming fear

- Removing obstacles

White Tara helps with the following:

- Compassion

- Divine love

- Enlightenment

- Life expectancy and longevity

- Protection

# *Zeus*

(Also known as Jupiter, "Lord of the Sky," "Cloud Gatherer," "Rain God," Zen, and Zeus the Thunderer)

*"If you embrace your true passion and are courageous to take the first steps to fulfill your dream, the courage will follow, and you will be forever empowered."*

*—Zeus*

Zeus is the sky and thunder god in ancient Greek religion who rules as king of the gods on Mount Olympus. Zeus's mythology and powers are similar to those of Indo-European deities like Jupiter, Perkūnas, Perun, Indra, Dyaus, and Zojz. Most famous among Zeus's powers was the lightning bolt he used to strike his enemies. He could also control the weather and summon storms when angry. Another power of his was the ability to shape-shift. He would use it to visit Earth and walk amongst humans, disguised as one of them.

The child of Cronus and Rhea, Zeus was the youngest of his siblings. In most traditions, he is married to Hera (his seventh and final wife), by whom he is said to have fathered Ares, Eileithyia, Hebe, and Hephaestus. According to theogony, Zeus's first wife was Oceanid Metis, by whom he had Athena. His infamous escapades resulted in many divine and heroic offspring, including Apollo, Artemis, Hermes, Persephone, Dionysus, Perseus, Heracles, Helen of Troy, Minos, and the Muses.

Zeus was respected as an All-father (a supreme being or god who rules over all others) who assigned roles to other gods. His symbols are the thunderbolt, eagle, bull, and oak. Zeus is depicted by Greek artists in one of three poses—standing, seated, or striding forward with a thunderbolt leveled in his raised right hand. He has been written about in literature throughout the ages, most famously in the *Iliad*, an ancient Greek epic poem attributed to Homer about the Trojan War and the battle over the city of Troy, in which Zeus plays a major role.

Zeus helps with the following:

- Confidence
- Empowerment
- Passion
- Shape-shifting
- Weather

# Guidance with Hecate

### A Story from Brittany R.

**I've been spiritual my entire life** but really started practicing and tuning my abilities at the end of 2022. I had been thinking of working with a deity but wasn't sure where to start. I kept getting signs about a deity named Hecate. I know it may sound silly, but I felt very drawn to her. I didn't know much about Hecate, other than that she helped people with shadow work.

The night to honor Hecate—November 16, the Night of Hecate—was coming up, so I decided to give an offering. I offered two eggs and a puff pastry with honey on top because that's what the internet said she and her dogs liked. I said, "This offering is for Hecate and her dogs. If you would like to work with me and guide me through my journey, please accept this offering." When I woke up the next morning, the eggs were gone but the pastry was still there. It was around 4:30 a.m., so I thought I'd give it extra time. I went to the gym, came home, and got ready for work.

By 6:30 a.m., I was in the kitchen making my coffee when I heard a knock at the door. Why was someone knocking at my door so early? I looked out the window, and no one was there. I checked the offering again, and the pastry was gone. I texted my husband later and asked if he could check the door camera to see what ate the eggs and the pastry. When he looked, he realized the camera was dead, and the last clip it took was me putting the offering on the front porch.

A couple days later, I did a guided meditation involving Hecate. I saw what she looked like before the person guiding the meditation even described her. Hecate started telling me about her and that she was there to help me. It was a very special session and I cried.

After that, I heard an owl hooting outside of my house for *two weeks straight*—same time every morning, 4:30 a.m. In addition, throughout the coming days, I listened to a playlist on random shuffle with over fifty-five hours of music on it, and I heard songs in a row that had either owls or meaningful lyrics.

Hecate is an amazing deity to work with. She has helped me work through dark shadows that I've suppressed over the years. She also helped protect me and showed me true patience and understanding.

I've noticed a lot of people are scared to work with deities because they don't understand or fear doing something wrong. But I think that stems from religious programming. True deities (or higher powers) know what you're capable of. In my experience, they are extremely loving, caring, understanding, and supportive. They will teach you hard lessons, but that's how we grow and evolve!

# Chapter 13

# Angels, Guardian Angels, Spirit Guides, and Animal Guides

*"The angelic purpose is to guide, comfort, and support us as we navigate our lives and go forth in our spiritual journeys."*

—*Nichole Bigley*

## Guardian Angels and Angels

Angels, guardian angels, and spirit guides are other members of our collective spirit teams. Some angels have spent all their time in heaven, and others come back and forth between heaven and Earth in the form of "Earth angels."

A while back, Archangel Michael informed me that our guardian angels are angels that we made agreements and contracts with before coming here to Earth. Because we've worked with guardian angels in other lifetimes, or alternate lifetimes, and have a relationship with them already, we decided to have them interact with us more regularly in our daily lives. Some believe that we are assigned a new guardian angel each lifetime, but I will take Archangel Michael's word that our guardian angels have worked with us many lifetimes over. It is just what resonates with me.

It is due to the agreement and contract we made before we came to Earth that guardian angels are able to intercede on our behalf, whether we are consciously aware or not. This is often why you hear of angels saving people from danger or other major situations in their lives. It is because we've already given them permission to do so. Our guardian angels are with us from birth until death. They usher us into the world and greet us when we cross over.

Angels of all forms—whether they be guardian angels, archangels, or other angelic forms—have a lighter and brighter energy than any other energetic being that I've worked with. This is one of the primary reasons I prefer to connect with and channel them. Not only is it seemingly easier to connect with them, it just feels *angelic* (for lack of a better word).

When I see angels in my mind's eye, they show up as light beings. However, when I am lucky enough to see them with my physical eyes, they often appear as bright white orbs or twinkly lights, very similar to Christmas lights on a tree. Sometimes they blink in and out, and other times they appear as fireworks.

The first time I saw an angel with my physical eyes was right after I had been attuned to reiki and had received my master certification. While I'd often sensed them around and had been able to pick up on their presence through my mind's eye, it was amazing to see them in the physical realm. As I looked across the room, a bright blue flashing orb appeared, and I instantly recognized the energy as that of Archangel Michael. Since then, any time Michael wants to make his presence known in a more impactful way, he will flash his blue light to get my attention.

Like Archangel Michael, other protective angels often make their presence known through blue lights. Green or purple angelic lights often represent healing, as in the case of Archangel Raphael. Yellow angelic light often brings angels related to divine guidance or direction. Pink angelic light angels emanate love. As mentioned in "Chapter 10: Archangels," rainbow colors or prisms represent a range of these angelic energies. Pure white lights are also angelic energy but don't denote a specific meaning other than that angels are with us to help in all ways. Personally, I have yet to see red or orange orbs or lights when angels are present, but that doesn't mean it doesn't happen. Those colors, however, in my experience, are usually reserved for auras or other associated energy. (Please refer to "Chapter 9: Your Spirit Team" for more information on chakras.)

Each angel has its own unique essence and is therefore a distinct species. Just like us, no two angels are the same, and their uniqueness is another example of how all energetic beings have their own resonance and spiritual DNA. Since they don't have material bodies, angels don't have specific genders, but they do tend to appear or feel either more masculine or more feminine depending on their focus areas or roles. This helps us identify them when they show up or are around us.

Angels also have an intellect and a will, just like human beings. However, unlike us, angels have made their permanent choice to serve God or Universal Source and, in doing so, to ultimately support us as we navigate our lives. At the moment of their creation, angels freely choose whether to accept or reject their mission, a choice locked into their will without remorse. The fact that angels are given one opportunity to make a choice like this may seem strange to us, but this is a misplaced understanding. Angels do not struggle to reason.

The following are additional facts and information about angels:

- When created, angels were infused with a perfect knowledge of things, including human nature. While they have not lived human lives (the exceptions here are the Archangels Metatron and Sandalphon), they do know far more about us than we do ourselves.

- Angels are organized into nine choirs. (See "Chapter 1: Christianity and Judaism" for more information about this.) This angelic hierarchy, so to speak, is based on their closeness and connection to God Source. It also means that some angels have greater knowledge than others and that each choir has an express purpose and each angel a unique role.

- Each angel was created for a specific task or mission. They received instantaneous knowledge of this mission at the moment of their creation.

- Angels are extremely active in human lives. The moment they decided to be in service to God was also the moment angels were determined to help us.

- Each human being has at least one guardian angel, if not more. Your guardian angel freely chose to accept you as their charge and vice versa. This is the contract you entered before you came here to Earth to live this lifetime.

- Angels are ubiquitous in that they don't move from location to location. They also are not restrained by time. Because angels are not physical beings, they do not have material boundaries or limitations. They are present wherever their will acts. Their presence, then, can be instantaneous.

- Angels communicate with one another by passing concepts from mind to mind. All angels can share their knowledge with other angels telepathically and among the various angelic levels. Angels interact with human beings through our psychic or intuitive senses, which can also be telepathic.

- Angels can prompt and guide the thoughts of human beings. However, they cannot violate our free will. (For more information on this subject, see page 159.)

- Angels can take information and bring an image or other thought into your mind in order to communicate with you. Remember that they are only able to do this in alignment with God or the Divine and only if there is a particular reason to do so. And it won't happen in every moment of every day.

- Angels do not have emotions the same way human beings do. They do experience an intensity that is similar to human emotions, but it isn't the same.

- Angels do not automatically know what is happening within our intellect or will, but they can surmise what is happening by watching our actions, reactions, and behavior. This is why giving them permission and being clear in our communication with them is so important.

- Human beings do not become angels when they die. However, human beings can eventually ascend, as in the case of ascended masters. Humans can also become vessels to deliver messages or conduct acts of kindness on Earth.

Understanding angels and guardian angels can help us be more aware not only of them, but also of the impact they have on our lives.

# An Angel Runner

*A Story from Debbie H.*

**In 2004 I was getting ready to get a divorce** after sixteen tough years of marriage, and I was about ready to file. We had two children together, and I had had enough of verbal abuse and was seeking Bible study classes to learn more about myself and gain the confidence I needed to start a new life. I was heavy into prayer at the time and had ongoing conversations with God. I felt very close to God, and I knew He would help me survive a divorce. I was also a runner.

Each and every morning, I would rise to jog five miles to have some alone time with God. We chatted on our morning routine, or at least I was the one talking. I always had signs He was listening, and I always felt connected to Source.

One morning, I was irritated at the events from the night before with my husband, so I went off, saying, "You know, God! This man I am married to has done this. And he has done that." And I continued to list the entire sixteen years of things I felt he had done wrong to me. Oh, the list was *long* ...

I got down the road a little, probably two miles into my run, and suddenly God started showing me images of all the things I had done wrong in my life. Oh yes. It was not exactly what I wanted to see at 6:00 a.m., but my mind began to flash my wrongdoings right in front of me. I began to weep and asked for forgiveness, as I knew God would forgive me.

I was about a mile away from home, and I saw a gentleman out walking toward me. I would usually cross the road to the other side. As a runner, you need to be very careful about your surroundings and use your instincts. But this morning, my instinct said, keep running on the same side of the road.

As the man approached me, he turned around and said, "Oh my goodness, can I run with you? I have been sick, and this is the first morning I got up to be outside, and you have inspired me to run. May I run alongside you?"

I eagerly replied, "Sure, come along. I run the same route every morning, but I have never seen you."

He shook his head up and down and was jogging my pace right beside me like he had always been a runner. I felt very comfortable with him, chatting about the weather for the day. We had a very short time together, but I came to his corner, and he remarked, "I need to turn here. Thank you for letting me jog with you for just a short way. You really made my morning!"

"I hope to see you again," I replied as I kept on running toward home.

He then turned to me and quietly retorted, "Oh, one more thing! God wants you to try forgiveness."

In shock, I questioned what he said: "What did you say?"

This angel replied, "God *wants* you to try forgiveness just like God has forgiven you!"

I kept running, and I never turned around because I knew this gentleman, who was an angel with a very powerful message, would not have been there. How did he know about the conversation I had just had with God? I never saw this gentleman again. It was a message I needed to hear for me to move into my next life after my divorce. I needed to forgive to move on.

I have never forgotten this special angel with the message that I needed to hear. "Forgive!" I no longer hold on to grudges. I got that divorce and am happily married now. My ex-husband and I are now friends, and that couldn't have happened without this powerful message of forgiveness.

Yes, I believe in angels. And I still talk to God every day! I hope someone who needed to hear this story is inspired to forgive too.

# Spirit Guides and Animal Guides

Spirit guides are souls that were once human and, after their spiritual growth and evolution, are now able to direct us while on the other side. These guides can come from different realms, dimensions, energy fields, or even galaxies and solar systems. They are the same level of consciousness as angels but exist in different realms. Spirit guides are also similar to ascended masters in that they were once human, but they aren't considered "holy" in the energetic sense, like the ascended masters.

People often have many spirit guides on their spirit team, as they help us to navigate primarily through periods of transition in our lives. Some are permanent and others are not. Spirit guides come into our lives when we need them, depending on what we are experiencing and how they can assist us based on our needs at that time. They are constantly encouraging us to trust our intuition and natural instincts, as well as to pursue what makes us happiest, because doing so feeds Universal Source.

Our spirit guides are as diverse as we are and often represent a lifetime, culture, or experience that we need to remember in order to strengthen our spiritual evolution.

Animal guides, also known as spirit animals, are on spirit teams for people who feel connected to Earth, relate to or practice a faith the spirit animal comes from, and/or have a deep love of animals overall.

The Universe often sends us animals in everyday life as well to get our attention. If you notice a recurring animal in your life, look into the meaning or symbolism behind it. When I decided to sell my home in Georgia and move to Ohio to be closer to family, I noticed that a single deer would often show up outside my new house in the city. The first time it happened, it was so surreal because it was the middle of the day and seemingly out of place. I embraced that moment and asked that if it was meaningful in some way, God continue to send it until I was able to better understand.

Over the next several days, I grew amazed as the one deer brought its friends and family, amassing up to nine deer at one point. I noticed that the deer only seemed to show up after I had gotten done interviewing someone on the podcast or had done some major clearing and healing work on a person. And when the deer or its family of deer arrived, it would just stand there and stare deeply at me. It is no coincidence that deer represent intuition, unconditional love, and gentleness, as well as safety, strength, and protection.

Deer never had a significant meaning to me up until this point. Now, whenever I see one, I stop and pay close attention to what I am thinking and feeling at that moment in time.

Scott shared his interesting story earlier about meeting his animal spirit guide, a leopard he named Shera. He read an article that suggested anyone could ask to see and meet their spirit animal by simply asking God or Spirit to provide. The morning after he asked, a leopard appeared on his right side in his mind's eye, sometimes sitting and other times walking next to him. He mentioned that Shera is so real to him that sometimes he unconsciously reaches his hand over to pet her head. He told me he believes that Shera's presence in his life at this time is to provide support, courage, and strength as he enters into a new phase of his life. Her presence provides great comfort to him.

As you can see from this chapter and throughout this book, we are literally surrounded by a huge number of spiritual beings. Many are involved with people and events we are unaware of, while others are solely committed to supporting, protecting, and guiding us through this life and into the next. Most of the time, we do not see them or their actions, but sometimes we do.

In either case, our purpose with this book is to remind you that you have a team of angels, archangels, sprit guides, and animals at your side day and night offering unconditional support and love. It is important to remember that, while they are here for us, there is an element of free will they must abide by. This means that, in order for you to interact more with your spirit team, you need to ask.

Are you ready?

# A Hawk with a Message

### A Story from Angie P.

**About a year ago, I had my spiritual awakening** and discovered I am clairaudient, which I now know was always there. I just never knew Spirit talks in your own voice! During that time, I was keeping everything to myself and scared to share my experiences with anyone.

One morning, I woke up and started to make coffee, as I do every day. I happened to look out the window, and there was a huge hawk in my backyard. I was startled but didn't want to draw attention to it. I went ahead with my day as usual—dropped the kiddos off at school, stopped at the grocery store. When I got back home about an hour later, I was surprised to find the hawk was still there, but in a different place, sitting on the top of our fence facing the opposite direction.

I felt as if he was waiting for me. I walked outside to snap a picture. He turned around to face me. He was huge, with a beautiful bright white chest of feathers. He stared directly into my eyes, and then I heard him speak: "I am here to remind you of your strength and resilience."

That message hit me, and I didn't even know I needed to hear it. I started getting very emotional, and then he said a few more things.

At first, I thought I was crazy—this seriously could not be happening. It was such an amazing experience. I had never "talked" to an animal before.

He showed up again right outside my office window a week later. If that's not a sign, I don't know what is! I realized that the hawk shows up whenever I need a reminder or a little guidance to be on the right path. He has visited me several times and continues to do so, while I'm driving, at the park, or randomly on light posts throughout the city. He even shows up in my meditations. As a matter of fact, he showed up on my walk just this morning with another message. I now know without a doubt he is my spirit animal.

# Part Four

# Connecting with Angels

Nichole Bigley

When angels visit us, we do not hear
the rustle of wings, nor feel the feathery
touch of the breast of a dove; but we
know their presence by the love they
create in our hearts.

—*Mary Baker Eddy*

# Chapter 14

# Understanding Your Psychic Senses

**W**e are all psychic. Whether you believe it or not, we are all born with intuitive senses, and they are as innate within us as our other physical, mental, emotional, and spiritual senses. Think about your psychic senses as mirrors to these other ones. Just as many of us can see, hear, smell, taste, and feel, we can also do this energetically on a spiritual or intuitive level.

You may hear people refer to the psychic senses as the "clairs." The word *clair* means "clear," and there are nine clairs, identified as clear hearing, clear knowing, clear feeling (of emotions), clear tasting, clear thinking, clear smelling, clear feeling (of sensations), clear touching, and clear seeing. Each of them has unique characteristics.

For example, clairvoyance, or clear seeing, is the most visual of the psychic senses. You receive pictures in the form of images in your third eye, also referred to as your mind's eye. If I ask you to picture or imagine an apple in your mind, can you see it? Is it red or green? Does it have a stalk or a leaf on it? Is the apple full or is there a bite taken out of it? Some people can picture this in their inner mind, but others cannot. They might be able to describe to you what it is supposed to look like, but they can't visualize it. This is a condition called aphantasia, which is a lack of the mind's eye, leading to the inability to visualize things mentally.

There are also people who don't have internal monologues or narratives with themselves; some people's thoughts are like sentences they "hear," and other people have abstract nonverbal thoughts and then have to consciously verbalize them.

I share this with you because if you've thought being "psychic" showed up in a certain way and that was a belief you held onto your whole life, up until now, you might not have realized that you are indeed intuitive! Spirit likes to connect and communicate with us however we naturally gravitate toward communicating or prefer to process and learn. For example, I am a very visual person. You can explain something to me verbally and I can track and follow, but often it isn't until I see it written down or shown visually in some other way that it "clicks" for me and I fully understand. So, it is not surprising that one of the biggest ways my guides and angels communicate with me is through my mind's eye, which makes me clairvoyant.

## Our Psychic Senses

Before we connect and communicate with our spirit team, it is important to better understand our psychic or intuitive senses. As you look through the descriptions below, see which of them matches experiences you have had. For those that do, it will give you a place to start to learn more.

*Clairaudience* or clear hearing is when you are able to hear voices or messages from the spiritual realm. You may hear them in the inner ear or physically hear them as well. For example, you may be driving and suddenly hear "slow down" even though you are the only person in the car. You might be clairaudient if you are naturally attuned toward sounds, music, or toning. One way that clear hearing shows up for people is that you repeatedly hear the same songs or musical lyrics. You may also experience ringing in one ear (in the absence of a medical condition), which means that a message is coming in from Spirit.

*Claircognizance* or clear knowing occurs when you experience a sudden knowing. You may have a strong sense of knowing information or what has or will happen. This is often referred to as the "sixth sense," "gut intuition," or even "mother's intuition." In other words, it can manifest as instincts. Mothers and their children, twins, or other people who have close bonds experience this often with each other.

*Clairempathy* or clear emotion is sensing other people's emotions, thoughts, or even symptoms. It is an awareness of emotional energy. Most humans are born with empathy, but some have a heightened sense of empathy and are particularly sensitive to their own and others' emotions. For example, you may feel a certain way and have no way of explaining why, especially if there is no reason for you to be feeling that way, such as a medical reason, specific experience that took place, or something else. It is important as a clairempath to understand how to balance your empathy, so as not to take on others' "stuff." The difference between clairempathy and clairsentience is that empaths can sense the emotion vs. physically feel it. (You can have both at the same time as well. If you've ever experienced a broken heart, that is both at play.)

*Clairgustance* or clear tasting is sensing or experiencing things through taste even without having that physical source of taste in your mouth. If you have this clair, then you might taste sweet, sour, salty, or spicy things. It could even be an unpleasant taste.

*Clairintellect* is clear thinking. This happens when your thoughts arise from your intuition. You may notice that words easily come when you're talking in conversations, but it feels like they are coming from a higher place. You may also experience thoughts coming in at random when you aren't thinking of anything in particular, or that profound solutions or epiphanies come at the right moment. You may be inclined toward clear thinking if you are left-brained or a linear thinker.

*Clairsalience* or clear smelling is when insights come through the perception of smell. An example of this is smelling your grandfather's tobacco pipe or your mother's favorite perfume. Angels are also known to send people the scent of flowers, especially roses, which have the highest vibration rate of any flower, reigning supreme at 320 MHz.

*Clairsentience* is clear physical feeling. (It differs from emotional feeling or clairtangency, which is clear touching.) You may feel the physical feeling in your body that others are experiencing. An example is if someone has a stomachache and you feel that same sensation or pain in your stomach as well. Another example is that you may feel your or someone else's emotional trauma that manifests in the body. I experience tingles up and down my spine when a message is particularly important for someone I am giving a reading to or if it is a message that resonates with me. People who can communicate with souls who have crossed over may feel the souls touching them on the top of the head, brushing a cheek, or holding their hand.

*Clairtangency* is clear touching, a form of extrasensory perception in which facts or impressions about a person or thing are received through contact with an object that retains an energetic impression. If you've gained insight about things or people by touching them, then you have this ability. This is also often referred to as psychometry or token-object reading.

*Clairvoyance* is clear seeing and the most visual of all the clairs. Visions may come in the form of vivid dreams, pictures, mental images, or mini movies that appear or play in your inner mind. These images may be literal or metaphorical. You may even be able to see colors of an aura. You are likely clairvoyant if you are a visual person and like to receive or process information that way.

| PSYCHIC SENSE / CLAIR | PHYSICAL, MENTAL, OR EMOTIONAL SENSE | EXAMPLES |
|---|---|---|
| *Clairaudience* (clear hearing) | Hearing | Hearing voices and sounds in the inner ear, including ringing, or hearing repetitive thoughts |
| *Claircognizance* (clear knowing) | Knowing | Having a strong sense of knowing information or what has or will happen, often referred to as "gut intuition" |
| *Clairempathy* (clear emotional feeling) | Feeling (emotions) | Feeling an emotion that comes out of the blue or is overwhelming, without a real reason to have it |

| PSYCHIC SENSE / CLAIR | PHYSICAL, MENTAL, OR EMOTIONAL SENSE | EXAMPLES |
|---|---|---|
| *Clairgustance* (clear tasting) | Tasting | Tasting things that are sweet, salty, spicy, sour, etc. without having eaten anything that would produce that taste |
| *Clairintellect* (clear thinking) | Thinking | Having epiphanies or key thoughts pop up at the right moments when needed |
| *Clairsentience* (clear physical feeling) | Feeling (sensations) | Experiencing changes in temperature or pressure; goosebumps |
| *Clairsalience* (clear smelling) | Smelling | Picking up "phantom" smells such as flowers, smoke, perfume, etc. |
| *Clairtangency* (clear touching) | Touching | Being able to pick up information about a person or object by touching or seeing them |
| *Clairvoyance* (clear seeing) | Seeing | Seeing flashes, pictures, or movies in the third eye (mind's eye); having visions in dreams or other ways; seeing auras, colors, repeating numbers, or symbols |

Each of us has a different relationship with each of the psychic senses. Just like some people are born naturally as great athletes, intellectual thinkers, or creative artists, and others have to work harder to get to that level, the same is true of our intuitive abilities. If we have a strong physical, mental, emotional, or spiritual sense, then that will likely be the mirror to our psychic sense(s). It will also be the one that our spirit team will use to communicate with us. Remember, Spirit speaks to us not only the way we receive and process information, but also in our own voice.

As mentioned in my story in Chapter 9, I will never forget the first time I heard Spirit speak "out loud" during that bright, sunny day at the park.

Years later, as I began to learn more about my own intuitive abilities, I asked a psychic where the voice came from. She explained that it was me, my own intuition or clairaudience. I had always thought it was my guardian angel or Archangel Michael. But upon reflection, the voice was definitely my own. I like to think that it was both my higher self and my guardian angel using my own voice to get my attention.

Since then, I've recalled a number of situations in which my own intuition seemed to come through verbally, whether it was a thought or an inner voice: "Don't trust them." "You can do it." "Take the job." "Slow down." You name it; either I or my guides and angels have said it. Our intuition is *always* guided by Source, our higher selves, or Spirit, nudging us in the best direction all along.

As you become aware of your psychic abilities, you'll discover that certain intuitive senses are easier for you to tap, and others may be more difficult. Pay attention to what psychic senses feel stronger to you, and focus on the sensory experiences to guide you. You will also more than likely evolve over time as you experience the clairs. Some might spend years working with one or a few psychic senses only to find that another one quickly surpasses them. It is as normal for us to grow and evolve as it is for psychic abilities to do the same.

This is certainly the case for me. It wasn't until recently that I started to experience physical sensations and the ailments of clients who come to me in sessions. When I was younger, I remember making a "wish list" of psychic abilities. One that wasn't on it? Experiencing how someone else felt physically, especially if they weren't feeling well. Fast forward several years later, and I've begun to experience physical symptoms of others. At first it began the day before, or if I was lucky, only a couple hours before I had a session. However, after realizing what was happening, I asked my guides and angels to only have it occur during the session itself. And for the most part, it only seems to occur now during sessions briefly and not before or after. This brings me to the importance of setting energetic boundaries.

## Energetic Boundaries

As we develop our psychic gifts, having strong, clear senses is important. The nine psychic senses are the best sources of input to provide us with the information we need in order to interpret messages from other frequencies such as our spirit team. We can enhance our ability to work with our intuitive senses by knowing what they are and how they work. We can also turn up or dial down the information we receive through them by keeping them highly tuned. However, keeping our clairs sharp without strong energetic boundaries can be problematic. As our intuitive abilities become more fine-tuned, boundaries are what keep us grounded. We are, after all, spiritual beings here having a human experience. Being balanced in both realms is key. Establishing boundaries prevents us from being overwhelmed or disconnected at best, or destabilized at worst.

Having clear energetic boundaries is our responsibility and our responsibility alone. The great news is that there are universal laws in place to help protect and guide us. One of those is that we have free will and choice. When I began to experience the physical symptoms of my clients, I had a choice. Did I still want to have this ability, and if so, did I require any adjustments? I recognized that my spirit team was giving me the opportunity to undergo things like headaches, nausea, etc. in order to quickly identify what the underlying ailment or issue of a client was and therefore be more efficient in helping the person. I no longer wanted to receive that information in advance of

Having clear energetic boundaries

is our responsibility and our

responsibility alone. The great

news is that there are universal

laws in place to help protect and

guide us. One of those is that we

have free will and choice.

the session but communicated that I was open to receiving it during the scheduled time if it was for that person's best and highest good. As mentioned earlier, the phrase "best and highest good" is a filter that removes your ego from the situation and from the desire to control the outcome.

Another example of setting clear energetic boundaries is when my guides and angels asked me to write about them and share about how people could connect with their own spirit teams. I had a lot going on at that time. I recognized that it wouldn't be possible without help. So, I asked, "If this is important and timely, make it happen by putting the right person and resources at the right time in front of me." Only then would I do it. I honestly thought it would take a few months, and by that time, things would have settled in my life. Imagine my surprise when it was only a couple days later that Scott emailed me and walked into my life. Regardless, the point is that my guides and angels made it happen, but it was an important and empowering lesson for me. Ask and you shall receive. And you always have a choice.

As in the above examples, boundaries are all about finding and setting that firm yet loving line. Once we decide where an energetic boundary needs to be (whether it is with a human being, our spirit team, or even the Universe) and communicate it, it is up to us to maintain it. It is important to know that sometimes our energetic boundaries can be either poorly maintained or set in the wrong place. For highly sensitive people, the way this manifests most often is through experiencing anxiety.

Setting and keeping energetic boundaries can be a lot of work, but luckily, we have a whole army of guides, angels, and even loved ones to help us. What follows is an exercise to help you open and embrace your psychic senses and also an exercise to help you set energetic boundaries with the human and spiritual realms.

# Intentional Exercise to Open Psychic Senses

Our psychic abilities are just like our other physical, mental, emotional, and spiritual senses in that we need to practice in order to strengthen or refine them. When I was a child, I asked my dad why we couldn't use our toes the way we used our fingers to grasp and hold things. He explained that over time, human beings didn't need them, so they weren't as flexible. I decided right then and there to practice moving each toe every night until I had mobility. (Yes, I fully admit I was a very curious and strange child.)

At first it was both frustrating and strange because I would just stare at a toe and will it to bend. I tried moving each one, but most wouldn't budge. I was so excited the first time each of my toes was able to fully bend! As a child, it made total sense to me why I wanted to be able to do this, but as an adult, I forgot the meaning behind it. It wasn't until I started writing this book that the angels reminded me that I did this. And why? To give an example of how focused and determined I was and that the same steps applied here. Have an intention and focus. Try. Let go. Try again. Later on in the book, these steps will be shared in more detail, along with additional exercises to practice how to connect and communicate with your spirit team. Before then, the following intentional exercise is designed to open you up to your intuitive abilities and is meant to be visualized in your mind's eye.

*If you are reading this in printed or e-book format, then take note of the following or record the steps on your phone to listen to your own voice and follow along.*

1. Pick a time of day—morning or night is best—when you are able to sit or lie down comfortably.

2. Close your eyes, and take some deep breaths in and out.

3.  As you quiet your mind, say to yourself or out loud:

    "I give the Universe permission to fully open and activate my psychic senses and abilities."

    "I ask that these open, activate, and integrate calmly and peacefully and in divine timing for my best and highest good."

    "I am fully open to receive, experience, and embrace my God-given and universal rights."

4.  Feel it! The really important part here is that you *feel* it down to your bones, that you not only state this, but that you push the intention and feeling out toward the Universe.

5.  "Thank you!"


Do this intentional exercise consistently and as often as you need to until your psychic senses begin to show up and/or become stronger. Just as I did as a kid wiggling my toes, you should try and do it daily at first. For those of you who are already familiar with your psychic senses, this practice will also help you open up abilities that you want to tap and that might not have become as present yet. Just customize and make it your own.

Earlier I shared the universal law of free will and choice. This is why this exercise is so important. You are giving the Universe permission to activate that which is already a part of you in a more meaningful and impactful way. As a teenager I read somewhere (I believe it was in a book by Linda Goodman) that you merely needed to ask the Universe in order to receive and open up your intuition. That night, as I lay in bed, I did a version of the above exercise. But what I didn't do was ask for it to occur in "divine timing." I flat out wanted to get from A to Z without going through all the other steps. Many of us are like this ... I asked the Universe to give me access to every psychic sense and to do it now and as intensely as possible.

There is a level of responsibility

that each of us has when we

begin to open up and learn about

the spiritual, specifically our

intuition and how to connect

with our spirit team.

That same night, I had a strange dream. It felt as if I were in someone else's body. I was at a party with other teenagers, and we were all drinking. A group of us got into an SUV. I was sitting in the back seat without a seat belt. As the four-wheel drive vehicle sped up on an exit ramp on the highway, the driver lost control and went into an embankment and down a ravine. Right before the car hit a tree and my body was flung forward, my last thought was "This is going to hurt."

In the morning, I recalled the intensity of the dream and also how strangely it stood out from other dreams. I felt as if I were actually there and remembered so many details. As I was getting ready for school, I heard on the radio that there had been an accident. It involved teenagers in a neighboring town who had gotten into an accident. The whole scene was exactly as it had happened in my dream, down to the number of people, the type of vehicle, and more. I was shocked because I had never before had a vision or premonition like this. And I was frustrated. I asked my angels why they would give me such a horrific experience, especially if there was nothing that I could do about it. After all, it had happened the same night I had the dream. What was the point if I couldn't stop it? They lovingly responded, "It is because you asked." They went on to explain that they were giving me the experience to show me that I had the ability, and did I want it? It was a very important lesson for me to learn. I went on to write down a wish list of what I was and wasn't open to experiencing psychically. I clarified that I was okay about receiving visions or premonitions, but only if there was something that I was supposed to do about them. Since then, I have very rarely had a premonition, and if I did, I knew that I was empowered to help in some way. This is just one example of how we can ask to receive and then have the opportunity to decide how via free will and choice.

I know that some of the stories I've shared don't sound pleasant, and they aren't meant to scare you, but there is a level of responsibility that each of us has when we begin to open up and learn about the spiritual, specifically our intuition and how to connect with our spirit team. Spirit promises that 90 percent of the time the spiritual experiences you have will be amazing and magical, and that 10 percent of the time is when you will go through something like a spiritual awakening or something deeper that requires you to work through it. More importantly, if we don't take the time and the pace we need, then we can't be surprised when such spiritual experiences show up because we try to cut corners, as I tried to do as a teenager.

It is up to you to decide what psychic senses you would like to experience, when you want them on or off, and what kind of information you would like to have come through. If you don't practice, then your senses will remain in their default settings. The following is an exercise designed to help you set those energetic boundaries.

## Exercise to Set Energetic Boundaries

Archangel Michael taught me when I was little to have what he calls "heaven hours" (instead of office hours). You can do this during or after a meditation, when you are grounded and your mind is clear. If you are like me and use prayer as your form of meditation, then you can skip straight to the exercise. The exercise is meant to be visualized in your mind's eye.

*If you are reading this in printed or e-book format, then take note of the following or record the steps on your phone to listen to your own voice and follow along.*

1.  Pick a place in your mind's eye that is calm and exudes what heaven is like to you. It can be floating in clouds, a crystal castle, a field of sunflowers, the top of a mountain—whatever brings you peace and joy.

2.  Take your time experiencing what this place is like. What do you hear? What do you see? What do you smell? Take it all in and in as much detail as you can.

3. As you look around, there will be a place for you to sit down. It may be a pile of pillows, chairs around a marble table, or something else. Walk toward that, sit down, and get comfortable.

4. When you sit down, you will be approached by your guides and angels. Take time here as well to experience what they are like. How many of them are there? Do they look like typical angels or humans? Or are they more like energetic light beings? There is no wrong answer. Enjoy the experience.

5. As your guides and angels sit down with you, a contract appears in front of you. Explain what you want and don't want to experience psychically. Do you lean more toward certain clairs than others and, if so, which ones? Do you want to open up your intuition on some levels and not others? Do you want to strengthen any and, if so, which ones? Do you want specific office hours such as times of the day or evening? Take the time to speak with them about what you want, and as you do, those items appear magically written on the contract in front of you. As you set up the terms, be very clear with your spirit team as well as yourself as to what you are willing to do or follow.

6. When you have said everything you want to say to your spirit team, ask them if there is anything that they would like you to know. Be silent and listen to what they do or say. Take note and acknowledge the information.

7. Before you get up to leave, be sure to thank them for their love, support, and guidance. Embrace them if you wish. They will be sure to pass along the terms of the energetic contract and boundaries with the rest of your guides, angels, and even loved ones on the other side.

# Ways to Strengthen Your Intuition

Now that you're more familiar with intuition overall and how it shows up, you can take the time to actively develop it if you are interested in doing so. One doesn't develop intuition simply through research or setting goals. Intuition is more noticeable or resonant when you are still and present, take time to reflect, and engage in more passive types of activities. It will take some time and observation, but you will become more aware of yourself and how your intuition speaks to you as you go.

The resources and methods listed on pages 130 and 334, which help get you into a state of oneness, can also help you develop your intuition. Some of those methods include practicing meditation; doing intentions and prayer; journaling or doing automatic writing; using healing modalities; clearing, balancing, and aligning your chakras; using crystals and essential oils; doing breathwork; and more. Additional things that can be done to strengthen your intuition include the following:

- *Take a chance on following your instincts.*

  When you become aware of your intuition and how it shows up for you, try following that insight or guidance and see what unfolds as a result. Seeing ways that your intuition manifests and trusting it help to reinforce that you ultimately know what is best for you. Further, trusting in yourself and your intuition not only builds confidence by empowering you, but also further amplifies your abilities through the energy of being in a state of gratitude.

- *Start doing daily energy scans.*

  One of the simplest ways to build your intuition is to make it a daily practice to check in with yourself and how you are feeling energetically on all levels—that is, mentally, physically, and emotionally. Many of us are used to overlooking the way we feel on these more subtle energy levels and just push through one situation to the next as the day goes on. But if we make a practice of being aware and acknowledging what our body,

274

mind, and heart are telling us, it gives a baseline to compare against as things unfold throughout the day. I like to do a check-in and gauge how I am feeling mentally, physically, and emotionally as I wake up in the morning. If things shift during the day, then it can be a helpful indicator that a message is coming through. The goal is to be more present and aware so that you can better pick up on the subtle messages you or the Universe might be sending.

- *Do a technology fast.*

With so many distractions coming at us from a myriad of places, we might not even know when our intuition is coming through because we are too busy bouncing from one thing to the next and not paying attention to ourselves. This is why being present and tapping into the state of oneness is so important.

Consider doing a technology detox. This could be done by shutting down all screens up to two hours before going to bed, not being on social media for a few days, taking a break from watching television or movies, or more. Freeing up your time to be digital-free gives your intuition a chance to show up as new messages or insights come into both your subconscious and your conscious awareness.

- *Ask your intuition questions.*

This is another simple way to tap into your intuition—be direct by asking it questions. Start by asking a question to yourself or out loud or even writing it down. Do any answers seem to pop up in your mind? Do you have a gut sense of knowing? Do you feel a certain way after asking the question? Keep track of anything that comes to you that could be a potential answer or guidance. If nothing comes up straight away, don't be discouraged. Sometimes the answer takes some time to come through. Just pay attention to what comes through—and how—in the coming days or weeks.

- *Start journaling.*

Writing can be a way to override your conscious mind and allow things to come to the surface. Experiment by sitting down once a day and writing what comes to your mind. Don't overthink it. Document things over time that seem like signs, synchronicities, or seemingly interesting "coincidences." (While mathematical law suggests events are random and bound to happen, I have come to believe what Albert Einstein once stated: "Coincidence is God's way of remaining anonymous.") See if there are things that repeat over time or things that connect the dots. These bread crumbs, so to speak, are how we are ultimately able to piece the larger picture together.

- *Keep an art journal.*

If journaling feels intimidating, or writing isn't a way you connect, consider keeping a visual journal instead through art. Create or draw your thoughts. This can help you unearth what is going on around or inside you.

- *Start a dream notebook.*

Dreams are an important way for our intuition to come through. Making small adjustments in your daily life and the way you pay attention can help you be more present in your dream life as well. This is sometimes referred to as lucid dreaming and gives you the ability to pick up on things in your dreams that you might have missed otherwise. Keep a notebook and pen by your bedside. As soon as you wake up, write down what you can remember from your dreams and see if anything resonates with you. If you can't remember what you dreamt, then jot down how you feel. Over time, you will begin to remember things more, and messages will become clearer.

- **Make a vision board.**

  A vision board doesn't always have to be about manifestation. In this instance, imagine if nothing were standing in your way—what are your biggest hopes and dreams? How do you feel? Giving ourselves permission to dream and leverage the imagination and creation parts of our abilities can help to activate our intuition. What feels right to you when you think about all the possibilities the universe has to offer? After all, the universe is infinite. What is part of your highest self and life? The possibilities are endless.

- **Practice with tools like tarot cards, oracle cards, or pendulums.**

  Using physical tools such as tarot or oracle cards or pendulums and even rosaries can help direct and provide answers if you feel like you're blanking intuitively. Spending time with guided tarot or oracle card pulls—or even just looking at one card at a time and thinking about what comes up when you see it—can help you uncover intuitive messages. Pendulums and rosaries are also easy tools to address questions.

  A pendulum taps into your own vibration and energy, so you are essentially channeling your own intuition through your higher self. To use a pendulum or rosary, first ask that the item be activated for your best and highest good. Hold the pendulum or rosary six to eight inches above the palm of your other hand. Ask for it to show you "yes." Then ask for it to show you "no." Results will vary for the individual. When I use a pendulum, it makes full circles for a "yes" answer and swings side to side for a "no" answer. However, for others, a pendulum may go clockwise for a "yes" and counterclockwise for a "no." After establishing "yes" and "no," ask a question that you know the answer to, such as "Is my name so-and-so?" Follow with any and all questions you would like answered.

Your intuition is always available

to you. It is up to you to work on

your abilities and to recognize and

acknowledge them as they unfold.

Using these tips, you should be

able to get a clearer sense of what

intuition looks like for you.

- **Act fast and with purpose.**

  Try not to overthink things. If you get an intuitive message, in the beginning, try to take note of it by writing it down so you don't forget, or make it a point to act promptly. If you start to think too much about the message—how it comes through, what it means, etc.—it can be easy to talk your way out of it, be in doubt, or lose the message altogether.


- **Be in gratitude.**

  Even if you doubt your intuition—the messages that come through or how it shows up for you—acknowledge and respect yourself for that thought and feeling. And then shift to one of gratitude. Be grateful that you have had the experience. Likewise, if there is no question about your intuitive experience or the messages that come through, be in gratitude for it.

  Gratitude is an energetic vibration and frequency that helps amplify our intuitive abilities. Say to yourself, "Thank you for showing up for me. Thank you for sending me messages. I am in deep gratitude."


Your intuition is always available to you. It is up to you to work on your abilities and to recognize and acknowledge them as they unfold. Using these tips, you should be able to get a clearer sense of what intuition looks like for you. If you decide to dive in deeper, there are numerous resources available out there, including practitioners who mentor and courses to choose from. Be sure to do your due diligence to research and vet the practitioner before committing to anything.

# Psychic vs. Medium vs. Intuitive

I almost didn't include this in the book; however, I know many of you would like to know the difference. There is much debate out there in the spiritual community about what is what and how to define the psychic senses and roles. The reason I was hesitant is because when defining things as human beings, we tend to put things into boxes. And when it comes to Source and energy, it isn't always quite so simple.

The title of my primary podcast, *A Psychic's Story*, came from my spirit team because there are so many myths and misconceptions about what a psychic is and who they are. The reason I used the word *psychic* is to inspire people to think differently and be open to all the ways we connect with Source and our spirit team, as well as other psychics' stories and how people got to where they are today. By hearing these stories about other people's experiences, we are less likely to feel alone in our own spiritual journeys.

Recently, a medium I don't know directly posted online: "Not every psychic is a medium, but every medium is a psychic. People don't understand the difference, but it helps to be educated. Psychics connect with incarnate souls (those living on Earth) and mediums connect with the discarnate (spirit world). Souls use mediums through the clairs to pass on their message." I normally don't respond to social media posts, let alone those that aren't directed at me, but I felt nudged by my spirit team to share my view.

It is true that not every psychic is a medium who directly speaks with souls who have crossed over. However, everyone has psychic or intuitive senses and abilities. You may not classify yourself as a psychic, but you are very much so. And as shared earlier in this chapter, the clairs are classifications of the psychic senses. Also, because we are all connected to Source, we have the ability to communicate not only with souls who have crossed over, but also with our spirit team, which is composed of archangels, ascended masters, spirit guides, loved ones, and more.

Technically, the following are the levels of spiritual abilities:

- Psychic—connecting to or reading energy outside of yourself

- Mediumship—connecting to souls or other energetic beings

- Intuition—your intuitive instincts, that inner voice or knowing

Regardless of whether someone defines themselves as a psychic, a medium, or an intuitive, or is called one by others, it means that a person can intuitively pick up on energy using psychic senses and intuitive abilities. A psychic can be a medium, a clairvoyant, an intuitive, a psychic intuitive, or even an energy healer. Try not to think too hard about it. There are so many titles out there, and ultimately, we are all psychic. It is only a matter of perspective.

While developing your psychic senses can dramatically impact your life and enable you to help others, those are not the most important benefits. As we develop our senses, whatever they may be, it provides a way to connect and work with your spirit team. I go into this more in the next chapter.

# Chapter 15

# Connecting with Your Spirit Team

---

*"Never fear, for angels are always with you. Forever by your side watching over and guiding you."*

*—Nichole Bigley*

---

B y this point, you have read about what and who your spirit team comprises, and you better understand them as well as your psychic and intuitive senses. This is where you apply that knowledge and tap into your intuitive abilities in order to connect with your angels and guides. Are you ready? The following are divine steps to strengthen your intuition and connect with angels.

### Trust

Trust is *knowing* that there is a divine energy and power and that all things are working out for your best and highest good. You don't have to "believe" because you are already in a state of being and absolute trust.

- Trust that Source gave you ultimate freedom and choice(s) in your life.

- Trust that you are surrounded by the Divine and are loved and protected at all times.

- Trust that you are worthy of love, peace, bliss, joy, happiness, and *all* that Source has to offer.

- Trust that your spirit team is *always* there and will help to guide you when you need it but also whenever you ask for it. Source makes sure you're constantly protected and nurtured by archangels, ascended masters, guardian angels, spirit guides, animal guides, and even loved ones on the other side.

- Trust that your higher self and intuition are available to tap at any time.

- Trust that you radiate the divine essence and life force with which you were born. This comes from Spirit and lives within your soul.

- Trust that when you're aligned with your higher self and in a state of oneness, you're able to clearly access your intuition.

*Say to yourself, "I trust that I am divinely loved, guided, and protected at all times."*

## Access

Access means being open to and tapping into the vibration of love and state of oneness. We come into this world connected to the Divine, and when we leave this world, we return back to it. As we live our lives, we often forget that this is our original state of BE-ing (or being). Love is the frequency that can help us to tap into our intuitive abilities as well as connect with the Divine. Throughout this book, a variety of methods and resources have been shared to help you get into oneness. Try them out and pick the ones that work best for you.

If you ever struggle with reaching this point, a simple yet powerful exercise is to recall a moment you experienced pure, unconditional love. For me, I remember my sister being born. When I held her for the first time, I immediately felt pure love and a bond that could never be broken. It wasn't because someone said she was my sister; it was an energy that connected us, that same energy and state that we all come from and are connected to. Think about what that moment or experience is for you. Can you see it? Can you feel it? Now embrace it by allowing that love to flow through you on all levels—emotionally, mentally, and physically. As that vibration and frequency emanate from within and around you, you immediately are connected to a state of oneness.

*Say to yourself, "I am constantly connected to Source. I am open to being in a vibration of love and a state of oneness. I can access my intuition at any time."*

## Ask

Ask is about asking the Universe and Source to help open you up and tap your psychic and intuitive abilities. It also means that while your angels and guides are always with you, by giving them permission to connect and interact with you, you help to strengthen and amplify that connection throughout your daily life. As human beings, we have free will and choice. By asking we give permission to set the wheels in motion and become more attuned to messages from the Divine. Again, our spirit team is always with us, but the saying "ask and you shall receive" is also at play. Ask yourself the following:

- Am I ready to develop my intuition?

- Am I open to embracing my spirit team so that they can continue to protect and guide me for my best and highest good?

- Am I willing to receive messages through my own intuition and spirt team that are for my best and highest good?

- Am I ready to make myself a priority? (By being in service to yourself, you become in service to others and the greater good of the community and the world at large.)

- What are my next steps?

*Say to yourself, "Universe, please help me develop my intuition and connect with my spirit team."*

## Act

Act is taking action after you ask yourself the above questions. It also means that you will act quickly and take action when you receive an intuitive hit from yourself or your spirit team. As mentioned in the section about ways to strengthen your intuition, try not to overthink things. Acting fast and with purpose can be as simple as being aware and acknowledging that you received a message or being in gratitude for an experience.

One day I was busy in between work calls and went to the refrigerator to grab a can of ginger ale. I automatically went for the first one in the beverage drawer; however, my intuition screamed at me to take one of the cans in the back. I debated with myself for a few moments and then reluctantly followed my intuition, telling myself it was silly. Later, I asked my guides and angels what the big deal was, and they explained that if I had taken the closest can, I wouldn't have wiped it down because I had been distracted. I would have gotten sick from something lingering on the lid. You never know what the ripple effect could be. I recommend to people all the time that they listen to their intuition when it whispers *and* when it shouts.

Taking action also confirms to the Universe and your spirit team that you want to continue to receive more of whatever "it" was. In addition, it strengthens your intuitive muscles, so to speak, along with your connection to your angels and guides.

# Creating Your Sacred Space

What is a sacred space? A sacred space can provide those who inhabit it with a sense of transcendence—being connected to something greater than oneself. Most people associate a sacred space with a religious institution or other place of worship or even a serene place outdoors. You can also have a sacred space within your home by dedicating a specific area for quiet time, prayer, meditation, or reflection. But in this instance, I am talking about creating a sacred space energetically within another dimension and reality. It is a place you can go to be at peace and at oneness with yourself and the Universe. And it is a safe space for you to tune into your intuition and connect with your spirit team.

To create a sacred space of your own, begin by writing down what *sacred* means to you. What does it stand for? What do you want to experience while there? How do you want to feel when in it? Take your time listing your desires and intentions for your sacred space.

When you are done with this step, begin to imagine the most magnificent, beautiful place that ever existed. If it were heaven, what does your sacred space look like?

When I was little, I created my sacred space by imagining a field of wildflowers as far as the eye could see—flowers so tall that their brilliant colors and petals blew in a soft breeze, a sky bright blue with not a cloud in it. I could hear birds singing but mostly nothing but an immense quietness. I also had a soft blanket that I would lie down on in the middle of the field of wildflowers and spend time looking up at the sky.

Your sacred space could be floating peacefully on a series of fluffy white clouds, on the top of a majestic mountain, at the bottom of a smooth ocean floor with abundant sea life around you, in a gorgeous castle made of crystals. Wherever it is, be sure to also dedicate a spot within your sacred place where you can sit or lie down—whether that be a seat, a table, or another area. Use your vivid imagination to create this special place for you. As you imagine it, state the intention that it is a sacred space for you and only you, where you are allowed to be your true, authentic self, a place where you can connect and align with your higher self as well as your spirit team. In it you are always divinely loved, protected, and guided.

I recommend that you spend several days imagining what your sacred place comprises—the idea is to take your time. Sit with how you feel and what you experience once there. Go to this place whenever you want to connect with your higher self or intuition but mostly to tap into the vibration and frequency of oneness.

## Meditation to Connect with Your Spirit Team

The following is a guided meditation designed to help you connect with the loving presence of your spirit team, angels, and guides. This practice will help you create a deep connection to the guidance system that is always within and around you—the energetic beings of love and light that are here to support you in all ways.

Before you begin the meditation, be sure to have a notebook or journal next to you. Following the meditation, you will practice a journaling exercise that helps stream of consciousness and your intuition to come through.

Your spirit team is always here for you. They often may not feel like they are present because you might not be aware of their presence, or you might not be inviting them in. But through this meditation, you can begin opening up your awareness to their existence and guidance by offering up the desire to have their presence be known.

Find a quiet, comfortable place. You can do this meditation seated in a chair or lying down, whichever is most comfortable for you. If you are seated, place your feet firmly on the ground with your palms facing upward. If you are lying down, be sure to not cross your legs and rest your hands by your side with palms facing upward. Begin to relax your body and its muscles one by one. Close your eyes and begin to focus your attention inward.

- Take a deep breath in.

- Breathe out.

- Breathe in.

- Breathe out.

- Imagine your sacred space. Take some time to visualize it or feel it. In it you are safe. You are loved. You are at peace.

- Set the intention now to contact your spirit guides and angels.

- Inwardly call on them with gratitude.

- Thank your guides for beginning to connect with you.

- Breathe in.

- Breathe out.

- Breathe in.

- Breathe out.

- Begin to open your awareness to their presence. Take your time.

- You may see them in your mind's eye.

- You may feel their energy around you like a warm embrace.

- You may receive a thought.

- You may hear them as a whisper.

- You may feel sudden emotions of peace or joy.

- You may have an inner knowing that they are there with you.

- Be open to how your intuition picks up on their presence.

- Breathe in and acknowledge their presence.

- On the exhale, extend your appreciation.

- Breathe in again, feeling their energy.

- Exhale with gratitude.

- If you desire, you can ask them to reveal their name or names to you now.

- Thank you, angels and/or guides, for revealing your name.

- Breathe in and listen.

- Breathe out.

- Now ask your guides if they have a message for you.

- Breathe in.

- Breathe out.

- Focus your energy on being present.

- Allow yourself to receive their spiritual insights and any messages of communication.

- Just be aware, be still, and listen.

- Breathe in.

- Breathe out.

- Breathe in.

- Breathe out.

- Now sit in stillness for a few moments, allowing yourself to receive beautiful messages from your spirit team.

- Be open to receiving anything and everything you need to know for your best and highest good. Be open to however and in whatever ways it comes through for you.

- Now that you've received information for your best and highest good say, "Thank you spirit team for supporting me. Thank you for revealing what I needed to know."

- When you are ready to take this experience further, gently open your eyes.

- Pick up your pen and notepad or journal, and start to write. "Thank you spirit team of divine love, light, and truth for sharing that with me. Please help me now write down additional wisdom for my best and highest good."

- Take the next five minutes to allow your pen to flow onto the page and let the voice of the Universe and unconditional love come through in all their glory.

- As you write, you are protected and guided in all ways.

- Take a moment to wrap up whatever it is you have been writing. Thank your spirit team for their support. Send them deep gratitude for connecting with and guiding you.

- Receive love and gratitude back from them into your heart.

- Take a deep breath and exhale.

- Take another deep breath in and thank your spirit team one more time for everything.

- "Thank you. So be it. *Amen.*"

Take some time to relax and process all that you experienced in the guided meditation and writing exercise before moving into any other activities. Reflect on all that occurred. If there were certain things that came up in the meditation, feel free to refer back to Chapters 10–12 on archangels, ascended masters, and deities.

You can use this meditation or practice any time you would like to call on your spirit team. Use it when you are looking for guidance or support in any area of your life. You can also use an abridged version of the meditation that follows by stating the names of any of the archangels, ascended masters, or deities mentioned throughout the book.

## Meditation to Call upon a Specific Being

Find a quiet, comfortable place. You can do this invocation seated in a chair or lying down, whichever is most comfortable for you. If you are seated, place your feet firmly on the ground with your palms facing upward. If you are lying down, be sure to not cross your legs and rest your hands by your side with palms facing upward. Begin to relax your body and its muscles one by one. Close your eyes and begin to focus your attention inward.

- Take a deep breath in.

- Breathe out.

- Breathe in.

- Breathe out.

- Imagine your sacred space. Take some time to visualize it or feel it. In it you are safe. You are loved. You are at peace.

- Set the intention now to connect with a specific archangel, ascended master, or deity. "I now call forth [state the name]."

- Inwardly call on this being with love and gratitude.

- Thank this being for beginning to connect with you.

- Now picture this energetic being standing in front of you within your sacred space.

- From your heart send them as much love as you can feel and imagine.

- Notice what happens next.

- Be open to the love returning to you. It is magnified manyfold.

- Keep sending and receiving this love.

- Monitor your breath as you inhale and exhale.

- Share anything that is weighing on you at this time.

- Share your deepest desires.

- Ask this being to intervene and give you guidance and direction. Know that the situation is in their loving hands, and they will work directly with Source to create a peaceful or healing situation for all involved.

- Notice any information that comes to you.

- Now sit in stillness for a few moments, allowing yourself to receive beautiful messages from this being.

- Be open to receiving anything and everything you need to know for your best and highest good. Be open to however and in whatever ways it comes through for you.

- Now that you've received information for your best and highest good, say, "Thank you [state the name] for revealing what I needed to know."

- When you are ready to take this experience further, gently open your eyes.

- Pick up your pen and notepad or journal and start to write. "Thank you for allowing me to experience that. Please help me now write down additional wisdom for my best and highest good."

- Take the next five minutes to allow your pen to flow onto the page and let the voice of the archangel, ascended master, or deity come through in all its glory.

- After your five minutes are done, take a moment to wrap up whatever it is you have been writing. Thank your spirit team for their support. Send them deep gratitude for connecting with and guiding you.

- Give thanks in your heart and let go.

- Take a deep breath and exhale.

- Take another deep breath in as you say, "Thank you. So be it. *Amen.*"

## Spiritual Hygiene

On my podcast, *A Psychic's Story,* I talk a lot about what I refer to as spiritual hygiene. I explain that you wouldn't skip showering or brushing your teeth for weeks or months on end, and neither should you skip your spiritual practices. In other words, spiritual hygiene involves intentional practices we adopt to cleanse and protect our energy bodies and energy field. (Refer back to Chapter 9 for more about the subtle energy bodies and chakras.) By prioritizing our spiritual hygiene, we can cultivate a positive and vibrant state of being.

Become mindful of how you manage your energy throughout the day. Prioritize activities that uplift and recharge you, such as spending time in nature, engaging in creative pursuits, or connecting with loved ones. My angels taught me to visualize my energy as a spiritual energy tank. Is that tank getting low? If so, fill it up. Practice saying no to energy-draining commitments that do not align with your spiritual priorities. Create a balance between work, rest, and play to prevent energy depletion.

Gratitude is a potent method for maintaining good vibrational energy. Each day, take a few moments to express gratitude for the blessings in your life. If you are into affirmations, they can also help reprogram your subconscious mind, replacing negative thoughts or beliefs with positive ones.

> *Repeat empowering affirmations like*
> *"I am deserving of all that the Universe*
> *has to offer me for my best and highest*
> *good. The possibilities are infinite."*

Surround yourself with people who uplift and support you. Seek out positive and like-minded communities, whether in person or online, where you can connect with others who are also on a path of spiritual growth and personal development. By engaging in meaningful conversations and shared experiences with supportive individuals, you can significantly enhance your spiritual hygiene and overall well-being.

Spiritual hygiene also entails creating a daily routine that fosters self-care, energy renewal, and resilience. By incorporating practices like meditation or intentions, you can elevate your energy levels, maintain emotional balance, and enhance your overall performance in life. The following are intentions to help you ground, clear, and protect your energy. You can do each intention separately or all three together. I recommend that you do these in a quiet place where you have time to relax and tune in, such as during a shower or bath or before going to sleep.

# Intentions and Prayers to Ground, Clear, and Protect

This is a guided visual intention to help ground, clear, and protect you. Use this daily to set, clear, and protect your energy, and return to it anytime you need to reground or realign with your higher self.

It is preferred for you to be seated or lying down in a place where you are free of all distractions as you read through the intentions.

You can also listen to the audio version of this intention on the "Intentions: Ground, Clear, and Protect" episode of *A Psychic's Story* podcast (available wherever you get your podcasts).

## *Ground*

*The following guided visual intention is designed to help ground you.*

- Get in a comfortable seated position, with your feet flat on the ground.

    o Take a deep breath in.

    o Exhale.

    o Take another deep breath in.

    o Exhale.

    o Take one more deep breath in.

    o Exhale.

- Continue to breathe in and out at whatever pace feels best to you.

- Imagine a gold light coming down from the heavens.

- As the warm glow descends toward your body, and gets closer and closer, feel an immense sense of peace and bliss.

- The golden light begins to enter through the top of your head.

- It slowly pulses in and out, emitting loving light and energy.

- As it moves slowly down through your body, you can't help but continue to feel peace and bliss, but also love—so much love.

- The light is now moving through your chest, down through your stomach area, and now into your hips, thighs, legs, and feet.

- When the light gets to your feet, imagine that this light starts to break off and grows, taking the form of roots.

- These roots—emanating such love and light—are anchored to your feet and begin to grow, moving down toward the floor.

- They move through the floor.

- They continue moving down, into the grass and dirt.

- The roots continue to push through layers and layers of Earth, going deeper and deeper: down, down, down.

- You can see layers of the Earth's crust as these roots continue to push through and on until they reach the center of Mother Earth.

- Once at the center, the roots take hold.

- Take three more deep breaths.

- Imagine the golden light pulsating in and out, grounding itself with Mother Earth.

- Say, "Thank you, Mother Earth, for giving and holding life."

- Say, "Thank you, Mother Earth, for providing an anchor and helping me to be grounded."

- Say, "As you give me life and light, I give you life and light."

- Say, "I'm in gratitude for all that you give—as I receive."

- Imagine the light, with the roots still anchored, beginning to travel back up from the center of Earth through the layers of crust, dirt, and grass.

- It slowly continues back up through the floor, reaching the bottom of your feet.

- When the light reaches your feet again, it pulsates in and out, filling you again with peace, bliss, and loving energy.

- It travels back up through your ankles, shins, knees, thighs, hips, pelvis, stomach, back, chest, hands, arms, shoulders, neck, and head.

- Your whole body and energy field are now filled with the glorious golden light.

- The light moves from the top of your head back up to the center of the universe.

- Once it arrives there, the light moves back down to the top of your head, quickly through your body, to the bottom of your feet and the center of Earth, and back. As it does so, take three deep breaths.

- Imagine this light is now connected to the universe and the center of Earth with your body, mind, and soul, grounded between and within.

- At any time during your day or evening that you want to feel grounded again, just imagine this beam of light connecting you to Earth and the astral plane, and you will immediately feel centered.

## *Clear*

*The following guided visual intention is designed to help clear and heal.*

- Take deep breaths in and out, focusing on your inhales and exhales.

- Continue to breathe in and out at whatever pace feels best to you.

- Take a moment to tap and tune in to how you're feeling:

  - Physically

  - Mentally

  - Emotionally

  - Spiritually or energetically

- Make a mental note of what you want to keep and what you want to clear and release.

- Starting at the top of your head, say the following:

  - I clear, align, and activate my crown chakra.

  - I am divine.

  - I am a spiritual being.

  - I am one with all that is.

  - I am infinite and boundless.

  - I am at peace.

  - I release anything that no longer serves me or is not for my best and highest good.

- Moving to your third eye, say the following:
    - I clear, align, and activate my third eye chakra.
    - I am insightful and intuitive.
    - I see clearly.
    - I think clearly.
    - I trust my decisions.
    - I expand my awareness.
    - I release anything that no longer serves me or is not for my best and highest good.

- Moving to your throat, say the following:
    - I clear, align, and activate my throat chakra.
    - I hear and speak the truth.
    - I live an authentic life.
    - My voice matters.
    - I have integrity.
    - I am open and honest.
    - I release anything that no longer serves me or is not for my best and highest good.

- Moving to your heart, say the following:
    - I clear, align, and activate my heart chakra.
    - I love myself and others.
    - I am an expression of love.
    - I am worthy of love.

- o   I forgive myself and others.

- o   I follow the voice of my heart.

- o   I release anything that no longer serves me or is not for my best and highest good.

- Moving to your solar plexus, say the following:

  - o   I clear, align, and activate my solar plexus chakra.

  - o   I feel my own power.

  - o   My potential is unlimited.

  - o   I honor myself.

  - o   I accomplish things easily.

  - o   I act with courage.

  - o   I release anything that no longer serves me or is not for my best and highest good.

- Moving to your sacrum, say the following:

  - o   I clear, align, and activate my sacral chakra.

  - o   I am creative and joyful.

  - o   I embrace my sexuality.

  - o   I honor my desires.

  - o   I am playful.

  - o   I deserve to enjoy life.

  - o   I release anything that no longer serves me or is not for my best and highest good.

- Moving to your root, say the following:
  - I clear, align, and activate my root chakra.
  - I am centered and grounded.
  - I love being in my body.
  - I have everything I need.
  - I am connected to nature.
  - I am safe.
  - I am loved.
  - I release anything that no longer serves me or is not for my best and highest good.

- Now say, "All of my chakras are now cleared, aligned, and activated. My aura and auric field are also cleared, aligned, and activated alongside my chakras."

- Take a big, deep breath in and out.

- As you exhale, release any remaining thoughts, feelings, emotions, or energy. Imagine handing them over to your guides and angels to be transmuted in love and light by the Universe.

- Say the following to yourself:
  - I call back any and all parts of my *self, being,* and *soul* that need to be reintegrated and reunited for my best and highest good.
  - As I call back my *self,* I feel fulfilled and at peace.
  - My soul's energy is being restored.
  - My spiritual tank is full.

- I welcome any vibrations, frequencies, sounds, colors, or energy that are needed for my best and highest good.

- I ask that anything I have released to be transmuted in love and light is replaced with love, peace, bliss, and joy.

- As I breathe in and out throughout my day, I will remain clear and my energy aligned and centered.

## Protect

*The following guided visual intention is designed to help protect.*

- As you breathe in and out, imagine that you are anchored to Earth's core. Say the following:

  - I am grounded.

  - I am cleared physically, emotionally, mentally, and spiritually—past, present, and future.

  - I feel centered and at peace.

  - My spiritual tank and energy are *full*.

  - I feel fulfilled on all levels.

- As you continue to breathe in and out, picture a bright white light descending toward your body.

- As it gets closer, it envelops you and both encases your physical body and surrounds your aura.

- This bright white light is an orb gently protecting and shielding you from any and all things that are not for your best or highest good.

- Say the following to yourself:
  - I place an angel in front of me.
  - I place an angel behind me.
  - I place an angel to my right.
  - I place an angel to my left.
  - I place an angel above me.
  - I place an angel below me.
  - Archangel Michael, my guides, and angels, please protect me in all ways.
  - Divinely guide and protect me throughout my day and evening.
  - Thank you, so be it, *amen.*

- At any time during your day or evening that you want to feel or call in protection, just imagine a bright white light surrounding you with Archangel Michael, your guides, and angels lovingly by your side.

In addition to the clearing intention, additional cleansing rituals include the following:

- *Salt Baths.* Take regular salt baths to cleanse your energy field. To do so, dissolve sea salt in warm water and soak for fifteen to twenty minutes, envisioning the salt drawing out any negative energy. As the water goes down the drain, picture it leaving your space.

- *Smudging.* Use sage, palo santo, or other cleansing herbs to purify your space and yourself. (Note that some people consider burning white sage cultural appropriation unless you are Native American. Others believe that if you are respectful, smudging is perfectly acceptable for those who do not come from Indigenous cultures.)

- *Sound Healing.* Use singing bowls, tuning forks, or healing music to harmonize and cleanse your energy. Allow the vibrations and frequencies to resonate with you, clearing any energetic blockages.

- *Visualization.* Envision a shower of pure white or golden light cascading down upon you, washing any negative energy and filling you with revitalizing energy. This is doubly effective if you do it while taking a shower, but it can also be done on its own.

## A Consistent Spiritual Practice

Committing to a spiritual life is the most empowering thing we can do for ourselves and our psychic development. At the heart of it all, we want to be the truest and most authentic version of ourselves. We know what it feels like to be in alignment with who we really are, to feel those magical moments of connection. Having consistent spiritual practices is an important way we can support ourselves in our soul's growth and spiritual journey. It becomes a way of life and the basis of a strong foundation that represents the process happening within us.

One of the easiest ways for people to start having a more consistent spiritual routine is what I call "bookending" your days. As you wake up in the morning, do your daily energy scan. This was written about in more detail on page 274. Check in with how you are feeling energetically on all levels—that is, mentally, physically, and emotionally. After you are done getting a baseline, transition into your daily prayers, intention, or meditation. For me, I state, "I ask my guides and angels to protect and guide me throughout my day. I ask to receive messages that are clear and succinct for my best and highest good. I am open to receiving information through my intuition and am grateful for the experiences that are to come." You can come up with your own prayer or intention and customize it to fit with what resonates with you.

During your day, be open to how you receive messages through your intuition. Jot down any experiences you have—nothing is too small. As things happen, be in appreciation for what unfolds.

In the evening, as you are going to bed, state something such as "Thank you to my spirit team for protecting and guiding me throughout my day." Now take the time to reflect on what happened. This is your opportunity to be in gratitude for whatever insights came or however you received them. But it is also your chance to ask your angels and guides for adjustments. Did you experience something that you want more of? Ask to receive more. Did something happen that you weren't too excited about? Ask for it to show up differently.

This is what it means to have your day "bookended." You start with a baseline and pay attention to how things shift throughout the day. You set an intention by asking and are open to what comes through and how. You act in the moment through recognition and gratitude. And then you reflect at the end of the day and ask for things to be adjusted next time.

If you want a more formal plan, start by creating a spiritual schedule for one week. Go slow and be easy on yourself. Set easy goals on the calendar each day.

*Select from activities, exercises, or methods shared throughout* Looking for Angels *or from the following:*

- Automatic writing
- Being in gratitude
- Breathwork
- Chakra work
- Church
- Clearing/cleansing practice
- Dream notebook
- Fitness (walk, yoga, dance, etc.)
- Grounding practice
- Intentions

- Journaling
- Meditation
- Music
- Prayer
- Protection practice
- Reiki (or other energy healing modality)
- Setting energetic boundaries
- Sound bath
- Spiritual book group
- Spiritual podcast

## Spiritual Schedule Template

|  | Sun. | Mon. | Tues. | Wed. | Thurs. | Fri. | Sat. |
|---|---|---|---|---|---|---|---|
| Morning |  |  |  |  |  |  |  |
| Afternoon |  |  |  |  |  |  |  |
| Evening |  |  |  |  |  |  |  |

There is a never-ending

*flow of light and energy*

that connects us with

the Universe.

It truly is

*infinite in all ways.*

By creating consistency in your life, you make your spiritual journey and growth a priority. You begin to see a natural shift take place, one that is empowering and healing. It signals to the Universe that you are ready.

## Your Spiritual Path and Journey

Everyone's path and spiritual journey is unique. Psychic and intuitive development often results in profound changes. It helps us connect with our angels and the Divine. As we become more spiritually awakened and aware, we open up to new things and experiences. We evolve and grow. As we do the work, our priorities shift. We become less concerned with the opinions of others. We witness phenomena that we might not have thought possible before. We experience miracles.

The number one thing holding people back in strengthening their psychic abilities is self-doubt. The most common misconception is the idea that intuitive abilities are rare, or special, or somehow supernatural. They are not meant for a chosen few; we *all* have these instinctual abilities.

Remember the divine steps: trust, access, ask, and act. Trust doesn't mean clinging to a false belief that everything will go our way. Instead, we trust that whether something happens or not, it is ultimately the best thing for us. Because, after all, our spirit team is always looking out for what is for our best and highest good. That includes us individually as well as collectively.

We may experience doubt often, especially early on in the process. But over time, we learn to hold on and trust for longer periods of time. Trusting allows us to be open to tapping into and accessing our intuitive abilities, which in turn enables us to ask for information and experiences. It is then up to us what we choose to do and what actions to take.

There is a never-ending flow of light and energy that connects us with the Universe. It truly is infinite in all ways. When we become awakened to this reality, we can stop looking for angels because we understand not only who they are and how to communicate with the Divine, but also what *we* are and how we are all connected, never separate, never alone.

# Chapter 16

# Our Spiritual Bill of Rights

W hen writing this book, my spirit team was adamant that I include what universal law dictates and what our spiritual rights entail. But before we get into that in more detail, I'd like to explain more about how the mind, body, and soul operate.

Think of God, Oneness, or whatever you'd like to call It as Source Energy. Source Energy is the source of all life and creation.

Our spirit is the divine essence, the part of us that is infinite, eternal, never changing, never ceasing. It is connected to the oneness from which all life comes, and to which all life returns. Out of oneness you were created as an individual soul, which has individual consciousness and operates as a bridge between your higher divine self and your physical self (e.g., a human being). In this way, our soul is connected through our energetic bodies—physical, mental, emotional, and spiritual. Think of the soul as a hard drive, a repository of all your lifetimes of experience, and as it grows, you grow. It knows and expresses divine will, love, and purpose. The essence of one's soul is love.

The "higher self" referred to throughout this book oversees and can express your soul's light and the light of the Divine through your words, thoughts, actions, and all that you are and do. When we refer to "being in alignment with the higher self," that is what it means, that we can express ourselves fully as we are meant to on the Earth plane. As your higher self, you carry out the purposes of your soul, instead of following the desires of your ego.

As you begin to become more aware that your soul is not separate from you or from Source, you expand your consciousness to experience your soul's light, wisdom, and love. Because our souls are made of light and are the embodiment of love, they are masters on their own plane, the soul plane. To grow and fulfill its higher purpose, your soul needs to become a master of the physical plane, Earth, on which you live. When people ask what their purpose is, this is one of the many reasons we are here on Earth and why the saying "We are spiritual beings having a human experience" resonates with so many.

With this arrangement, our spirit and our body use our soul to connect with each other. The soul operates as the "glue" that helps the spirit connect to and with the physical body and other energetic bodies. To better understand this, imagine God, Oneness, or Source as energy within a power plant. Your spirit is the local transformer where the energy from the power plant comes from. That energy gets integrated down to a voltage and into neighborhoods, and then houses, which represent your human body. Your soul operates as the fuse box within the house, feeding energy where it needs to go, such as your aura, chakras, and other energy points.

Governing and overseeing all of this are other beings, and in place are universal laws to protect us and keep things moving smoothly.

All souls and spiritual beings have inalienable rights through the universal law of oneness. These rights include the following:

- To be connected to God, Source, or the Divine

- To be free, which includes free will and choice

- To have freedom of thought and soul expression without judgment

- To feel and be safe

- To feel and experience unconditional love

- To be heard

- To experience and have peace

- To be healed

These universal laws are governed through higher powers, and checks and balances are also placed for all energetic and spiritual beings to abide by. In addition, legitimate spiritual practitioners and lightworkers will honor the universal laws and spiritual rights by maintaining and implementing the following guiding principles and professional standards of care:

- *Treat everyone with respect.* All souls, wherever they are in their spiritual journey or life, are to be treated professionally and respectfully by practitioners.

- *Act with pure intentions.* Practitioners should never use their abilities or gifts to manipulate or coerce others for their individual benefit. This includes using fear to sell services or products.

- *Never proactively reach out (especially without explicit permission).* This is called "informed consent" because the practitioner is expected to provide clear explanations of the benefits or risks prior to someone's participation in any spiritual service. Unfortunately, this does not always happen as thoroughly as it should. Note that if verbal consent is not possible, then the practitioner must request it from a person's higher self.

- *Always close or sever energetic connections.* After any and all sessions, practitioners are expected to close or sever connections made with other energetic beings on all levels, including emotionally, physically, spiritually, and mentally—past, present, and future.

- *Maintain privacy.* All souls retain the right to privacy. This includes both human and spiritual privacy. Practitioners are not allowed to share details about someone else, the discussions had, or energetic information shared with anyone else without explicit permission.

Keep these spiritual laws and our Bill of Rights in mind as you continue along your spiritual journey. You are always being guided and protected.

# Chapter 17

# Angel Stories

In addition to the other angel
stories throughout this book,
we compiled some experiences
submitted by listeners of
the top-charted spiritual
podcast *A Psychic's Story.*
Thank you to everyone
for sharing!

# Seeing a Seraphim

### *A Story from Branson M.*

**I grew up in a haunted house,** so I was really scared of everything as a kid because I was sensitive. There were some tragedies that happened in the house before my family moved in, such as a suicide that involved drugs and alcohol with the prior residents. It really was a tragic story.

Growing up, I wouldn't sleep in my own bedroom because I would hear chatter and distinct arguments between two voices that clearly were not physically there. I would also see shadow people run in the hallways. But I mostly felt somebody looming over me, and I often felt faint.

As you can imagine, I slept with my grandmother a lot of times because I was too scared to sleep in my own bed. After a while, I started praying, "God, I don't want to be scared of anything anymore." I would always pray, and after a while, I started seeing this being. I didn't understand what I was seeing at the time, nor did I understand what angels looked like. I always thought they would be huge, winged beings like in the Bible.

What I saw instead were eyeballs that were floating and spinning really fast in circles. I didn't know how to describe them as a kid, so I would tell my grandma they looked like "floating tornado eyeballs I see everywhere when I'm trying to go to sleep."

She took me to the doctor, and the doctor told her that my eyes were fine, and maybe it was just my imagination. After that, I stopped telling her that I saw the eyes, but I still see this angelic being to this day.

Now that I'm older and on my spiritual path, I've spoken to a few mediums, and they all say that this type of angel is called a seraphim angel. I have never heard this angel speak, and I've never communicated with him, but he is always there. Since I began meditating, his image is a little bit clearer to me. If you just look up the seraphim angel, the angel I see looks exactly like that. I feel very protected now.

# An Angel in Human Form

### *A Story from Jenni M.*

**In 2022 three close friends died,** and I was incredibly depressed. I have always felt like an outcast in my family, especially with my mom and sister, who are best friends. But my mom decided to take me and my sister to Maui, Hawaii. One night we went to a club, and while my mom and sister were dancing with guys, I sat at the bar and had some drinks. A few hours later, we left.

As we got in our rented Jeep, we had a heated argument. My mother and sister started a tirade about how I had issues and am "crazy," and they said other very hurtful things. I decided right then that I was over with this life; I did not want to live anymore. I could not continue to make it in this environment at all.

When we got back to the hotel, I knew I did not want to go back to the room with them, so I threw the key at them and went into the lobby bathroom. I cried in the bathroom stall, saying to myself, "I just don't want to live, and I don't know how I'm going do this. I cannot live anymore."

Then I heard a voice. It was two o'clock in the morning. It said, "Are you okay?"

It startled me, and I thought that maybe I should not be there in the bathroom that late. I walked out of the bathroom, and I saw this lovely lady with long dark hair parted in the middle, wearing a muumuu-type dress. I noticed her name tag, Jenni, which is my name.

I said, "I'm sorry. Should I not be in here? I'll leave right now."

And she said, "No, no, don't worry. Please don't worry." Then she looked me right in the eyes and said, "They were very cruel to you. They are very cruel to you."

I was shocked because no one up to that point had ever acknowledged, seen, or witnessed the cruelty that I've gone through.

I answered, "They are, aren't they?"

And she responded, "Yes, they are. Why don't you go ahead and follow me?"

I followed her to the front desk, and she began tapping on the hotel computer and said, "Let's get you a room tonight."

And I said, "Oh no, that's okay."

She said, "No, no, no, this is best. I don't want you going back to that room with them."

I said, "Okay, but I don't have any money."

She said, "Don't worry. Let's just find you something. Why don't you give me your other last name?"

And I didn't think about this until later, but I don't know how she knew that I had another last name, that I had been going by my stepdad's last name. So, I gave her my real dad's last name.

"Perfect," she said. "They won't look for that name. Let's go!" She grabbed the key, and she took me up to this beautiful room that overlooked the ocean. It was much bigger than the room my mother and sister were sharing.

After I woke up the next morning, I decided to write Jenni a letter to thank her for giving me the room that I couldn't pay for and the peace and quiet that came with it.

I went down to the front desk with my folded-up letter and said, "I'd like to leave this letter for Jenni."

The woman at reception asked, "Jenni?"

I replied, "Yes, Jenni, who works here."

And she said, "We don't have a Jenni who works here."

I stated, "Well, yeah, you do. She's got long brown hair. She probably works the night shift."

The woman said, "No, we do not have a Jenni here."

So, I said, "Yes, she wears a muumuu, has long brown hair, and helped me last night."

321

She replied, "No, that's not our uniform, miss; this is what we wear." And she pointed to her khaki Bermuda shorts and Hawaiian-type shirt. "I've been a manager here for five years and have never known a Jenni to work here."

I said, "What about a different department; you must have a Jenni, maybe in food services?"

"No, like I said, we're a pretty tight group. I've worked here a long time, and unless it was before my time here, we don't have a Jenni."

At this point, I was slightly hungover and completely freaking out. Like, what the heck? I asked around with the food services staff and housekeepers. And I still could not find a Jenni.

I went back to the front desk to give the girl the key to the room, and I asked, "So there is really no Jenni. Maybe she goes by a different name?"

"No, I'm really sorry." She was looking at me like I was just nuts.

Then, after the shock settled in, I knew that Jenni was an angel and that it was possible I would have really hurt myself if not for her and how kind she was to me.

I think that in times when we don't see a way out, someone will intervene from our higher soul family to let us know that we are loved, validated, and acknowledged for exactly who we are. That's my angel story.

*If you or someone you know is struggling or in crisis,*
*please reach out to a mental health professional.*
*If you are based in the United States, visit*
**988lifeline.org**
*or*
*call or text 988.*

# An Energetic Miracle

### A Story from Kelly S.

**My first angel experience** was about ten years ago. I was reading the book *A Course in Miracles*, and at the same time, I was reading *A Return to Love*, which is based on *A Course in Miracles*. I was saying a lot of the things that Marianne Williamson said to say, like, "Please let me see this situation differently," over and over again.

At that time, my marriage was falling apart, and I was asking for help from my angels. Then I experienced a miracle. And I can only say that it was a miracle because it immediately changed my perception of what was happening in my life.

I believe they were angels because I only had the feeling that they were. I didn't see anything, but I felt it, and what I felt could not be described as an earthly feeling. I can only describe it as pure, pure love that came into my body and changed my whole perception of what was happening in my life.

After that, my marriage completely turned around like a miracle. This is not something that we worked at. It just, boom, changed. I can only say that, ten years later, my husband and I are extremely happy and joyful. The experience and energy entirely changed our perception, and I think his view changed because mine did. And we're able to live literally happily ever after, weirdly like.

# Messages to Prepare for Mom's Passing

### *A Story from Yessenia R.*

**A lot of the intuitive messages I receive** come to me in dreams. Back in 2017, we moved out of the house I grew up in and into a whole new city and home. One night I dreamt of an angel, and the only thing the angel said was "Pay attention because you are going to receive a message."

A few weeks later, I dreamt about my maternal grandfather, who died when I was five years old. Although I don't have a lot of memories of my grandfather, I always felt we had a special connection. I always knew that I'd name my son after him.

The night that my grandfather came to me in my dream, he said, "I'm coming for someone—be prepared." It felt so real, and as soon as I woke up, I told my mom about my dream. I interpreted the message to mean that my grandpa was coming for my grandma. Years had gone by since my grandpa died, and my grandmother never remarried. So, it seemed logical that that would be the order of things.

Fast forward to several months later: I had dreamt my mom and I were in a big, beautiful church. We had the church all to ourselves. We were walking around admiring the beauty of the church. After a while, my mom kept disappearing, and I was desperately trying to find her. Then the main doors to the church opened, and all I could see was clouds and a bright light. My mom started to walk into the light, and I tried to go but couldn't move. I kept screaming for her to take me with her, but she just smiled, walked into the light, and disappeared.

I woke up with so much emotion and tears in my eyes. I told my mom about the dream and asked her to take me with her if she were to pass. By the end of that year, we found out my mom had terminal cancer. The doctor gave her three months to live. My mom kept saying that she just wanted to make it to the New Year. She loved the holidays.

My mom passed away on January 2. She got her wish and spent the last Thanksgiving, Christmas, and New Year's with all her children. Since then, I have had a lot of premonition dreams. Thank you for letting me share my story.

# Angels in the ICU

### A Story from Andrea K.

**I've always felt my intuition,** but I never had a spiritual awakening or had worked to strengthen my intuitive gifts. But in June of 2021, that all changed.

It was a sunny summer day, and my three kids were playing in the backyard. My youngest, who was three years old at the time, had decided to climb onto our patio table. She fell back onto the concrete patio and hit her head. We immediately suspected a concussion and took her to urgent care, which led to a trip to the emergency room. After a CT scan, it was determined that she had a brain hematoma and a small skull fracture. She was admitted into the ICU so they could keep a close eye on her for a few days and decide after some time if surgery would be necessary.

As a mother, this was heart-wrenching and of course spun me into unimaginable worry and fear. So, I began to pray. After several hours, when we were all settled in the ICU, I prayed even more ... just lay next to my daughter, eyes closed, and prayed.

During one of these times of prayer, I felt very relaxed, and a sense of peace came over me. I then had a vision in my third eye that I was not lying next to my daughter in her bed but was now sitting in a chair away from the bed, just watching her. From the right corner of the room, a bright light started to pour in toward her bed. And suddenly, I could *feel* angels and see them (again, all in my third eye). The angels were huge, and I could feel their presence, their strength, their love. I could feel their thick white wings and just knew that these were archangels. They surrounded my daughter's bed and stayed for what felt like several minutes. They didn't speak but were just there ... to comfort, heal, and bring peace. After this, they came in several more times over the next week or so. Even after we were home, they would appear in her room around her little toddler bed. She didn't end up needing surgery and made a full recovery!

I didn't tell anyone, not even my husband, about this angel experience for quite a while. I just kept it to myself, and when I did start to share with others, I was always brought to tears. It was just such a powerful, overwhelming experience to feel their presence and strength that I get emotional talking about it. Pure love!

They say that spiritual awakenings can sometimes happen in a difficult situation such as this, and that's definitely the case with me. The angels came to bring healing to my daughter and to also start me on my spiritual journey of finding my gifts.

# Repeating Numbers

### *A Story from Heather D.*

**All of us have looked at the clock** and seen the same number over and over again, and most of us believe they are signs from our spirit guides or angels and call them "angel numbers."

Oftentimes, we look up the meanings of these numbers in a book or discount them altogether. However, the story I am about to tell you will give you a fresh perspective and leave you with proof that not only are there messages behind these numbers, but also if you pay attention enough, they may change your entire life. My experience will show you that there is, without a doubt, more behind the repeating numbers you've been seeing. You just have to talk back to them.

It was a day like any other. I was driving home from work, noticing my favorite number all around me. My favorite number was appearing on license plates and billboards; everywhere I looked, I saw my favorite number. I wondered what the angels were trying to tell me. The thing is, when you see your favorite numbers, it could be a sign that you're on the right path. It could be a sign that tells you to keep on going, but on this day, it was totally scrambled. It wasn't making any sense at all. Was I not on the right path?

The only way to know was to ask the angels myself. So, at the next red light, I tuned in, and I got the gut instinct from my angels to play the lottery. I thought, "How cliché is that?" Angels asking a psychic to play the lottery. I thought about it for a little bit and decided that I'd listen to them—I was going to play the lottery. I literally said out loud to the angels: "If I win this, it will for sure strengthen our bond, and I will know, without a doubt, that I am talking to you, and I will never doubt what you give me again."

I went into the store, and I went to buy a lottery ticket, but the next day, I checked the numbers and realized I hadn't won. I started to cry. To be honest, I was heartbroken that the angels had let me down. When I asked them why, they said I did not lose. They said that I needed to look at the numbers that did come up. They said that the numbers were related to someone with whom I needed to spend more time, someone who needed me.

The numbers that did come up on that day were one, nine, five, and nine. I thought, "Wow, 1959! That could actually be someone's birthday. But whose?"

Later that day, I asked my mom. She was the first person that I thought of. "Mom, what year were you born?"

She replied, "1959."

I was flabbergasted and so excited. I could not believe it. I told her, "The angels want us to spend more time together!"

When I asked how she was doing, she replied, "I'm pretty good, but I just broke a rib."

I asked, "How the heck did you do that? Who breaks a rib?"

She said, "Oh it's a long story. I'll tell you about it later." Then we just chatted, and throughout that week, I made sure to contact her every day. The week after that, I received the news my mom had cancer.

I really didn't think anything of it, but soon I realized the message I got through the lottery was the angels letting me know that I truly did need to spend time with her. Because it wasn't even three weeks after her diagnosis that she passed away. She went to be with the angels, who proved to me beyond a shadow of a doubt that they were with her and also me. I am so grateful to the angels for sending me the numbers because I got to spend more time with my mom.

I hope that by sharing my story, I help you to see these signs in your life. Maybe the next time you see repeating numbers, you'll get an intuitive hit to do something or to reach out to someone. Then, perhaps, you can start seeing the beautiful messages that may be waiting for you behind the numbers.

# Part Five

# Guides and Resources

*If you are reading this in printed or e-book format, then take note of the following or record the steps on your phone to listen to your own voice and follow along.*

*Chapter 18*

# Meditations, Intentions, and Prayers

To further assist you in your spiritual journey, we have included the meditations, intentions, prayers, and other key resources presented throughout the book in this section as well. You can review the background of each by referring to its respective chapter.

### *Includes the following:*

Meditation to Become Present with Oneness

Meditation to Connect with Your Higher Self

Intentional Exercise to Open Psychic Senses

Exercise to Set Energetic Boundaries

Meditation to Connect with Your Spirit Team

Meditation to Call upon a Specific Being

Intentions and Prayers to Ground, Clear, and Protect

Spiritual Schedule Template

# Meditation to Become Present with Oneness
## *From Chapter 9, page 130*

**The following intention** to become present with oneness takes only a few minutes a day. It doesn't matter when or how you do this intention—before bed, in the shower, or while you're walking outside. The possibilities are endless. The steps are as follows:

- Get in a comfortable and relaxed position.

- If you are sitting or lying down, close your eyes. If you are walking outside in nature, taking a shower, or doing something similar, please keep your eyes open.

- Breathe in deeply.

- Breathe out deeply.

- With each breath, feel each inhale and exhale with your entire body.

- You are present. You are calm. You are peaceful.

- As you feel more and more relaxed with each breath, take a moment to release—either mentally, physically, or emotionally—anything that might be weighing on you.

- If you'd like, you can visualize handing whatever that thought, physical sensation, or emotion is over to your guides and angels. Ask your spirit team to take it from you and transmute it into love and light.

- As you breathe in and out and release, ask your higher self, guides, and angels to bring forth and integrate within you whatever is needed for your best and highest good. (The phrase "best and highest good" is a filter that removes your ego from the situation and from the desire to control the outcome.) Love. Peace. Bliss. Joy. Happiness. Hope.

- When you're ready, imagine that your feet are anchored and rooted to the ground. From your feet, an energetic grounding cord begins to grow, moving down slowly toward the center of Mother Earth.

- As this grounding cord travels down in a column of golden white light, it anchors to the center of the Earth.

- The divine love of Mother Earth radiates from Earth's core back up the column of light until it reaches the tips of your toes and the bottom of your feet, sweeping up your legs, thighs, tailbone, and hips, clearing out any stagnant energy it comes across.

- As this energy pulsates through you, it continues to move up your spine, nourishing your entire body, physically, mentally, emotionally, and spiritually.

- Breathe in and out.

- This golden white light is Universal Source, the I Am presence, and spreads along the energetic neurological branches that are the Tree of Life within you.

- Breathe in and out.

- This light and energy expand in love through your stomach, all the way up until they reach the center of your chest and sacred heart.

- Your entire heart fills with love, and as it does, you allow any further resistances in your physical, mental, emotional, and spiritual bodies to fully release.

- Breathe in and out.

- You are now in a total state of peace and ease—past, present, future, now.

- Breathe in further and continue to receive the increasing flow of Earth's energy as it regenerates every cell of your body and BE-ing.

- Let go of any thought that you are separate from Earth or God.

- As your breath softens, the golden white light works its way toward your shoulders and neck, moving up your face and to the front and back of your head.

- Resting a moment on your forehead and third eye, the Source Energy pulsates and tingles, clearing anything out that no longer serves you.

- Your breath feels even lighter as the energy moves to the top of your head and out in a beam of golden white light upward to the sky, universe, and Source.

- This golden white light is connecting you to God, to oneness.

- A gentle waterfall of love and light beams back down toward you, filling up your whole self.

- Breathe into the welcoming embrace of both God and Mother Earth. As above, so below.

- You rest in perfect communion.

- As you continue to breathe in and out deeply, notice the power of oneness, Earth, and your higher self and how it completely fills your energetic body, mind, heart, and soul. The circle of light expands within and around you.

- Release the illusion that you are alone or that you must do anything alone.

- Notice how your heart is one with your energetic body.

- Recognize how the air you are breathing is part of NO-thing and everything at the same time.

- Notice how you are one with All That Is, a perfect state of oneness and BE-ing.

# Meditation to Connect with Your Higher Self

## *From Chapter 9, page 140*

**There are many ways you can connect with your higher self.** The easiest way I have found is to get into a state of BE-ing and oneness, have a pure and clear intention, and make a request. Then be open to how and what comes through.

If you want to practice and have a more detailed approach connecting with your higher self, you can do the following:

- Get in a comfortable position.

- Relax your shoulders, close your eyes, and take some deep breaths.

- As you breathe in and out each time, contract and relax all the muscles in your body, getting into a deeper state of rest.

- Once you've done this a few times, become aware of your breath, allowing it to flow in and out effortlessly.

- Allow further relaxation and presence as you continue to breathe.

- Begin to focus on your heart space and imagine a moment when you experienced unconditional love. Hold onto this feeling.

- Ask your guides and angels to envelop you in love and light, bringing in healing and protective energy that surrounds you on all levels.

- Feel that state of safety and protection.

- Call upon your higher self, your oversoul, to be present and come closer. Say, "I call in my higher self. I ask to connect with and be in alignment with you, to receive information and messages clearly and succinctly for my best and highest good."

- Imagine a part of yourself is coming closer and closer toward your body and energetic space.

- Continue to be as present as possible and use all of your awareness and senses—physical, mental, emotional, and spiritual— to pick up sensations, messages, or information.

- Ask to be given a signal of what it feels like when your higher self is present or communicating with you.

- When you feel your higher self is present, you can begin to ask questions.

- As the energy flows through you, do not doubt or judge what you receive.

- Tune back in with your heart and feel what resonates.

- When you feel like your time with your higher self is complete, imagine releasing it back to Source.

- Come back to your body through your breath.

- Place your hands wherever you feel led—your heart, forehead, stomach area, or elsewhere.

- Thank your higher self and your spirit team for this amazing experience.

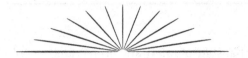

# Intentional Exercise to Open Psychic Senses
## *From Chapter 14, page 268*

**The following intentional exercise** is designed to open you up to your intuitive abilities and is meant to be visualized in your mind's eye.

1. Pick a time of day—morning or night is best—when you are able to sit or lie down comfortably.

2. Close your eyes, and take some deep breaths in and out.

3. As you quiet your mind, say to yourself or out loud:

   "I give the Universe permission to fully open and activate my psychic senses and abilities."

   "I ask that these open, activate, and integrate calmly and peacefully and in divine timing for my best and highest good."

   "I am fully open to receive, experience, and embrace my God-given and universal rights."

4. Feel it! The really important part here is that you *feel* it down to your bones, that you not only state this, but that you push the intention and feeling out toward the Universe.

5. "Thank you!"

I am fully open to

*receive, experience,*

*and embrace*

my God-given and

universal rights.

# Exercise to Set Energetic Boundaries

## *From Chapter 14, page 272*

**You can set your energetic boundaries** during or after a meditation, when you are grounded and your mind is clear. If you use prayer as your form of meditation, then you can skip straight to the exercise. The exercise is meant to be visualized in your mind's eye.

1.  Pick a place in your mind's eye that is calm and exudes what heaven is like to you. It can be floating in clouds, a crystal castle, a field of sunflowers, the top of a mountain—whatever brings you peace and joy.

2.  Take your time experiencing what this place is like. What do you hear? What do you see? What do you smell? Take it all in and in as much detail as you can.

3.  As you look around, there will be a place for you to sit down. It may be a pile of pillows, chairs around a marble table, or something else. Walk toward that, sit down, and get comfortable.

4.  When you sit down, you will be approached by your guides and angels. Take time here as well to experience what they are like. How many of them are there? Do they look like typical angels or humans? Or are they more like energetic light beings? There is no wrong answer. Enjoy the experience.

5. As your guides and angels sit down with you, a contract appears in front of you. Explain what you want and don't want to experience psychically. Do you lean more toward certain clairs than others and, if so, which ones? Do you want to open up your intuition on some levels and not others? Do you want to strengthen any and, if so, which ones? Do you want specific office hours such as times of the day or evening? Take the time to speak with them about what you want, and as you do, those items appear magically written on the contract in front of you. As you set up the terms, be very clear with your spirit team as well as yourself as to what you are willing to do or follow.

6. When you have said everything you want to say to your spirit team, ask them if there is anything that they would like you to know. Be silent and listen to what they do or say. Take note and acknowledge the information.

7. Before you get up to leave, be sure to thank them for their love, support, and guidance. Embrace them if you wish. They will be sure to pass along the terms of the energetic contract and boundaries with the rest of your guides, angels, and even loved ones on the other side.

# Meditation to Connect with Your Spirit Team

## *From Chapter 15, page 288*

**The following is a guided meditation** designed to help you connect with the loving presence of your spirit team, angels, and guides. This practice will help you create a deep connection to the guidance system that is always within and around you—the energetic beings of love and light that are here to support you in all ways.

- Take a deep breath in.

- Breathe out.

- Breathe in.

- Breathe out.

- Imagine your sacred space. Take some time to visualize it or feel it. In it you are safe. You are loved. You are at peace.

- Set the intention now to contact your spirit guides and angels.

- Inwardly call on them with gratitude.

- Thank your guides for beginning to connect with you.

- Breathe in.

- Breathe out.

- Breathe in.

- Breathe out.

- Begin to open your awareness to their presence. Take your time.

- You may see them in your mind's eye.

- You may feel their energy around you like a warm embrace.

- You may receive a thought.

- You may hear them as a whisper.

- You may feel sudden emotions of peace or joy.

- You may have an inner knowing that they are there with you.

- Be open to how your intuition picks up on their presence.

- Breathe in and acknowledge their presence.

- On the exhale, extend your appreciation.

- Breathe in again, feeling their energy.

- Exhale with gratitude.

- If you desire, you can ask them to reveal their name or names to you now.

- Thank you, angels and/or guides, for revealing your name.

- Breathe in and listen.

- Breathe out.

- Now ask your guides if they have a message for you.

- Breathe in.

- Breathe out.

- Focus your energy on being present.

- Allow yourself to receive their spiritual insights and any messages of communication.

- Just be aware, be still, and listen.

- Breathe in.

- Breathe out.

- Breathe in.

- Breathe out.

- Now sit in stillness for a few moments, allowing yourself to receive beautiful messages from your spirit team.

- Be open to receiving anything and everything you need to know for your best and highest good. Be open to however and in whatever ways it comes through for you.

- Now that you've received information for your best and highest good say, "Thank you spirit team for supporting me. Thank you for revealing what I needed to know."

- When you are ready to take this experience further, gently open your eyes.

- Pick up your pen and notepad or journal, and start to write. "Thank you spirit team of divine love, light, and truth for sharing that with me. Please help me now write down additional wisdom for my best and highest good."

- Take the next five minutes to allow your pen to flow onto the page and let the voice of the Universe and unconditional love come through in all their glory.

- As you write, you are protected and guided in all ways.

- Take a moment to wrap up whatever it is you have been writing. Thank your spirit team for their support. Send them deep gratitude for connecting with and guiding you.

- Receive love and gratitude back from them into your heart.

- Take a deep breath and exhale.

- Take another deep breath in and thank your spirit team one more time for everything.

- "Thank you. So be it. *Amen.*"

# Meditation to Call upon a Specific Being

## *From Chapter 15, page 292*

**The following is a guided meditation** designed to help you connect with a specific being. This practice will help you create a deep connection to the guidance system that is always within and around you—the energetic beings of love and light that are here to support you in all ways.

- Take a deep breath in.

- Breathe out.

- Breathe in.

- Breathe out.

- Imagine your sacred space. Take some time to visualize it or feel it. In it you are safe. You are loved. You are at peace.

- Set the intention now to connect with a specific archangel, ascended master, or deity. "I now call forth [state the name]."

- Inwardly call on this being with love and gratitude.

- Thank this being for beginning to connect with you.

- Now picture this energetic being standing in front of you within your sacred space.

- From your heart send them as much love as you can feel and imagine.

- Notice what happens next.

- Be open to the love returning to you. It is magnified manyfold.

- Keep sending and receiving this love.

- Monitor your breath as you inhale and exhale.

- Share anything that is weighing on you at this time.

- Share your deepest desires.

- Ask this being to intervene and give you guidance and direction. Know that the situation is in their loving hands, and they will work directly with Source to create a peaceful or healing situation for all involved.

- Notice any information that comes to you.

- Now sit in stillness for a few moments, allowing yourself to receive beautiful messages from this being.

- Be open to receiving anything and everything you need to know for your best and highest good. Be open to however and in whatever ways it comes through for you.

- Now that you've received information for your best and highest good, say, "Thank you [state the name] for revealing what I needed to know."

- When you are ready to take this experience further, gently open your eyes.

- Pick up your pen and notepad or journal and start to write. "Thank you for allowing me to experience that. Please help me now write down additional wisdom for my best and highest good."

- Take the next five minutes to allow your pen to flow onto the page and let the voice of the archangel, ascended master, or deity come through in all its glory.

- After your five minutes are done, take a moment to wrap up whatever it is you have been writing. Thank your spirit team for their support. Send them deep gratitude for connecting with and guiding you.

- Give thanks in your heart and let go.

- Take a deep breath and exhale.

- Take another deep breath in as you say, "Thank you. So be it. *Amen*."

# Intentions and Prayers
# to Ground, Clear, and Protect

## *From Chapter 15, page 296*

**This is a guided visual intention** to help ground, clear, and protect you. Use this daily to set, clear, and protect your energy, and return to it anytime you need to reground or realign with your higher self.

## *Ground*

*The following guided visual intention is designed to help ground you.*

- Get in a comfortable seated position, with your feet flat on the ground.

  o Take a deep breath in.

  o Exhale.

  o Take another deep breath in.

  o Exhale.

  o Take one more deep breath in.

  o Exhale.

- Continue to breathe in and out at whatever pace feels best to you.

- Imagine a gold light coming down from the heavens.

- As the warm glow descends toward your body, and gets closer and closer, feel an immense sense of peace and bliss.

- The golden light begins to enter through the top of your head.

- It slowly pulses in and out, emitting loving light and energy.

- As it moves slowly down through your body, you can't help but continue to feel peace and bliss, but also love—so much love.

- The light is now moving through your chest, down through your stomach area, and now into your hips, thighs, legs, and feet.

- When the light gets to your feet, imagine that this light starts to break off and grows, taking the form of roots.

- These roots—emanating such love and light—are anchored to your feet and begin to grow, moving down toward the floor.

- They move through the floor.

- They continue moving down, into the grass and dirt.

- The roots continue to push through layers and layers of Earth, going deeper and deeper: down, down, down.

- You can see layers of the Earth's crust as these roots continue to push through and on until they reach the center of Mother Earth.

- Once at the center, the roots take hold.

- Take three more deep breaths.

- Imagine the golden light pulsating in and out, grounding itself with Mother Earth.

- Say, "Thank you, Mother Earth, for giving and holding life."

- Say, "Thank you, Mother Earth, for providing an anchor and helping me to be grounded."

- Say, "As you give me life and light, I give you life and light."

- Say, "I'm in gratitude for all that you give—as I receive."

- Imagine the light, with the roots still anchored, beginning to travel back up from the center of Earth through the layers of crust, dirt, and grass.

- It slowly continues back up through the floor, reaching the bottom of your feet.

- When the light reaches your feet again, it pulsates in and out, filling you again with peace, bliss, and loving energy.

- It travels back up through your ankles, shins, knees, thighs, hips, pelvis, stomach, back, chest, hands, arms, shoulders, neck, and head.

- Your whole body and energy field are now filled with the glorious golden light.

- The light moves from the top of your head back up to the center of the universe.

- Once it arrives there, the light moves back down to the top of your head, quickly through your body, to the bottom of your feet and the center of Earth, and back. As it does so, take three deep breaths.

- Imagine this light is now connected to the universe and the center of Earth with your body, mind, and soul, grounded between and within.

- At any time during your day or evening that you want to feel grounded again, just imagine this beam of light connecting you to Earth and the astral plane, and you will immediately feel centered.

## *Clear*

*The following guided visual intention is designed to help clear and heal.*

- Take deep breaths in and out, focusing on your inhales and exhales.

- Continue to breathe in and out at whatever pace feels best to you.

- Take a moment to tap and tune in to how you're feeling:

    o Physically

    o Mentally

    o Emotionally

    o Spiritually or energetically

- Make a mental note of what you want to keep and what you want to clear and release.

- Starting at the top of your head, say the following:
  - I clear, align, and activate my crown chakra.
  - I am divine.
  - I am a spiritual being.
  - I am one with all that is.
  - I am infinite and boundless.
  - I am at peace.
  - I release anything that no longer serves me or is not for my best and highest good.

- Moving to your third eye, say the following:
  - I clear, align, and activate my third eye chakra.
  - I am insightful and intuitive.
  - I see clearly.
  - I think clearly.
  - I trust my decisions.
  - I expand my awareness.
  - I release anything that no longer serves me or is not for my best and highest good.

- Moving to your throat, say the following:
    - I clear, align, and activate my throat chakra.
    - I hear and speak the truth.
    - I live an authentic life.
    - My voice matters.
    - I have integrity.
    - I am open and honest.
    - I release anything that no longer serves me or is not for my best and highest good.

- Moving to your heart, say the following:
    - I clear, align, and activate my heart chakra.
    - I love myself and others.
    - I am an expression of love.
    - I am worthy of love.
    - I forgive myself and others.
    - I follow the voice of my heart.
    - I release anything that no longer serves me or is not for my best and highest good.

- Moving to your solar plexus, say the following:
    - I clear, align, and activate my solar plexus chakra.
    - I feel my own power.
    - My potential is unlimited.
    - I honor myself.

- o  I accomplish things easily.
- o  I act with courage.
- o  I release anything that no longer serves me or is not for my best and highest good.

- • Moving to your sacrum, say the following:
  - o  I clear, align, and activate my sacral chakra.
  - o  I am creative and joyful.
  - o  I embrace my sexuality.
  - o  I honor my desires.
  - o  I am playful.
  - o  I deserve to enjoy life.
  - o  I release anything that no longer serves me or is not for my best and highest good.

- • Moving to your root, say the following:
  - o  I clear, align, and activate my root chakra.
  - o  I am centered and grounded.
  - o  I love being in my body.
  - o  I have everything I need.
  - o  I am connected to nature.
  - o  I am safe.
  - o  I am loved.
  - o  I release anything that no longer serves me or is not for my best and highest good.

I welcome any vibrations,

frequencies, sounds,

colors, or energy

that are needed

*for my best and*

*highest good.*

- Now say, "All of my chakras are now cleared, aligned, and activated. My aura and auric field are also cleared, aligned, and activated alongside my chakras."

- Take a big, deep breath in and out.

- As you exhale, release any remaining thoughts, feelings, emotions, or energy. Imagine handing them over to your guides and angels to be transmuted in love and light by the Universe.

- Say the following to yourself:

  - I call back any and all parts of my *self*, *being*, and *soul* that need to be reintegrated and reunited for my best and highest good.

  - As I call back my *self*, I feel fulfilled and at peace.

  - My soul's energy is being restored.

  - My spiritual tank is full.

  - I welcome any vibrations, frequencies, sounds, colors, or energy that are needed for my best and highest good.

  - I ask that anything I have released to be transmuted in love and light is replaced with love, peace, bliss, and joy.

  - As I breathe in and out throughout my day, I will remain clear and my energy aligned and centered.

### Protect

*The following guided visual intention is designed to help protect.*

- As you breathe in and out, imagine that you are anchored to Earth's core. Say the following:

  - I am grounded.

  - I am cleared physically, emotionally, mentally, and spiritually—past, present, and future.

  - I feel centered and at peace.

  - My spiritual tank and energy are *full*.

  - I feel fulfilled on all levels.

- As you continue to breathe in and out, picture a bright white light descending toward your body.

- As it gets closer, it envelops you and both encases your physical body and surrounds your aura.

- This bright white light is an orb gently protecting and shielding you from any and all things that are not for your best or highest good.

- Say the following to yourself:

  - I place an angel in front of me.

  - I place an angel behind me.

  - I place an angel to my right.

  - I place an angel to my left.

- I place an angel above me.

- I place an angel below me.

- Archangel Michael, my guides, and angels, please protect me in all ways.

- Divinely guide and protect me throughout my day and evening.

- Thank you, so be it, *amen.*

- At any time during your day or evening that you want to feel or call in protection, just imagine a bright white light surrounding you with Archangel Michael, your guides, and angels lovingly by your side.

# Spiritual Schedule Template

## *From Chapter 15, pages 306-307*

**During your day, be open to** how you receive messages through your intuition. Jot down any experiences you have—nothing is too small. As things happen, be in appreciation for what unfolds.

Set an intention by asking to be open to what comes through and how. You act in the moment through recognition and gratitude. And then you reflect at the end of the day and ask for things to be adjusted next time.

If you want a more formal plan, start by creating a spiritual schedule for one week. Go slow and be easy on yourself. Set easy goals on the calendar each day.

> *Select from activities, exercises, or methods shared throughout* Looking for Angels *or from the following:*

- Automatic writing
- Being in gratitude
- Breathwork
- Chakra work
- Church
- Clearing/cleansing practice
- Dream notebook
- Fitness (walk, yoga, dance, etc.)
- Grounding practice
- Intentions

- Journaling
- Meditation
- Music
- Prayer
- Protection practice
- Reiki (or other energy healing modality)
- Setting energetic boundaries
- Sound bath
- Spiritual book group
- Spiritual podcast

## Spiritual Schedule Template

| | Sun. | Mon. | Tues. | Wed. | Thurs. | Fri. | Sat. |
|---|---|---|---|---|---|---|---|
| **Morning** | | | | | | | |
| **Afternoon** | | | | | | | |
| **Evening** | | | | | | | |

# Chapter 19

# Calling upon a Specific Archangel, Ascended Master, or Deity

God, Universe, and Source (GUS) and your spirit team are always with you and available to you. As mentioned on pages 292 and 348, you can also call upon a specific archangel, ascended master, or deity if you are looking for guidance or support that requires a particular area of focus. The following pages were compiled so you can easily refer to these spiritual beings and their specialties.

In addition to the meditations, intentions, and prayers provided before this section, you can also state the following to yourself or out loud.

*"I call upon you*

*[mention the archangel,*

*ascended master, deity].*

*I am looking for your love,*

*guidance, and support with*

*[describe the circumstance or*

*situation]. I ask for help now*

*and all that is for my best and*

*highest good. Thank you!"*

As you do this, trust your intuition. Do you feel divinely led to close your eyes, breathe in deeply, place your hand over your heart, or something else? Don't worry about the words or methods—your intention of your prayer is the most important part. GUS and your spirit team will know your intention and will respond in kind. No request is ignored. It may take some time to deliver results, but they always come through for us.

You can live a heaven on Earth starting right now. You don't have to wait for the rest of humanity to awaken. That is God's gift to you right now, along with your free will and choice. Your spirit team is enacting that plan by supporting you, through you—one person at a time.

These categories are generally associated with each being. If you don't see the circumstance or situation you need, pray for guidance as to who can best help.

# A

## Accomplishments and goals
- *Archangel Metatron*

## Agriculture
- *Hecate*

## Alchemy
- *Archangel Uriel*
- *Merlin*

## Alignment
- *Archangel Metatron*
- *Archangel Michael*

## Angel communication
- *Archangel Gabriel*
- *Mary*

## Animal communication
- *Archangel Ariel*
- *Archangel Gabriel*

## Arts
## (music, dance, and poetry)
- *Apollo*

## Ascension
- *Archangel Sandalphon*
- *Serapis Bey*

## Awakening
- *Archangel Sandalphon*
- *Serapis Bey*

---

# B

## Balance (in all things)
- *Buddha*

## Beautiful thoughts
- *Archangel Jophiel*

## Bravery, courage, and strength
- *Archangel Michael*

---

# C

## Careers
- *Archangel Chamuel (overall)*
- *Archangel Gabriel (communications, journalism, marketing, and writing)*

**Children**

- *Apollo (health and education)*
- *Artemis*
- *Mary*

**Comfort (during stressful times and situations)**

- *Archangel Azrael*

**Commitment and dedication**

- *Archangel Michael*

**Communication**

- *Archangel Gabriel*
- *Saint Francis*

**Compassion**

- *Archangel Zadkiel (and mercy)*
- *Green Tara*
- *Kwan Yin*
- *White Tara*

**Concerns about the future**

- *Archangel Jeremiel*

**Confidence**

- *Zeus*

**Connection (to heaven)**

- *Archangel Azrael*

**Conscious connection**

- *Archangel Raziel*

**Courage and confidence to speak up**

- *Archangel Gabriel*

**Creative endeavors and inspiration**

- *Archangel Jophiel*

**Creative insights, problem-solving, and solutions**

- *Archangel Uriel*

**Crossroads (and liminal spaces)**

- *Hecate*

**Crystal work**

- *Merlin*

## D

**Detachment**

- *Buddha (from suffering)*
- *Saint Franics (from people, places, or things)*

**Devotion**

- *Mary Magdalene*

**Divine love**

- *White Tara*

## E

**Emergency help (physical or spiritual)**

- *Green Tara*

**Empowerment**

- *Archangel Raguel*
- *Zeus*

**Energetic boundaries**

- *Archangel Raguel*

**Energy clearing and purification**

- *Melchizedek*

**Energy healing work**

- *Archangel Raphael*
- *Merlin*

**Energy or space clearings**

- *Saint Germain*

**Enlightenment**

- *Kwan Yin*
- *White Tara*

**Environmentalism**

- *Artemis*

**Esoteric knowledge and higher levels of information**

- *Archangel Raziel*
- *Melchizedek*

## F

**Faith**

- *Jesus*

**Feminine power**

- *Artemis*

**Feng shui and interior decorating**

- *Archangel Jophiel*

**Fertility and/or feminine energy and strength**

- *Isis*
- *Mary*

**Forgiveness
(of self and others)**

- *Archangel Zadkiel*
- *Jesus*
- *Saint Padre Pio*

# G

**Grace**

- *Mary Magdalene*

**Guidance and support
for healers**

- *Archangel Raphael*

# H

**Happiness and joy**

- *Archangel Haniel*
- *Buddha*

**Harmony and order**

- *Archangel Haniel*
- *Archangel Raguel*
- *Archangel Zadkiel*
- *Isis*
- *Jesus*
- *Mary*

**Healing**

- *Apollo (animals
  and people)*
- *Archangel Ariel
  (animals, environment,
  and people)*
- *Archangel Azrael
  (depression, grief,
  and sadness*
- *Archangel Michael
  (all aspects of the
  mind, body, and soul)*
- *Archangel Raphael
  (animals and people
  on all levels)*
- *Archangel Raziel*
- *Archangel Zadkiel
  (all aspects of the
  mind, body, and soul)*
- *Ganesh*
- *Isis (energetic healing
  on all levels)*
- *Mary
  (healing power)*
- *Saint Francis (animals
  and environment)*

**Hope and peace**

- *Jesus*

**Households**

- *Hecate*

# I

**Inner peace**
- *Buddha*

**Insight and guidance**
- *Green Tara*

**Intellect or wisdom**
- *Archangel Raphael*

**Intuition**
- *Artemis*

# J

**Justice**
- *Archangel Raguel*
- *Ida-Ten*

# K

**Kindness to self and others**
- *Kwan Yin*

# L

**Life expectancy and longevity**
- *White Tara*

**Life purpose**
- *Archangel Chamuel (and direction)*
- *Archangel Metatron*
- *Archangel Michael*
- *Saint Francis (and direction)*
- *Saint Germain (and direction)*

**Life reviews and making life changes**
- *Archangel Jeremiel*

**Love (self-love and love for others)**
- *Archangel Chamuel*
- *Mary*

# M

## Magic

- *Archangel Ariel*
- *Archangel Raziel*
- *Archangel Uriel*
- *Hecate*
- *Isis*
- *Merlin*

## Manifestation

- *Archangel Ariel*
- *Archangel Jophiel*
- *Archangel Raziel*
- *Archangel Uriel*
- *Melchizedek*
- *Saint Germain*

## Mediumship (communicating with those who have passed)

- *Archangel Gabriel*

## Memory enhancement and recall

- *Archangel Zadkiel*

## Mercy

- *Archangel Zadkiel*
- *Kwan Yin*
- *Mary Magdalene*

## Miracles

- *Jesus*

## Moon energy

- *Archangel Haniel*

## Motivation for a healthy lifestyle

- *Serapis Bey*

## Music (sending messages and healing through it)

- *Archangel Sandalphon*

# N

## Nighttime (and the moon)

- *Hecate*

# O

## Organization and recordkeeping

- *Archangel Metatron*

## Overcoming fear

- *Green Tara*

## Overcoming unhealthy situations (people, places, or things)

- *Serapis Bey*

# P

## Passion for oneself or others

- *Saint Padre Pio*
- *Zeus*

## Peace (personal and global)

- *Archangel Chamuel*
- *Saint Francis*
- *Serapis Bey*

## Persecution due to religious and/or spiritual beliefs

- *Ida-Ten*

## Poise and grace

- *Archangel Haniel*

## Positive energy

- *Ida-Ten*

## Positive thoughts

- *Archangel Jophiel*

## Prayers and signs (delivering and answering)

- *Archangel Sandalphon*

## Prevention of negative thoughts

- *Archangel Azrael*

## Prioritization

- *Archangel Jophiel*
- *Archangel Metatron*

## Projects (artistic, creative, science, or writing)

- *Archangel Gabriel*

## Prophecy or divination

- *Apollo*
- *Merlin*

## Prosperity and abundance

- *Ganesh*

## Protection

- *Archangel Ariel*
- *Archangel Michael*
- *Ida-Ten*
- *Isis*
- *Kwan Yin*
- *White Tara*

## Protection against evil

- *Apollo*

## Protection from psychic attacks

- *Melchizedek*

## Psychic abilities

- *Archangel Haniel*
- *Archangel Raphael*
- *Archangel Raziel*
- *Merlin*

## Psychic dreams, visions, and interpretations

- *Archangel Jeremiel*

## Psychic information and protection

- *Saint Germain*

# R

## Relationships

- *Archangel Chamuel*

## Releasement of fear and worry

- *Archangel Jeremiel*

## Removal of egoic thoughts

- *Archangel Zadkiel*

## Removal of obstacles or blockages

- *Ganesh*
- *Green Tara*

## Resolution and mediation of conflict and disputes

- *Archangel Raguel*

# S

### Safety (unborn babies and mothers)

- *Archangel Sandalphon*

### Service (being in service to others)

- *Archangel Sandalphon*

### Shape-shifting

- *Zeus*

### Soul purpose

- *Archangel Metatron*
- *Archangel Michael*

### Soul transitions from life on Earth to the other side

- *Archangel Azrael*
- *Archangel Jeremiel*

### Space clearing

- *Archangel Raphael*

### Spirit releasement

- *Archangel Raphael*
- *Melchizedek*

### Spiritual awakenings and evolution

- *Mary Magdalene*

### Spiritual growth

- *Saint Padre Pio*
- *Serapis Bey*

### Spiritual growth and understanding

- *Archangel Uriel*
- *Buddha*

# T

**Time management**

- *Archangel Metatron*

**Transcendence and enhanced awareness**

- *Ganesh*

**Travel**

- *Archangel Raphael*
- *Ganesh*
- *Hecate*

**Truth**

- *Ida-Ten*

# W

**Weather**

- *Archangel Uriel*
- *Zeus*

**Wildlife**

- *Artemis*

# U

**Understanding and mercy**

- *Mary*

**Understanding eternal life**

- *Mary Magdalene*

# Chapter 20

# Index of
# Spiritual Beings

The spiritual beings mentioned throughout the book are not a comprehensive list of all of the archangels, ascended masters, or deities. Readers are encouraged to do their own research and have fun tapping in and calling upon their spirit team members.

*archangels, † ascended masters, ‡ deities*

# Glossary

## A

**Angel (modern-day)**

An energetic spiritual being who helps bridge the connection to the Divine and acts as a messenger of God, Universe, and Source (GUS).

**Angel (religious)**

In Hebrew, Greek, and Arabic, the root word for *angel* is translated as "messenger." Judeo-Christian and Muslim traditions state that angels are created beings and not related to humans. Tasked with interacting with humans' physical work in a variety of ways, they can appear as bright lights or be perceived in human form.

**Animal guide or animal spirit**

An animal with whom a human has a connection. Also referred to as spirit animal.

**Apocrypha**

A term that means "hidden" and relates to religious books and writings that, while not recognized as sacred or accepted core writings, are viewed as offering valuable religious teachings. Most religions have apocryphal books and writings in addition to their sacred books.

**Archangel**

An order of angels, comprising energetic spiritual beings with specialized functions, that oversees other angels. Archangels have never been incarnated (except for Archangels Metatron and Sandalphon), and they are extremely powerful and one of the closest sources of energy to the Divine. The number of main archangels varies from three-four to seven-fifteen, depending on the religious or spiritual belief.

**Ascended master**

A notable spiritual teacher, healer, or prophet who previously walked the Earth as a human, or another planet as another living being. The ascended master gained mastery during the reincarnation cycle and, after death, decided to support humans from the other side.

**Ascension**

A term used for spiritual awakening or the enlightenment process that involves the expansion of the heart, mind, and soul.

**Aura**

An emanation of the emotional, mental, and spiritual levels that forms an energy field around the body of a living being.

---

# B

**Bodhisattva**

A key concept in Buddhism that refers to someone who has been enlightened and is on the path to Buddhahood.

---

# C

**Call upon**

To ask a spiritual being for guidance or help.

**Canonized books**

Sacred texts in the Judeo-Christian tradition that have been approved as the true word of God. There are sixty-six canonized books, comprising the Hebrew Bible (Old Testament) and New Testament.

**Celestial hierarchy**

The traditional hierarchy of angels developed by Pseudo-Dionysius, a Greek author and theologian of the late fifth century. Ranked from highest to lowest, the nine categories of angels are seraphim, cherubim, thrones, dominions, virtues, powers, principalities, archangels, and angels.

**Chakra**

An energy center of spiritual power in the human body.

**Clair**

A spiritual term meaning "clear."

**Clairaudience**
Clear hearing.

**Claircognizance**
Clear knowing.

**Clairempathy**
Clear emotional feeling.

**Clairgustance**
Clear tasting.

**Clairintellect**
Clear thinking.

**Clairsalience**
Clear smelling.

**Clairsentience**
Clear physical feeling.

**Clairtangency**
Clear touching.

**Clairvoyance**
Clear seeing.

**Clairvoyant**
Someone who can perceive information, things, or events beyond typical sensory contact.

**Cleanse/cleansing**
A spiritual term used for purifying, clearing, and recharging energy, which helps to sharpen intuition. Sometimes the word *clear* (*clearing*) is used interchangeably.

**Clear/clearing**
A spiritual term used for purifying, cleansing, and recharging energy, which helps to sharpen intuition. Sometimes the word *cleanse* (*cleansing*) is used interchangeably.

# D

**Dark night of the soul**

Used to describe an extremely difficult or painful period of one's life or a time of spiritual desolation. This is something that happens when a situation or disaster seems to invalidate the meaning life had before.

**Deity**

A supernatural being who is divine or sacred and is often worshipped.

**Divine**

Relating to or coming directly from God (primarily) or a god. As "the Divine," this is often used as an alternative reference to God.

**Divine light**

Energy or light that comes directly from God (primarily) or a god.

**Divinity**

The state or quality of being divine.

**Dualism**

The view that the mind and the body comprise two separate realms or substances: the thinking substance (mind) and the extended substance (matter).

---

# E

**Electromagnetic spectrum**

The range of frequencies of electromagnetic radiation and their respective wavelengths.

**Energy healing**

A technique to restore the balance of energy and support physical, mental, emotional, and spiritual well-being.

**Entity**

Something that has a separate or distinct existence or conceptual reality.

# F

**Frequency**
> The rate at which a vibration occurs.

---

# G

**God**
> In Christianity and other monotheistic religions, God represents the supreme being, creator, and ruler of the universe. When the term appears lowercase (god), it means an aspect of the creator and often represents a superhuman being that is worshipped.

**Goddess**
> An aspect of God the creator that represents female energy and/ or identity.

**Ground/grounding**
> A technique that involves doing activities that electrically reconnect someone to the earth. Also referred to as earthing.

**Guardian angel**
> A spirit that watches over and protects a person, animal, or place.

**GUS**
> God, Universe, and Source.

---

# H

**Healer**
> Someone who seeks to restore the balance of energy and support physical, mental, emotional, and spiritual well-being.

**Higher self**
> An eternal, omniscient, and conscious being who is one's real self (e.g., true self). Also referred to as oversoul.

# I

**Incorporeal**

Having no material body or form.

**Intention**

An idea, purpose, or plan that someone intends to carry out. Acting with intention means acting with full consciousness.

**Intuition**

An instinctive ability to directly gain knowledge or cognition. Intuition mirrors the physical, mental, and emotional senses of people and animals.

---

# J

**Judeo-Christian Bible**

A term used for the sixty-six books of the Bible. Both the Christian and Jewish faiths tend to accept the Hebrew Bible (Old Testament), but only Christians accept the New Testament.

---

# K

**Kabbalah**

An esoteric method, discipline, and school of thought in Jewish mysticism. It translates to "something received" and can be spelled a total of twenty-four ways. (In Christianity it tends to be spelled with a *C*, in Judaism with a *K*, and in spiritualism with a *Q*). The ancient Judaic mystical text refers to secrets of divination and manifestation with symbols and numbers.

# L

## Light

A spiritual term used to represent the Divine. It brings forth illumination, understanding, wisdom, and healing.

## Lightworker

Someone who feels led to help people, animals, and Earth through spiritual energy.

---

# M

## Meditation

A practice that involves focusing or clearing one's mind.

## Medium

Similar to a psychic, a medium relies on intuitive abilities to gather information about a person, animal, place, or thing, but mediums can also tune into spirit energy. They often rely on the presence of nonphysical energy outside themselves for the information being read. Most mediums focus on making connections with and delivering messages from people who are no longer living to those who still are.

## Meridians

Pathways in which energy travels. Meridians are also referred to as *nadis*, a Sanskrit word translated as "tubes," "channels," or "flow."

---

# N

## Nonvisual frequencies of energy

Broader wavelengths in the electromagnetic spectrum outside of what the human eye can see. Examples include infrared, microwaves, radio waves, sound waves, ultrasound, ultraviolet, and X-rays.

# O

**Oneness**

A state of being unified or whole with God, Universe, and Source (GUS).

**Other side**

The perceived afterlife, as a supernatural realm, inhabited by the spirits of deceased people.

---

# P

**Paranormal**

Phenomena or events that are beyond the scope of normal scientific understanding.

**Paranormal investigation**

The discipline of studying angels, ghosts, and other spiritual energies or beings.

**Prayer**

An act of communication, request for help, or expression of thanks, usually addressed to God.

**Psychic**

Someone who can sense, tune into, or read energy beyond typical sensory contact. Psychics rely on intuitive ability to gather information about a person, animal, place, or thing.

---

# Q

**Quantum physics**

An area of study of the physical properties of nature at the scale of atoms and subatomic particles (under one micron, one-fiftieth of a human hair).

**Qur'an**

Islam's holy book, viewed as a reiteration of the previous revelations (Judeo-Christian books) written in Arabic.

# S

**Scientific Revolution**

The series of events in the sixteenth and seventeenth centuries that marked the emergence of modern science with discoveries by scientists John Locke, Isaac Newton, and others. The resulting developments in mathematics, physics, astronomy, biology, and chemistry transformed society's views about nature and how the world works, presenting a mechanistic view of the physical world.

**Soul**

The essence or spiritual or immaterial part of a person or animal that confers individuality and humanity. It is often considered to be synonymous with the mind or self.

**Soul energy or spirit energy**

The energy of one's soul or spirit. These terms are often used interchangeably to indicate one's consciousness or expression and have a close affiliation with one's emotions.

**Soul journey**

A path of spiritual growth that allows someone to connect with their higher self, explore their passions, and align with their purpose. It is a journey toward spiritual enlightenment and awakening that helps one to realize their unique potential.

**Source**

Used in lieu of denominational phrases like God, it is interchangeable with the Divine or Universe.

**Source Energy**

A source from which energy can be obtained.

**Spirit**

The force believed to give life. Also referred to as the nonphysical part of a person that is the seat of emotions and character (e.g., the soul).

**Spirit guide**

An energetic being that acts as a guide or protector to a living, incarnated individual.

**Spirit releasement**

The process of releasing stagnant energy from a person's or animal's body or aura.

**Spirit team**

Composed of enlightened beings, including animal guides, archangels, ascended masters, guardian angels, deities, spirit guides, and loved ones from the other side. The spirit team assists humans by offering guidance, support, and clarity to life situations and the soul's journey.

**Spiritual awakening**

An experience of one or more profound shifts in consciousness that brings a greater understanding of life and the interconnectedness of all things.

**Spiritual being**

A supernatural, incorporeal being.

**Spiritual hygiene**

Intentional, routine practices to cleanse and protect energy bodies and energy fields.

**Spiritual vibration**

The concept that all matter in the universe is made up of energy that vibrates.

**Subtle body**

Etheric energy that begins at the physical body and radiates outward in different layers that connect and surround a person. The focal points are called chakras and are connected by meridians that are connected to the aura.

**Subtle energy**

Composed of life force.

**Subtle energy bodies**

Assumed energy points within the human body that cannot be viewed by the naked eye.

**Subtle energy system**
Composed of three components: chakras, meridians, and aura.

**Supernatural**
An order of existence beyond the visible, observable universe.

---

# T

**Telepathy**
The communication of thoughts or ideas by means other than the known senses.

---

# U

**Universe**
Another name for a supreme being or higher power. It is all existing matter and space considered as a whole and interconnected. In some spiritual circles, it also represents consciousness.

---

# V

**Vedas**
The four holy books of Hinduism: Rig Veda, Sama Veda, Yajur Veda, and Atharva Veda. Also referred to as the Shruti ("that which is heard"), these writings are believed to include revelations of unquestionable and eternal truth.

**Vibration**
A state of being.

**Vibrational energy**
A pervasive life force.

# References

## Chapter 1     Christianity and Judaism: A Starting Point

1.  Kevin Corrigan and L. Michael Harrington, "Pseudo-Dionysius the Areopagite," in *Stanford Encyclopedia of Philosophy (Winter 2019 edition)*, ed. Edward N. Zalta, last modified April 30, 2019, https://plato.stanford.edu/archives/win2019/entries/pseudo-dionysius-areopagite/.

2.  Matthew Fox and Rupert Sheldrake, *The Physics of Angels* (New York: Monkfish Publishing, 2014).

3.  Cristobal Almanza, "Explanation and Hierarchy of the 9 Choirs of Angels [Infographic]," *Soulpainter* (blog), September 30, 2015, https://soulpainter.com/2015/09/explanation-and-hierarchy-of-the-9-choirs-of-angels-infographic/.

4.  Rick Kirby, "Who Is the Angel of the Lord?," Christianity.com, June 12, 2020, https://www.christianity.com/wiki/angels-and-demons/the-angel-of-the-lord.html.

5.  Michael S. Heiser, *Angels: What the Bible Really Says about God's Heavenly Host* (Bellingham, WA: Lexham Press, 2018).

6.  Archangel Michael is mentioned in Jude 9, Revelation 12:7–8, and Daniel 10:13, 21. Archangel Gabriel is mentioned in Daniel 8:16, 9:21 and Luke 1:19, 1:26–27.

7.  1 Enoch 22–28.

8.  Hope Bolinger, "What Are Archangels in the Bible, and How Many Are There?," Christianity.com, February 8, 2022, https://www.christianity.com/wiki/angels-and-demons/what-are-archangels-in-the-bible.html.

9.  Stephanie Hertzenberg, "What Is the Name of Each Archangel?," Beliefnet, accessed November 15, 2022, https://www.beliefnet.com/inspiration/angels/what-is-the-name-of-each-archangel.aspx.

10. Isaiah 6:1–7, Ezekiel 1:1–24.

11. Heiser, *Angels*, 24.

12. Daniel 9:21, Revelation 14:16.

13. David Jones, *A Very Short History of Angels* (New York: Oxford University Press, 2011), 41.

14. Genesis 19:10–11.

15. Acts 12:7.

16. Acts 12:10, 5:9.

17. Matthew 28:2.

18. 2 Kings 19:35.

19. Acts 12:23.

20. Michael Pennock, *This Is Our Faith: A Catholic Catechism for Adults* (Indianapolis: Ave Maria Press, 2018).

21. "Why We Call Him 'The Angel Doctor,'" *The New Theological Movement* (blog), January 28, 2013, http://newtheologicalmovement.blogspot.com/2013/01/why-we-call-him-angelic-doctor.html.

22. Michael J. Plato, "C. S. Lewis and Billy Graham on Angels," *Southern Baptist Journal of Theology* 25, no. 2 (2021): 143–59, https://equip.sbts.edu/publications/c-s-lewis-and-billy-graham-on-angels/.

23. Helmut Hornung, "Comets Play a Role in the History of Civilization," Phys.org, November 11, 2013, https://phys.org/news/2013-11-comets-role-history-civilization.html.

24. Marilynn Carlson Webber and Dr. William D. Webber, "The Warrior Angels," in *The Big Book of Angels*, ed. editors of Beliefnet (New York: Rodale Books/Beliefnet, 2002), 270.

**Chapter 2     More on Archangel Metatron**

1.  *Encyclopaedia Britannica Online*, s.v. "Metatron," last modified September 8, 2022, https://www.britannica.com/topic/Metatron.

2.  *New World Encyclopedia*, s.v. "Metatron," accessed September 23, 2022, https://www.newworldencyclopedia.org/p/index. php?title=Metatron&oldid=1086467.

3.  *Encyclopaedia Britannica Online*, s.v. "Metatron."

4.  *New World Encyclopedia*, s.v. "Metatron."

5.  Chris Heath, "The Epic Life of Carlos Santana," *Rolling Stone*, March 16, 2000, https://www.rollingstone.com/music/ music-news/the-epic-life-of-carlos-santana-89485/.

6.  Ibid.

7.  Agustin Gurza, "Santana and Spiritualness," *Chicago Tribune*, December 12, 2002, https://www.chicagotribune.com/news/ ct-xpm-2002-12-12-0212120261-story.html.

8.  Heath, "The Epic Life of Carlos Santana."

9.  Gurza, "Santana and Spiritualness."

10. Don Lattin, "$30 Million Awarded Men Molested by 'Family Priest'/ 3 Bishops Accused of Stockton Coverup," SFGATE, July 17, 1998, https://www.sfgate.com/news/article/30-Million-Awarded-Men-Molested-by-Family-3001550.php.

11. Michael Rezendes, "Church Allowed Abuse by Priest for Years," *Boston Globe*, January 6, 2002, https://www.bostonglobe.com/ news/special-reports/2002/01/06/church-allowed-abuse-priest-for-years/cSHfGkTIrAT25qKGvBuDNM/story.html.

12. "Pope Sends First E-mail Apology," *BBC News*, November 23, 2001, http://news.bbc.co.uk/2/hi/europe/1671540.stm.

## Chapter 3    *Islam: A Reconfirmation*

1. Musharraf Hussain, "Basic Beliefs of Islam—Books," University of Nottingham, January 26, 2016, YouTube video, 7:37, https://youtu.be/b2loXW4jI20.

2. Warren Larson, "Islam's 7 Articles of Faith," Zwemer Center for Muslim Studies, accessed September 12, 2022, https://www.zwemercenter.com/guide/islams-seven-articles-of-faith/.

3. Omar Suleiman, *Angels in Your Presence* (Leicestershire, UK: Kube Publishing Ltd, 2021).

4. Diane Morgan, *Essential Islam: A Comprehensive Guide to Belief and Practice* (Santa Barbara, CA: ABC-CLIO, 2010), 45.

5. Zohair Abdul-Rahman, "In Pursuit of Conviction III: Do You Really Believe in Angels?," Yaqeen Institute for Islamic Research, updated April 6, 2021, https://yaqeeninstitute.org/read/paper/in-pursuit-of-conviction-iii-do-you-really-believe-in-angels#:~:text=Believing%20in%20the%20angels%20allows,not%20been%20written%20for%20you.

6. Ibid.

7. Hussain, "Basic Beliefs of Islam—Books."

8. Omar Suleiman, "Angels in Your Presence," Yaqeen Institute for Islamic Research, video series, accessed November 20, 2022, https://yaqeeninstitute.org/series/angels-in-your-presence.

9. "Duties of Angels," Islam.org, accessed September 16, 2022, https://www.islam.org.uk/beliefs-overview/angels/duties-of-angels/.

10. "The Major Angels and Their Duties," Questions on Islam, accessed September 23, 2022, https://questionsonislam.com/article/major-angels-and-their-duties.

11. Whitney Hopler, "Archangel Azrael," Learn Religions, updated August 25, 2018, https://www.learnreligions.com/meet-archangel-azrael-124093.

12. *Encyclopaedia Britannica Online*, s.v. "Isrāfīl," May 7, 2020, https://www.britannica.com/topic/Israfil.

13. "The Major Angels and Their Duties."

14. Whitney Hopler, "Kiraman Katibin: Muslim Recording Angels," Learn Religions, updated August 11, 2017, https://www.learnreligions.com/kiraman-katibin-muslim-recording-angels-124021.

15. Suleiman, *Angels in Your Presence*, 89–93.

---

*Chapter 4      Hinduism: Angel-Like Beings*

1. "Hinduism," History.com, accessed November 4, 2022, https://www.history.com/topics/religion/hinduism.

2. "Hindu Sacred Books," The Heart of Hinduism, accessed October 10, 2022, https://iskconeducationalservices.org/HoH/tradition/doctrine-and-scripture/hindu-sacred-books/.

3. Ibid.

4. *Encyclopaedia Britannica Online*, s.v. "Smriti," October 4, 2013, https://www.britannica.com/topic/Smriti.

5. "The Smritis," The Divine Life Society, accessed November 5, 2022, https://www.sivanandaonline.org//?cmd=displaysection&section_id=572.

6. Joshua J. Mark, "Bhagavad Gita," in *World History Encyclopedia*, last modified June 15, 2020, https://www.worldhistory.org/Bhagavad_Gita/.

7. Whitney Hopler, "Guardian Angels in Hinduism," Learn Religions, updated April 27, 2019, https://www.learnreligions.com/guardian-angels-in-hinduism-124346.

8.  Shoba Narayan, "May Hanuman Be with You," *The Big Book of Angels*, ed. editors of Beliefnet (New York: Rodale Books/Beliefnet, 2002), 105.

9.  Dharma Speaks, "Hinduism: Why So Many Gods?," May 2, 2017, YouTube video, 10:32, https://youtu.be/m3iiJ7hAUaU.

10. Jay Lakhani, "What Does Hinduism Say about Angels?," Hindu Academy, January 25, 2021, YouTube video, 1:27, https://youtu. be/9pChBC1MKmg.

11. Jayaram V., "Hinduism Beliefs about War," Hinduwebsite.com, accessed November 15, 2022, https://www.hinduwebsite.com/ hinduism/h_war.asp.

12. "New Angles on Angels," *Hinduism Today*, September 1, 1992, https://www.hinduismtoday.com/magazine/ september-1992/1992-09-new-angles-on-angels/.

---

### Chapter 5    Buddhism: A Matter of Reality

1.  "The Global Religious Landscape: Buddhists," Pew Research Center, December 18, 2012, https://www.pewresearch.org/ religion/2012/12/18/global-religious-landscape-buddhist/.

2.  "Buddhism," History.com, July 22, 2020, https://www.history.com/ topics/religion/buddhism.

3.  Charles Prebish, Dzogchen Ponlop Rinpoche, and Joan Sutherland, "Is Buddhism a Religion?," *Lion's Roar*, January 4, 2019, https:// www.lionsroar.com/is-buddhism-a-religion-november-2013/.

4.  Ibid.

5.  Ibid.

6. "The Diamond Sutra—The Eleventh Section," The British Library, accessed October 18, 2022, https://www.bl.uk/onlinegallery/ttp/ sutra/accessible/section11.html.

7. John Pendall, "The Reality of Things: Does Not Apply," *The Tattooed Buddha*, accessed November 1, 2022, https://thetattooedbuddha. com/2016/03/28/the-reality-of-things-does-not-apply/.

8. Ajahn Sumedho, "Buddhist Angels," Amaravati Buddhist Monastery, April 30, 2022, YouTube video, 57:07, https://youtu.be/ Rxop7FiplEY.

9. "Deva," Tibetan Buddhist Encyclopedia, updated December 14, 2015, http://tibetanbuddhistencyclopedia.com/en/index.php/ Deva.

10. "Deva," Encyclopedia of Buddhism, accessed November 1, 2022, https://encyclopediaofbuddhism.org/wiki/Deva.

11. James B. Apple, "Bodhisattva," in *Oxford Bibliographies Online*, last modified December 19, 2012, https://www.oxfordbibliographies. com/view/document/obo-9780195393521/obo-9780195393521- 0048.xml.

12. James Dinwiddie, "What Are Angels?," *bdbuddha* (blog), March 23, 2014, https://bdbuddha.com/2014/03/23/what-are-angels/.

13. Sheng Yen, "The Legacy of Chan: Lesson 6: The Bodhisattva Path," DharmaNet, accessed November 2, 2022, https://dharmanet.org/ coursesM/26/chan6.htm.

14. Kosho Uchiyama, "What Is a Bodhisattva?," *Tricycle*, 2016, https:// tricycle.org/magazine/what-bodhisattva/.

15. Michael Sunderland, "Zen Reflection of the Day: Modern Bodhisattvas," a Few Words, Medium, October 27, 2020, https://medium.com/afwp/ zen-reflection-of-the-day-modern-bodhisattvas-37db308c2dad.

### Chapter 6    Where Did the Angels Go?

1. Ibn Taymiyyah, *Kit̄ab al-nubuww̄at*, vol. 1 (Riyadh: Maktabat Aḍwā' al-Salaf, 2000), 194–95.

2. Ibid., 195.

3. Rex Hauck, ed., *Angels: The Mysterious Messengers* (New York: Ballantine Books, 1994), 37–38.

4. Neha Sahgal, Jonathan Evans, Ariana Monique Salazar, Kelsey Jo Starr, and Manolo Corichi, "Religion in India: Tolerance and Segregation: Religious Beliefs," Pew Research Center, June 29, 2021, https://www.pewresearch.org/religion/2021/06/29/religious-beliefs-2/.

5. "Belief in Angels and Heaven Is More Common Than Belief in the Devil or Hell," AP-NORC Center for Public Affairs, July 2023, https://apnorc.org/projects/belief-in-angels-and-heaven-is-more-common-than-belief-in-the-devil-or-hell/.

6. *St. Thomas Aquinas: Summa Theologiae*, vol. 9. (New York: Blackfriars/McGraw-Hill Book Company, 1964), part 1, question 63, article 7.

7. Fox and Sheldrake, *The Physics of Angels*, 103.

8. Ibid., 104.

9. Rob Picheta, "Nobel Prize for Quantum Physicists Who Explained Particles' 'Spooky Behavior,'" *CNN*, October 4, 2022, https://www.cnn.com/2022/10/04/europe/nobel-prize-physics-winner-2022-intl-scn/index.html#:~:text=Clauser%20and%20Anton%20Zeilinger%20have,announced%20in%20Stockholm%20on%20Tuesday.

10. Michael Lipka and Claire Gecewicz, "More Americans Now Say They're Spiritual but Not Religious," Pew Research Center, September 6, 2017, https://www.pewresearch.org/fact-tank/2017/09/06/more-americans-now-say-theyre-spiritual-but-not-religious/.

11. "In U.S., Decline of Christianity Continues at Rapid Pace," Pew Research Center, October 17, 2019, https://www.pewforum.org/2019/10/17/in-u-s-decline-of-christianity-continues-at-rapid-pace/.

12. Gregory Smith, "About Three-in-Ten U.S. Adults Are Now Religiously Unaffiliated," Pew Research Center, December 14, 2021, https://www.pewforum.org/2021/12/14/about-three-in-ten-u-s-adults-are-now-religiously-unaffiliated.

13. "The Changing Global Religious Landscape," Pew Research Center, April 5, 2017, https://www.pewforum.org/2017/04/05/the-changing-global-religious-landscape/.

14. Michael Levitt, "America's Christian Majority Is on Track to End," NPR, September 17, 2022, https://www.npr.org/2022/09/17/1123508069/religion-christianity-muslim-atheist-agnostic-church-lds-pew.

15. Claire Gecewicz, "'New Age' Beliefs Common among Both Religious and Nonreligious Americans," Pew Research Center, October 1, 2018, https://www.pewresearch.org/short-reads/2018/10/01/new-age-beliefs-common-among-both-religious-and-nonreligious-americans/#:~:text=Overall%2C%20roughly%20six%2Din%2D,%25)%20and%20astrology%20(29%25).

16. Frank Newport, "Most Americans Still Believe in God," *Gallup*, June 29, 2016, https://news.gallup.com/poll/193271/americans-believe-god.aspx.

17. Scott Guerin and Nichole Bigley, "Angel Encounters Survey V1," November 15, 2022–January 10, 2023, distributed by Testable (https://www.testable.org/).

## Chapter 7    Scientific Perspectives

1. Newport, "Most Americans Still Believe in God."

2. Peter Cooper, "Almost Half of Us Believe in Guardian Angels," *Ipos*, September 6, 2009, https://www.ipsos.com/en-uk/almost-half-us-believe-guardian-angels.

3. Sahgal et al., "Religious Beliefs."

4. Guerin and Bigley, "Angel Encounters Survey V1."

5. Renaud Evrard, "Everybody Knows Parapsychology Is Not a Real Science: Public Understanding of Parapsychology" (presidential address, Parapsychological Association and Society of Scientific Exploration SEE-PA Connections Conference, 2021).

6. Tony Phillips, ed., "Discovery of 'Arsenic-Bug' Expands Definition of Life," NASA Science, December 2, 2010, https://science.nasa.gov/science-news/science-at-nasa/2010/02dec_monolake.

7. Becky Oskin, "Intraterrestrials: Life Thrives in Ocean Floor," *Live Science*, March 14, 2013, https://www.livescience.com/27899-ocean-subsurface-ecosystem-found.html.

8. "Visible Light: Eye-Opening Research at NNSA," National Nuclear Security Administration, October 17, 2018, https://www.energy.gov/nnsa/articles/visible-light-eye-opening-research-nnsa.

9. "Sound Waves: What Is Sound?," PASCO, accessed October 5, 2022, https://www.pasco.com/products/guides/sound-waves.

10. "Cameras vs. the Human Eye," Cambridge in Colour, accessed October 10, 2022, https://www.cambridgeincolour.com/tutorials/cameras-vs-human-eye.htm.

11. Diane Curriden, "Science Suggests That Auras Do Exist," *Santa Ynez Valley News*, January 24, 2013, https://syvnews.com/lifestyles/columns/abundant-health/science-suggests-that-auras-do-exist/article_bd6d4fcc-65f1-11e2-bf2d-0019bb2963f4.html.

12. Valerie Hunt, *Infinite Mind: The Science of Human Vibrations of Consciousness* (Malibu, CA: Malibu Publishing Co., 1996).

13. "Equipment," Paranormal Investigations of Rockland County, accessed October 19, 2022, https://www.pirc-ny.com/equipment.

14. Abdul-Rahman, "Do You Really Believe in Angels?"

---

### Chapter 8  Psychological Perspectives

1. Andrew Newberg, Abass Alavi, Michael Baime, Michael Pourdehnad, Jill Santanna, and Eugene D'Aquili, "The Measurement of Cerebral Blood Flow during the Complex Cognitive Task of Meditation: A Preliminary SPECT Study," *Psychiatry Research Neuroimaging*, April 10, 2001.

2. Dean I. Radin and Diane C. Ferrari, "Effects of Consciousness on the Fall of Dice: A Meta-Analysis," *Journal of Scientific Exploration* 5, no. 1 (1991): 61–83.

3. Dean I. Radin and Roger D. Nelson, "Evidence for Consciousness-Related Anomalies in Random Physical Systems," in *Parapsychology* (New York: Routledge, 2017), 385–400.

4. Dean Radin, *The Conscious Universe* (San Francisco: Harper, 1997), 144.

5. Dean Radin, Marilyn Schlitz, and Christopher Baur, "Distant Healing Intention Therapies: An Overview of the Scientific Evidence," *Global Advances in Integrative Health and Medicine* 4, no. 1 (2015): 67–71, https://doi.org/10.7453/gahmj.2015.012.suppl.

6. Neeta Mehta, "Mind-Body Dualism: A Critique from a Health Perspective," *Mens Sana Monographs* 9, no.1 (January 9, 2011): 202–09.

7.  Gregg Henriques, "What Is the Mind?," *Psychology Today*, December 11, 2011, https://www.psychologytoday.com/us/blog/theory-knowledge/201112/what-is-the-mind.

8.  Linda Glaser, "Understanding the Mind," Cornell University Department of Psychology, March 8, 2016, https://psychology.cornell.edu/news/understanding-mind.

9.  Nexus Void, "Carl Jung: Metaphysics of the Psyche," July 23, 2019, YouTube video, 22:03, https://youtu.be/fV0UkQAUsXI.

10. Carl Gustav Jung, *Synchronicity*, trans. R.F.C. Hull (Princeton, NJ: Princeton University Press, 1960), 104.

11. Ibid., 105.

12. Nexus Void, "Carl Jung."

13. Hunt, *Infinite Mind*.

14. Eileen Kennedy-Moore, "Imaginary Friends," *Psychology Today*, January 31, 2013, https://www.psychologytoday.com/us/blog/growing-friendships/201301/imaginary-friends.

15. "Hallucinations," Health Library, Cleveland Clinic, last modified June 26, 2022, https://my.clevelandclinic.org/health/symptoms/23350-hallucinations.

16. Cassandra Vieten and David Lukoff, "Spiritual and Religious Competencies in Psychology," *American Psychologist* 77, no. 1 (2022): 26–38, https://doi.org/10.1037/amp0000821.

# Nichole Bigley

**For the last twenty-three years, Nichole Bigley** has been transforming lives, including her own.

At an early age, she remembered being in heaven before coming to Earth and has spoken with angels ever since. As Nichole got older, she realized that not everyone had the same types of memories or angel encounters and learned to keep them close to her heart.

After receiving an urgent message from her spirit team, Nichole launched the top-charted spiritual podcast *A Psychic's Story*, which receives millions of downloads a year, with listeners in all 195 countries. Now Nichole shares her and others' spiritual experiences to help them not feel alone.

To help the next generation shift their vibration, develop their intuition, and become more empowered, Nichole created a spinoff podcast for kids and teens, *A Psychic's Story: Kids' Edition.* Her global podcast *Supernatural Matters* dives into the surreal, helping people determine what is natural or supernatural.

*Looking for Angels: A Guide to Understanding and Connecting with Angels* is Nichole's first book with coauthor Dr. Scott Guerin. For more information about the book, visit *lookingforangelsbook.com.*

Each year Nichole helps thousands of people worldwide with their spiritual journeys, teaching them how to connect with the Divine and discover and lean into their life purpose. In addition to conducting intuitive sessions and creating content for and hosting her three podcasts, Nichole is currently working to launch spiritual courses and retreats and go on speaking tours designed to motivate and inspire others to find and embrace their truths. Discussions with networks and streaming services are also underway on several TV show concepts.

To learn more about Nichole, visit *apsychicsstory.com* or Instagram, Facebook, TikTok, X, or YouTube: @APsychicsStory.

# About the Authors

## Scott Guerin, PhD

**The driving force behind Dr. Scott Guerin's life** has been his passion for unraveling the mysteries of God, Universe, and Source, and the intricate tapestry of their relationship with humanity. A distinguished author, educator, and retired healthcare professional, Scott is committed to the exploration of spiritual development.

With two master's degrees and a doctorate in human development with a focus in spiritual development, Scott's journey has been a remarkable one that delves into the profound realms of the human spirit. His popular *Angel in Training* series describes how society has begun to shift from organized religion to spirituality. Through it, Scott shares his own experiences over decades of pursuing a spiritual life, resulting in two books, *A Spiritual Journey* and *12 Lessons,* that document his journey to spiritual freedom. His conclusion is that we are all angels in training—eternal, connected, and capable beyond belief.

Scott's twenty-three-year tenure as an adjunct professor in psychology at Kean University in New Jersey allows him to impart wisdom and knowledge to countless eager minds, helping them foster a deeper understanding of human psychology and spirituality.

Scott's insights into spiritual development have been covered in top publications such as the *Chicago Tribune, Population Health Management, Thrive Global, U.S. News and World Report, Real Simple,* and many more.

To learn more about Scott or take his free spiritual course, *Where Are You In Your Spiritual Journey?*, visit *angelintraining.org* or follow him on Instagram: @scottguerinauthor.

Made in the USA
Las Vegas, NV
23 November 2024